Mark Hallock is one of the most imp[...] modern day to revitalize dying churc[...] s the rare gift of this proven practitione[...] only to assess replanting, but how to do it effectively. This gem is unwaveringly biblical as well as immensely practical. *Replant Roadmap* is sure to become the practical how-to guide to lead this next generation into this noble work. I heartily commend the author and this excellent book!

Brian Croft, Senior Pastor, Auburndale Baptist Church; Senior Fellow, Church Revitalization Center, The Southern Baptist Theological Seminary

Mark Hallock is a seasoned and respected veteran at replanting churches. This replanting work is a valuable and critical strategy for furthering the gospel and bringing new life into once thriving churches. Having led or personally participated in several church replants, I commend Mark's book to you as a valuable roadmap in replanting.

Brian Howard, Network Director - U.S. West, Acts 29 Church Planting Network

I'm so thankful for what God is doing through Mark Hallock! *Replant Roadmap* is the real deal written to help restore his glory to many tired, broken churches. I pray God will use this book to lead your church to become a leader-developing, leader-deploying church that will do the same.

Jim Misloski, Developing Leader Catalyst, Missouri Baptist Convention

There is a need for more pastors like my friend Mark Hallock who has faithfully done the work of replanting churches. Pastors who are committed to their calling as replanters; men who are bringing gospel-centered life back to dying churches. The insights and wisdom of "Replant Roadmap" equip pastors to see gospel lighthouses that were once dim, burn brightly again for Christ in their communities. Mark brings personal and practical steps to seeing Jesus continue to build and "replant" His church today. My hope is that many Legacy Churches and just as many Kingdom building churches will partner in this vision of the *Replant Roadmap* for the glory of God's name to the ends of the earth.

Tyler Powell, Groups Minister, The Village Church, Flower Mound, TX; former Assessment Director, Acts 29 Church Planting Network

This is a book that meets an enormous – and immediate - need for the American Church in the early 21st century. Where many often see only despair and death in local churches, Mark Hallock sees the potential for new life, vibrant gospel ministry and the extension of God's kingdom. And this is not merely ministry theory; Pastor Hallock provides a field-tested strategy that actually works for re-planting churches. I can't recommend *Replant Roadmap* enough!

Dr. Scott Wenig, Professor of Applied Theology, Haddon Robinson Chair of Biblical Preaching, Denver Seminary

For several years, I've watched in admiration as Mark Hallock replanted Calvary Church from a dying church into a vibrant, multiplying movement of churches. I'm thankful he's now written up his replanting strategy in book form so all of us can learn from it. If you're a pastor considering replanting or a member of a church that needs a new start, Mark is a guide you can trust. Inside this book is real hope that your church's best days are ahead.

    Hunter Beaumont, Lead Pastor, Fellowship Denver Church; Board Member - U.S. West, Acts 29 Church Planting Network

There are many things to commend about this book. First, this book is written with one goal in mind. It isn't about how to grow your church. It isn't about how to find a comfortable pastorate. It isn't about taking the next step on the pastoral ladder. This book is about the glory of God. What does it look like to surrender our callings as pastors to the glory of God above our own comfort? Mark Hallock instructs us well in this area. Second, I love that this book is written by a guy that is in the midst of doing the work of making disciples and replanting churches. This book is filled with personal stories, testimonies, and difficulty. You are not about to read a book that is just theory, this book has grown out of a movement of God. My prayer is that God would use this book to reorient your heart and your church to what it looks like to prioritize His glory above all other things.

    Brad O'Brien, Pastor, Jesus Our Redeemer Church, Baltimore, MD; Assessment Coordinator - Replant, North American Mission Board

Some books give you great theory and theology on why the local church and its revitalization matter so much. Other books give you some instruction in how we can practically help local churches get back to health and thrive again. It is extraordinary when you find a book that does both in a super compelling and helpful way. Mark Hallock is uniquely wired to both paint a beautiful picture for why church replanting matters so much, and also how exactly we can all do that in a way that will succeed. If you are looking for a book that is written by a true practitioner that has replanted a church, that thought its best days were behind it, and now is thriving once again, than you have found it. I personally have seen what Mark writes about in this book work to bring a church back to life, and I have seen how it is the core of who he is and what he is passionate about. I am truly excited to see the ways God will use the book to give hope and direction to thousands of churches and leaders who love their church and want to see them thrive again.

    Ryan Kearns, Executive Pastor, Stonegate Church, Midlothian, TX

Mark addresses a vital topic in the church today. In too many communities the modern church is in decline. Jesus is calling young leaders to re-imagine how we build the Church and reach our communities, taking advantage of these unique opportunities. Mark's passion to replant churches is contagious and this book presents practical, Biblical steps for those who want to be involved in this essential movement. It's obvious he writes not only from a solid theological framework, but also from hands on experience from within his own church and re-planting network. He lives out what he writes. Read it, reflect on it and apply it.

Mike Work, Executive Pastor, Sun Valley Community Church, Gilbert, AZ

The only thing that exceeds the reach of Mark's expertise of the local church is the depth of his affection for her. With personal vulnerability and clarity from the Scriptures, Mark's love for Jesus and understanding of the Church shine brightly through the pages of *Replant Roadmap* and will increase both in his readers.

Jason Helveston, Pastor, Park Community Church - Logan Square, Chicago, IL

In an age when church planting is a primary focus of denominations, networks, and local churches, we may all too often neglect the vital importance of helping a dying church find life again. *Replant Roadmap* is a timely handbook providing practical steps and clear strategies to help the Sending Church enter the world of replanting churches. Mark Hallock brings together a wealth of experience and a deep desire to see God's church flourish across the globe.

Vince Black, Lead Pastor, The Town Church, Ft. Collins, CO

Since churches plant churches, churches should "replant" churches! Mark is a road warrior who not only has a great heart for God, but also His bride, including the godly leaders who are called to this great calling of replanting. Mark is a proven shepherd, revitalizer and replanter who has been in the trenches of this work. What an incredible roadmap that will serve pastors and churches which, if followed, could lead to a movement of restoring dying churches to new life across America.

Dave Howeth, Send City Missionary, Denver, CO, North American Mission Board

REPLANT
roadmap

Mark Hallock

 ACOMA PRESS

Dedicated to the Elliot family. All of you. Thank you for trusting God and taking a leap of faith on a crazy youth pastor. The best is yet to come...

CONTENTS

ACKNOWLEDGMENTS

No book project is possible without the generous help of many others. I have been so blessed by the help and assistance of so many who helped make this book what it is. While I wish I could thank every single person who helped in some way with this book, unfortunately, space will not allow for it. However, I do want to take a moment and thank a few specific people.

I want to thank my wonderful wife, Jenna, and my children Zoe and Eli. Thank you for the grace and encouragement you so regularly extended to me throughout the writing of "the big book."

Thank you to Jeff Declue, my brother in Christ and faithful partner in the trenches of replanting and revitalization.

Thank you to Tamsen Sear, a gifted, joyful and servant-minded sister in Christ, who also happens to be an amazing editor.

Thank you to Erica Myeni who added so much to this project, specifically in helping me think through how to make it as useful and accessible as possible for pastors and leaders.

I also want to give special thanks to Dan Hallock, Kevin Hanly, Al Barrera, Deral Schrom, Dan Freng, Scott Iken, Gabe Reed, Matt Whitt, Brad O'Brien, Scott Thistlethwaite, Ricardo Cardenas, Matthew Hunt, Jessica Evans, Tiesha Von Kaenel, Evan Skelton, Jianna Kellems, Karen Henkelman, Jim Misloski, Tim Witmer, Frank Cornelius, the Calvary Englewood Pastors/Elders, Deacons, and staff, our awesome revitalization interns and residents, my Calvary Family of Churches' brothers and sisters, and finally, Mark Clifton and the NAMB replant team.

I praise God for the gift it is to serve alongside each of you. *Soli Deo Gloria.*

FORWARD

It was a parched land unable to sustain life without life-giving water... And
the enemy had sabotaged the wells. In fact, the wells that once brought life,
hope and a future to a dry and thirsty land were completely stopped. But
then, the son of the one who dug the wells sought to reclaim the land from
the enemy and dug again those very same wells. The wells that still contained
life-giving water. The wells that could change the entire landscape. Of
course, this is the story of Isaac digging again his father Abraham's wells
recorded in Genesis 26:18, "And Isaac dug again the wells of water that had
been dug in the days of Abraham his father, which the Philistines had
stopped after the death of Abraham."

We are living in a day when thousands of life-giving wells have been
sabotaged by the enemy. These wells that still contain the living water have
been stopped up by the very one who seeks to rob God of his glory. And yet,
we are living in a day when God, for his glory, is raising an entire generation
of young Isaac's who are coming along and unstopping those wells. At a time
when as many as 4,000 churches across North America close their doors
every year, God is answering the prayer of those who are praying for his
church. Brave young leaders are the answer to this prayer as they embrace
dying and dysfunctional churches. Rather than turning away from them,
ignoring them, marginalizing them, or even criticizing them, these young
men are being *called to them*. And, they are being called there to dig again
those wells and to find again the truth of the gospel that remains. This is
happening over and over in rural America, in the heart of our cities, and in
our suburbs. It is happening in a way we've never seen before. For God's
glory, dying churches are indeed coming back to life. These wells once again
are providing water.

In this book, Mark Hallock gives sound, biblical advice on how to get living water flowing from these wells again. Speaking from the heart of experience and the call of God on his life to embrace and reclaim dying churches, Mark speaks as one who has done it. He speaks as one who has walked with others who have done it, and he speaks as one who wants to walk with you as you do it. This book is practical, informative, groundbreaking and, most importantly, this book is founded on solid biblical principles.

Mark has written a timely book for the family of God. If you have a heart to reclaim dying churches and if you want to be part of resurrecting wells so life-giving water can spring forth once again, then I commend this book to you.

Mark understands that replanting a dying church is a divine activity. It is not a work of man. And yet, it pleases God to use our effort as part of his work. Our effort in replanting is needful, but it is not effectual. The only effectual way to replant a church is for the Holy Spirit to do a work. And the Holy Spirit does his work in replanting as we are faithful and obedient to the command of our Lord. This book will help you be obedient to that command, and it will give you the tools, the insight, and the motivation you need to do what you can and to rely upon the Holy Spirit to do what He will do when we are faithful to this task. For his glory and our joy, we are digging again these wells. We are replanting dying churches.

Mark Clifton
National Director - Replant
North American Mission Board

INTRODUCTION

One of the great joys and privileges of my life is being able to sit down with pastors and church leaders in plateaued or declining churches and encourage them, to remind them that God is not done with their church.

In a day and age when what seems to be valued most in many church circles is big numbers, cool buildings, and over the top programs, it can be incredibly discouraging to be part of a church that has none of these things, a church that from the world's perspective is less than impressive. Add to that the reality that many of these churches are struggling to simply survive. If you've never been part of a church like this, it may be hard for you to imagine just how tiring and hopeless things can seem at times.

Will things ever get turned around for our church? Do we need to just close the doors for good? Is there any hope? What can we do? Is God done with us? These are the types of questions men and women, pastors and lay leaders, are wrestling with everyday in the thousands of declining and dying churches in North America and beyond.

It is because of churches that I wrote this book. But, my burden is not only to help dying churches; it is to help equip healthy churches to come alongside them in this effort.

I believe that churches must plant churches for the sake of gospel advancement in our world. And at the same time, I believe churches must replant churches. Dying churches cannot experience transformation on their own. They need help from Jesus-loving, Kingdom-minded, mission-focused congregations, congregations that share this burden to see forgotten, tired, declining churches reclaimed for the glory of God. This book was written as a tool for this endeavor.

Our congregation, Calvary Church, in Englewood, Colorado was once in a place of near death, considering closing our doors for good, until God brought us new life, until he provided vibrancy through Spirit-empowered revitalization and renewal. Since then, in his kindness, the Lord has allowed our congregation to replant several other dying congregations. And, what a joy it has been to see God do what only he can do for his glory—to breathe new hope, fresh passion, and renewal into a dying church that it might reach its community once again with the power of the gospel.

In this book, my hope is to lay out much of what we at Calvary have learned in this journey of replanting dying churches. I will be the first to say that we have made many mistakes and still have much to learn, but hopefully, some of what is shared in these pages can help equip and encourage leaders who desire to get "into the game" of replanting. Praise God, there is much being written today about church revitalization and replanting, but this book is designed to mobilize those who want to get to work. I realize it is scary and will take a huge leap of faith, but I believe our awesome God will lead you and empower you every step of the way. Here's why: As passionate as we may be to help dying churches, the Lord is far more passionate about it. This is *his* bride, *his* blood-bought people. This is *his* church, which *he* has saved for *his* glory. For these reasons, I believe the Lord is the most passionate church replanter in the universe! And, he invites us to join him in this endeavor. There is no time to waste. The time is now.

WHO THIS BOOK IS WRITTEN FOR

While I hope that any person interested in learning more about replanting dying churches can benefit from this book, there are three primary audiences I have in mind.

Audience #1: Pastors and Leaders of Potential Sending Churches

The primary audience I have in mind for this book are the pastors and key leaders of a healthy congregation who seek to come alongside dying congregation as a Sending Church. I regularly meet with leaders like this who are interested in the actual nuts and bolts of effectively replanting a church. This book serves as a "roadmap" to help guide and direct these leaders not only to do the work of replanting, but to do it in a strategic, biblical, God-honoring manner.

Audience #2: Replanters in Training

For any dying church to be replanted, it takes a humble, joyful, godly replanter to lead the charge. The truth is, we can have all the vision in the world, but unless churches are intentionally equipping and raising up replanters, we will never see a replanting movement happen. Leadership development is critical, and I believe this book can be a helpful tool in the development of replanters themselves. Ideally, I think this book will be most helpful for a team of pastors and leaders from a Sending Church to read and study together with their potential replanter. Together they can engage and implement the strategies discussed in these pages.

Audience #3: Those Who Want to Learn More about Replanting

I know there are many who are neither part of a potential Sending Church, nor are potential replanters themselves, but who desire to learn more about the work of replanting. This book also provides an overview of the need for this important ministry as well as some of the practical ways they might get involved.

HOW TO USE THIS BOOK

There are a variety of ways you may choose to read this book. Here are a few of them:

Read it straight through.

I sought to write this book in a fairly systematic way for the sake of clarity and helpfulness. The book moves from the need for replanting, to a biblical understanding of replanting, to the practical steps it will take to lead a replant. Because of this, reading it straight through may be the most helpful way to work through the material.

Read the introductory chapters.

The first three chapters of this book are designed to give a basic overview and introduction to replanting, helping to lay the foundation for the rest of the book. For someone who is more interested in simply getting a basic introduction to replanting, working through the first three chapters would be beneficial.

Read specific chapters that are of interest.

You may want to jump around a little bit when reading this book, which you can easily do. For instance, you may want to learn more about starting a replanting residency in your church (Chapter 5) or how to best support and encourage a replanter and his wife as they do the work of replanting (Chapter 11). While there is an intentional movement between the chapters, each chapter can stand on its own.

Read it alone or in a group.

You may want to work through this book on your own, but I have also formatted the material for groups to work through together, discussing what they are learning chapter-by-chapter. In fact, I have provided discussion questions at the end of each chapter to assist you in this. If your church is seriously considering the potential of replanting a church, I recommend that your pastors and key leaders to read and discuss this book as a group. Not only will it will enhance your learning and application of the material; it will make the journey more enjoyable!

SPEND TIME WITH THE APPENDICES...SERIOUSLY.

I realize that in many books, the appendices are simply an optional "add-on" for the hardcore reader. This book is different. As you can see, there are a TON of appendices in this book! And, this has been done intentionally. Many of these appendices could have easily been put into the main body of this book; in fact, many of them were at one point. However, including these as appendices makes these key resources much more accessible.

Some of these appendices address common questions about replanting. There are also several "how-tos" including how to shepherd older members as a young replanter, how to develop a new church membership process in a replant, how to navigate financial challenges, how to start a replanting residency, how to engage replanting in either an urban or rural context, and many more.

You will also notice a glossary at the end of the book, which defines some of the key words and phrases used throughout the material. For your convenience, I have *highlighted** these terms the first time they appear.

WHAT I HOPE YOU WILL GET OUT OF *REPLANT ROADMAP*

I realize we are all busy, and it is a commitment to read any book in a thoughtful and thorough manner, let alone a book as long as this one. But, let me share why I think this book is worth your time and what I hope you will gain from it.

Goal #1: You will gain a greater awareness of the epidemic we are facing.

As you will read in the coming pages, the current state of many churches in North America is not a good one. Churches are closing their doors at a faster pace than at any other time in our history. I praise God for the many new churches that are being planted. But, if truly we want to push back the darkness in our communities, we must also do all that we can to restore dying churches to health and vibrancy.

Goal #2: You will grow deeper in your understanding of what replanting is and isn't.

In light of the great need, I will also defend replanting as one of the most strategic pathways to meeting it. In some circles, there is much confusion as to what replanting actually is. In fact, revitalization and replanting are often seen as synonymous terms for the work of leading declining churches back to health. Certainly, I believe both revitalization and replanting are vital, and can both be very effective strategies depending on the context and need. But, I hope to show that they are, in fact, two different things, two different approaches to church renewal.

Hear me well. I don't believe that replanting is the only option for declining churches, nor do I believe it is always the best option. There are many factors to consider before a dying church should pursue being replanted. In the same way, there is much to consider before a healthy church chooses to help replant a congregation in need. However, for a church near death which desires not simply to survive but to thrive as a mission-minded, community reaching, disciple-making congregation in their community, replanting is one of the best options.

Goal #3: You will be encouraged and even inspired to help dying churches.

One thing I can tell you is that wherever you live, whatever community you find yourself in, there are almost assuredly churches in need of help and hope nearby. Churches that love Jesus and want to reach the community with the gospel, but are struggling to just stay alive—these churches are everywhere. I hope God will use this book to lovingly push you toward helping one of these churches in some way.

It may be in leading your congregation toward the replanting of one of these churches in need. It may be in starting a residency program in order to raise up and equip a future replanter. It may be committing yourself to fervently pray for struggling churches in your community on a consistent basis. Whatever it might be, I hope you are encouraged and even inspired to help in some way.

Goal #4: You and your church will be better equipped to replant a dying church.

It can be tough to find practical help when it comes to replanting churches well. When I say "well" I mean in a way that is marked by humility and love as well as strategic, courageous leadership. I hope this kind of help is what you find in this book, help that is practical, rooted in the Word, and trustworthy as you walk the road of replanting.

Toward this end, I've tried to offer ideas and strategies that are easy to apply and carry out in a variety of contexts. In fact, we have seen these work effectively in both rural and urban contexts because nothing in this book is built on anything other than the simple, straight-forward teaching of God's

Word. You see, effective replanting is not based on the latest trend or passing fad; it is based on the character of our sovereign God, empowered by the Holy Spirit, rooted in his unchanging Word.

HERE WE GO!

Are you ready for this? I pray the Lord will challenge, encourage, and equip you through this book. I pray you will be able to apply what you read here in a manner that is helpful in your own context. I pray it will be a source of joy for you and your walk with the Lord as well. May our great God be pleased and may Jesus be made famous as together we seek to help dying churches come alive and thrive once again!

Chapter 1

A MOVEMENT IS NEEDED

It seems like yesterday that I was sitting with one of my best friends in the parking lot of Calvary Baptist Church in Englewood, Colorado. At the time, Calvary was a church of 30 sweet folks who loved Jesus but were weary and ready to close the doors of the church for good. They needed serious help. They needed help that had to come from the Lord himself. You see, Calvary had once been a healthy, vibrant congregation that multiplied and sent members out to plant other churches. Several churches in the Denver-Metro area exist today because at one time Calvary had the vision, passion, and faith to plant new congregations. However, over the years, like so many other churches, Calvary slowly began to decline. The community around the church began to change. Families began to move away. Older members were passing away. A few pastors came in who were more focused on their own agenda than God's. And sadly, over time, Calvary began to die. But the Lord wasn't done with this church.

As I sat with my friend that day, I knew full well, as crazy as it seemed, that the Lord was calling my wife and I to go to this dying church and by God's grace, see it come back to life for his glory. As though it were yesterday, I remember my friend looking at me in that parking lot and saying, "Are you sure you know what you're doing?" I looked back at him and said, "No. I don't know what I'm doing. In fact, I really have no idea as to what I'm doing. But one thing I can't deny is this. I can't deny that God is calling me to lead and love this congregation. And I can't deny that I believe the Lord can bring this church back to life." With a little smirk and a laugh, my buddy looked at me and kindly replied, "You are nuts."

This wasn't the last time someone called me "nuts" for going to Calvary to pastor this dying congregation. I've heard it from a number of people on numerous occasions. Many of these folks didn't mean to put me down in any way, they simply looked at the obstacles ahead for this little church and believed leading Calvary back to health was next to impossible. To be honest, I have come to embrace being called, "nuts." The truth is, I am! I would say that everyone of us who is passionate about church replanting is a little nuts. We're nuts because we are crazy enough to believe that God is not done with dying churches. We're nuts enough to believe that God has not given up on most churches that many of us would have given up on a long time ago. We're nuts because, just like in the Bible, we believe that God would take a seemingly impossible situation and use it for his glory. We're nuts because we believe that he loves dying churches and receives much glory when dying churches come back to life and vibrancy...and that he invites us to be part of it!

The truth is, you can hardly blame people for calling folks like us nuts. When you look at recent statistics on the health of the church, and Christianity in general, in North America, things don't look so great. Chew on these stats for a few moments:

- According to the Hartford Institute of Religion Research, more than 40 percent of Americans "say" they go to church weekly. As it turns out, however, less than 20 percent are actually in church. In other words, more than 80 percent of Americans are finding other things to do on weekends.[1]

- Each year, nearly 3 million more previous churchgoers enter the ranks of the religiously unaffiliated.[2]

- Barna Group researcher, David Kinnaman, estimates 60 to 80 percent of those raised in the church today in our country will no longer be active in their faith or consider themselves church members by the time they are in their mid-20s.[3]

- Thom Rainer speculates that between 8,000 to 10,000 churches are currently closing their doors every year in North America.[4]

Let me give you a snap shot of the state of churches within one major denomination, the Southern Baptist Convention, which is the largest protestant denomination in North America:

- North American Mission Board research has determined that in recent years, the Southern Baptist Convention has been losing around 900 churches every year.[5]

- Seventy-seven percent of the cities these 900 churches are in have more than 100,000 residents and 90 percent of those churches are in growing communities -- striking down the presumption that declining churches are only in rural or declining areas.[6]

- On average, 17 Southern Baptist churches shut their doors for good every Sunday, leaving underserved and unreached neighborhoods in cities across North America.[7]

- 10-15% of churches in the SBC are healthy and multiplying, 70-75% are plateaued or declining, and 10-15% are at or near risk.[8]

These statistics, among others, are very sobering. What we see is that not only are we in need of new, healthy churches in North America, but we are in desperate need of replanting declining and dying churches. So, what exactly are we talking about when we talk about church replanting?

CHURCH REVITALIZATION VS. CHURCH REPLANTING: WHAT'S THE DIFFERENCE?

*Church revitalization** and *church replanting** are probably terms you have heard at some point and are familiar with on a basic level. But how are they distinct? What's the difference between the two? You may find an in-depth look at the contrast in **Appendix V**, but let's start with a short comparison, beginning with church revitalization.

Many of us could take an educated guess on what church revitalization is all about. Hopefully we know it's more than just changing the carpet in a sanctuary or adding some new worship songs! The reality is revitalization is needed in almost every church in our country today.

In church revitalization, the hope and intent is to help a church that is plateaued or declining get healthy again so that it can become a unified, vibrant, disciple-making congregation on mission to reach their surrounding community with the gospel. Revitalization is a work only God can do through the power of the Holy Spirit as he works in the heart of a church and its members. Typically in a revitalization context a church knows they need help, but they may be unaware of just how *much* help they need. This type of church still has some fight left in them. They have a functional building and enough money and people that they are able to hold out several more years without hitting the panic button. While money, people, and a building can all be great blessings to a church in need of revitalization, these can also help to create a false sense of security that prevents a church from making the necessary changes to become healthy and growing again. In contrast to replanting, the congregation we are describing has no intention of becoming a new or different church; however, it does desire to hire a pastor who will help lead them back to health and vitality.

There are differing mentalities among the congregants within a declining church like this. There are probably some who are saying, "We've really got to do something now! We've got to make some major changes or we're going to die." There may be others who are saying, "Meh, things aren't great, but we're doing okay." Most likely there is probably a third group of folks who are saying, "We're just fine. We don't need to change anything. Are you kidding me? Things are great!" These are typically three of the different types of mindset among the church members of this struggling church. As you can imagine, a church revitalization brings with it great challenges, but also potential opportunities for great Kingdom work.

WHAT IS CHURCH REPLANTING?

Contrary to what you may have heard, church replanting is not the same thing as church revitalization. There are important distinctions. Think of it this way: Church replanting is a specific strategy or approach to church revitalization. Broadly speaking, if church revitalization is concerned with helping plateaued or declining churches experience new life and vitality, church replanting is one of the most biblical, God-honoring, and effective strategies for actually making it happen. For the purposes of this book, we will define church replanting as the process by which members of a dying congregation discern God's leading to joyfully submit their church's current and future ministry to an outside *Sending Church** and its leadership, working together to begin a new church for a new season of gospel ministry in their community.

Church replanting is a very unique ministry. In church replanting, the focus is on congregations that are not simply declining, but dying. And they know it. These are congregations that have reached a point where they realize they are not only sick and unhealthy, but they are nearing their death. Churches are first identified as needing to be replanted when they humbly and honestly acknowledge that they are at risk of closing their doors once and for all within two to five years if major changes are not made. These congregations do not simply have a metaphorical cold that needs a little help to get healthy again, but rather they have some form of cancer with major surgery and treatment needed to survive. As a result, these congregations have come to a point of humble surrender. They are no longer concerned with fighting battles over such things as the color of the carpet, whether we sing hymns or praise songs, or whether the pastor preaches in a suit or jeans. They have come to a point of humble surrender, saying, *"Lord, whatever you want to do with our church, we are all in. This is Your Church, not ours. We want to do whatever it takes to not simply survive, but thrive for the sake of the gospel, for the sake of this community."*

Pastor and church replanting strategist, Jeff Declue, gives a helpful analogy of what replanting is like. Imagine that you were given a beautiful plant. Everyone that came to your house complimented you on its size, health, vibrancy, the breath taking fragrance. Now one day you noticed the plant was changing. Its leaves were turning pale yellow and the plant looked slightly withered. You didn't forget to water it. Maybe someone else watered it too much. Maybe it isn't getting enough light. You love this plant and you will do whatever it takes to save it. If you don't act now it is going to die.

Quickly you get the plant into a new pot where you can get back to the basics. You get food with some quality nutrients. You now can make sure it is getting ample sunshine and water. Deep green color starts to return to the leaves and its strength starts to return. It takes time but it *is* coming back to life. Now replace the flower in a pot with a church in a community. This is a picture of church "replanting."

As Christians, we need to lock arms and fight to stop the trend of dying churches in our communities. The task of church replanting then is to come alongside these dying congregations and lovingly and joyfully shepherd them back to health, mission, and multiplication. Al Mohler, President of The Southern Baptist Theological Seminary in Louisville, Kentucky writes:

> One of our central tasks in the present generation is to be bold in our vision of replanting churches — helping existing churches to find new vision, new strategic focus, new passion for the gospel, new hunger for the preaching of the Word, new love for their communities, and new excitement about seeing people come to faith in Jesus. Replanting churches requires both courage and leadership skills. A passion for replanting a church must be matched by skills in ministry and a heart for helping a church to regain a vision.[10]

Indeed, the need for church replanting is great, as is the opportunity and potential. Sadly, many churches will close their doors for the final time this next Sunday. As I mentioned earlier, in the Southern Baptist Convention alone, 17 churches will close their doors for the final time this next Sunday. And the next week, another 17 will close. And another 17 the next week. This should break our hearts! Many of these are churches made up of sweet saints who love Jesus, love the Bible and love people, but have perhaps lost vision and hope for what God can do in and through them. They are sheep that need a pastor-shepherd who can know them, feed them, and lead them with passion, joy, and hope into the future. So where do we go from here?

A REPLANTING PATHWAY

Once a church comes to the place of humble surrender and desires to be replanted for the sake of the gospel and the glory of God, what's next? Practically, what are next steps at this point to begin the replanting process? How does a healthy church and its leaders come alongside and help guide a dying congregation from where they are now to a place of renewed hope and vibrancy through a replanting strategy? We will spend the rest of this book going into great detail answering these questions. But at this point, let me offer a brief overview of the primary replanting pathway we will be considering throughout this book. This pathway is one that is biblical, pastoral, missional, respectful of history, loving of people, gospel-driven, and I believe, God-honoring. This is a pathway that is doable and reproducible. It is a pathway that can give thousands of churches hope that indeed God is not done with them.

Here's the replanting pathway I would like to propose in a nutshell. Notice there are three primary components to this pathway—When the dying congregation joyfully chooses to be replanted, they agree to:

1. Surrender all day-to-day decision making to an outside transition team, ideally from a Sending Church.

2. Engage strategic outside ministry partners.

3. Call a trained replanting pastor.

What does this pathway look like practically? First, as noted above, the church needing to be replanted has already said, "We surrender. We recognize this is the Lord's church and to move forward in a healthy way, there needs to be fresh leadership. We joyfully submit to an outside *transition team** that can guide us into the future." This transition team could be a group of pastors, elders, deacons or other lay leaders from a Sending Church, like yours. It could be a group made up of pastors and leaders from different churches in the community. It could be a group of *denominational leaders**. It might be a combination of all the above. Whoever these individuals are, the dying church has agreed to give up day-to-day decision making and oversight to this outside group of leaders. They have gladly surrendered to this group to help guide them and lead them into the future. While each of these transition team options can be effective for churches that need to be replanted, this book will lay out the replanting strategy for a transition team from a particular Sending Church, rather than a group of various outside leaders.

Secondly, the congregation, along with their outside transition team, begins to engage outside ministry partners and churches, inviting them to be part of this new, exciting replanting vision. The reality is that no declining church can get healthy on its own. Declining churches need healthy churches to come alongside them, to encourage them, help share resources with them, and joyfully serve as partners in this new work and to point out the unhealthy habits they have developed. Radical cooperation is needed. Just as a replanted church may need a cane to lean on as it regains its strength, a replanting or Sending Church needs to have a vision to depend on the churches around it until the dying church can stand on its own again. This is the beauty of the body of Christ in action and makes much of Jesus and the gospel!

Thirdly, the congregation recognizes they need a pastor who is trained in, equipped for, and has a heart for replanting. Because replanting is a unique ministry, it takes unique leadership, including a unique type of pastor. This church needs a pastor who is a visionary shepherd. This is a pastor who is burdened to reach the lost in the community and who is willing to do whatever it takes to lead this dying church to engage the surrounding community with the love of Christ. At the same time, this congregation needs a pastor who truly loves shepherding people, both young and old, who respects and honors the history of the congregation and understands the unique dynamics of replanting ministry. Where does this church find such a pastor? In most cases, this replanting pastor will be identified and appointed by the outside transition team from the Sending Church that is helping to oversee the entire replanting process for this congregation. Working with the declining congregation and potentially denominational leaders, the transition team will seek to find a *replanter** who they believe is a good fit for leading this particular congregation back to health and life.

Can you imagine what would happen if we began to see large numbers of dying churches begin to pursue this kind of replanting pathway? I can tell you from experience, more and more churches are choosing to trust the Lord and take a leap of faith in this very direction. Many once dying churches are now becoming healthy again, engaging their communities and reaching the lost with the power of Christ in new and exciting ways. Children's Sunday School classrooms that had been empty for years are now filled with laughter and singing from little ones each and every Sunday morning. Baptism tanks that had been dry and unused for years are now being filled regularly as lost men and women experience new life in Jesus. Neighborhoods that for years had not even taken notice or cared that a church had been there are now taking notice, being impacted in countless ways through new outreach ministries making a real difference in the community. It's happening! The Lord is doing this kind of replanting work all over our country and world for his glory and the joy of his Church.

WE'RE NOT TALKING ONE REPLANT HERE... WE'RE TALKING A MOVEMENT

As excited as I get at the thought of even one dying church being replanted for the sake of the gospel, the truth is, in order to reach the masses of people in our world that don't know Christ, *one replant is not enough.* Two are not enough. Ten are not enough. Even a hundred new church replants are not enough! Our vision as the church in North America must be to see hundreds and even thousands of churches replanted for the glory of God. What we need is a *replanting movement.* A cyclical movement of churches replanting churches that replant churches.

Now, what exactly do I mean by a movement? What is a replanting movement? On the most basic level, movements are about *mobilizing people behind a shared purpose.* Movements happen in our world all the time. Movements happen in the world of business, or technology, or food, or entertainment, or even in the Church. When you look at the spread of the gospel through the early church in the book of Acts, what you see is a movement...a gospel movement infused by the Holy Spirit that changed the world, one life, one church, one community, at a time.

I don't know about you, but I get excited dreaming about a new kind of movement in the church today. A church replanting movement. A movement where God does what only he can do through his people. A movement where God uses ordinary, faithful pastors, church leaders, and lay people to bring declining and dying churches back to life. A movement that mobilizes God's people behind the shared purpose of replanting dying churches for the glory of God. A movement where churches that seem to have no hope and no pulse come back to life by the Spirit of God in such a way that they not only survive, but thrive to the point of replanting other dying congregations. Yes, we need to plant new churches. We need to plant many new churches in order to take the gospel to areas where people are far from Christ. But at the same time, if we as the Church of Jesus Christ are going to truly push back the darkness, and go from a posture of defense to a posture of offense in our mission to take the light of Christ into a dark world, we must be as intentional and purposeful in our church *replanting* efforts as we are in our church planting efforts. It is not an either/or, but rather, a both/and. Now is the time. Now is the time for a church replanting movement. Are you in?

FOUR PRIORITIES OF A CHURCH REPLANTING MOVEMENT

So what would be the marks of a church replanting movement? How would we know if we are in the midst of this type of movement of God? What would be the priorities of churches and church leaders who seek to join God in his work of bringing hope and new life to dying churches? Let me offer what I believe to be four essential priorities of this kind of replanting movement.

Priority #1

Together as churches and church leaders, we must pursue our joy in Jesus, seeking to make him non-ignorable in North America and to the ends of the earth.

First and foremost, we must desire to be churches and church leaders where Jesus is our greatest treasure and where together we passionately pursue our joy in him. As we pursue our joy in him, our hope, prayer and mission must be to see many others in our communities find their joy in him. Of course we know that we are surrounded by people we know and love who, though seeking true joy and satisfaction in their lives, are knowingly or unknowingly *ignoring* the only one who can actually give true satisfaction to them: Jesus Christ.

This is why our shared desire in this movement of church replanting must be to make Jesus non-ignorable in North America and to the ends of the earth. For this to happen, we must be men and women known by our passionate love for Jesus, for his Word, and for people. We must be churches and church leaders zealous for and committed to persistent prayer, seeking the face of God in all things. This is not a movement with the goal of trying to be the coolest or biggest churches in town. This is a movement about God and for God. This is a movement about desperate men and women begging the Lord to do what only he can do. This is a movement that desires to see the impossible become possible; namely dying churches infused with new life and vibrancy, becoming healthy, faithful, and reproducing churches for the sake of gospel advancement.

Priority #2

Together as churches and church leaders, we must do whatever it takes to make disciples who make disciples and replant churches that replant churches.

Jesus has called us to *be* his disciples, but it doesn't stop there. He has called us to *make* disciples who make disciples—joyful, passionate disciples! Along with making disciples who make disciples, we must be churches that replant churches. Disciples are made in the context of the local church, not apart from it.

It doesn't matter if you live in a major city or in a small, rural town; every one of our communities is in desperate need of gospel-centered, Word-saturated, outward-focused, people-loving churches. Not a few of these kinds of churches, but many of these churches. Because of this, we need a movement in which local churches are committed to aggressively coming alongside and replanting dying churches that will become replanting churches themselves.

There must be an urgency in all of this. For this kind of movement to happen, it means we need churches that don't simply talk the talk, but walk the walk when it comes to doing whatever it takes to replant churches. We need churches and church leaders who are humble and willing to set aside personal preferences for the sake of reaching those far from Christ. We need churches who are willing to die of themselves for the sake of those in their communities who are lost and broken. We must be willing to do whatever it takes to get the gospel out, by the grace of God and the power of his Spirit.

Priority #3

Together as churches and church leaders, we must practice humble, radical, cooperation for the sake of gospel advancement.

I truly believe we as churches are always at our best when we link arms and pursue ministry together. Just as there is no such thing as a lone ranger Christian, there is no such thing as a lone ranger church. Or at least there shouldn't be. We can't do this alone, which is why a replanting movement must be made up of churches and leaders who practice humble, radical cooperation. A replanting movement must have churches and leaders who intentionally pursue the joyful sharing of any and all kinds of resources (people, money, programs, etc.) whenever and however we can.

In a true replanting movement, this kind of cooperation will not be a burden, but a joy! A movement like this is not about one church or one church leader and the advancement of their own kingdom. This type of movement is centered on the one Hero, Jesus Christ, and the advancement of his Kingdom for his glory.

Priority #4

Together as churches and church leaders, we must be committed to one another for the long haul.

Ministry is hard. It is hard in all kinds of ways and for all sorts of reasons. And because ministry is hard, not only must we practice humble, radical cooperation, but we must be committed to one another for the long haul, by the grace of God and the power of the Spirit. This is what families do, or at least the best families. The healthiest families. As Christians and as churches, we are the family of God. This means through good times and bad times, mountain tops and valleys of church replanting, we're the family of God. We are a family committed to love and encourage and sharpen one another, journeying together in this challenging yet vital ministry for the long haul.

This type of commitment to one another as churches that replant churches, is essential if we are to see a true movement take place.

CAN YOU IMAGINE?

Can you imagine what the Lord could do in North America and to the ends of the earth if we were to link arms and live out these four priorities together as churches and church leaders?

Can you imagine the hundreds, even thousands, perhaps millions of lives transformed by the gospel?

Can you imagine the churches we would see replanted, moving from near death to health and vibrancy?

Can you imagine the many spiritually dry communities that would be transformed as the gospel begins to move in power through a newly replanted congregation?

Can you imagine how non-ignorable Jesus would become in towns and cities where the majority of people are currently ignoring him?

Can you imagine how much glory God would get?

Can you imagine a movement like this?

Now is the time for a church replanting movement. *Are you in?*

FOR FURTHER REFLECTION

Discussion Questions

1. As you think of the area surrounding your church, how has it changed in the last five years? The last 15 years? The last 50 years? How has your church met & dealt with those changes?

2. What would your church be like today if nothing had changed over the last 50 years? What would it be like if things had changed too much and too frequently?

3. As you think of struggling churches, what are some of the dead areas that you can think about and pray that God will bring back to life?

4. Chapter 1 mentioned three primary components to church replanting—1) *surrender all day-to-day decision making to an outside transition team, ideally from a Sending Church; 2) engage strategic outside ministry partners; and 3) call a trained replanting pastor.* Which do you think will be the biggest challenge? Which are you most excited about?

Ways to Pray

- Pray for the replanting pastor that God is raising up to send out from your church.

- Pray for God to guide you to the dying church He wants you to replant.

- Pray for that church to be open & receptive to new gospel strategies.

- Pray for both the sending & dying churches during the transition.

Chapter 2

WHY WE MUST REPLANT CHURCHES NOW

"I'm just not convinced that replanting churches is a good way to go. I've seen so many churches that 'say' they want to get healthy, but when it comes down to it, they're not willing to do what it really takes to get there. I mean, come on Mark, do you really believe replanting churches is a wise use of time, money, and other resources? Wouldn't it be more effective to just let these dying churches die?"

This was a conversation I had recently over coffee with a pastor friend of mine. I wish I could say this conversation was the only one of its kind, but I hear these concerns regularly from pastors and church leaders all over the country. Is my friend right? Is this replanting thing a waste of time? Is it worth all of the sacrificial energy and resources and prayer we put into it? Are we just being unwise here? Is it better to just let these churches die? Are there better places to put our funds and efforts? These are good questions that deserve thoughtful answers. Let me share some of my thoughts on this by offering seven reasons why I believe my friend (whom I love dearly) is wrong. These are seven reasons why I believe it is absolutely critical that we as the church of Jesus Christ begin to actively and intentionally pursue the replanting and revitalization of dying churches in our communities.

REASON #1: GOD'S PEOPLE IN DYING CHURCHES NEED ENCOURAGEMENT, NOURISHMENT AND FRESH VISION.

First of all, God's people in dying churches need **encouragement**. Typically when you step inside a dying church, you will quickly see folks who are *tired*. They're exhausted. They've probably lost passion and zeal. It's not that they desire to be dispassionate about the Lord, the church, and the lost. It's just that they've been going so hard for so long that they're simply worn out. It's been a difficult season for that church, and likely the season has been a long one. This church needs encouragement - lots of loving encouragement.

Secondly, God's people in dying churches need **nourishment**. The Lord's sheep need nourishment. Sheep rely on receiving healthy food from a good shepherd, a pastor who faithfully preaches and teaches the Word of God. John 21:15 says, "When they had finished eating, Jesus said to Simon Peter, 'Simon, son of John, do you truly love me more than these?' 'Yes Lord,' he said, 'You know that I love you.' Jesus said, 'Feed my lambs.'" It's the responsibility of a replanting pastor to feed the flock of God good food for the renewing of their hearts and minds that they might move out on mission in their community with joy and strength in the Lord. This is why raising up and training faithful replanting pastors is so critical to seeing churches replanted in a healthy, biblical way. Jeremiah 3:15 reads, "The Lord declares, I will give you shepherds after my own heart who will lead you with knowledge and understanding." Dying congregations need replanting pastors who can shepherd them well, nourishing them with the food of God's Word, while leading them with knowledge and understanding.

Thirdly, God's people in dying churches need **fresh vision**. Many times these churches have lost vision. As a result, they have lost hope and passion for what the Lord can do in and through their congregation. They need fresh vision and new hope. They need to be loved and led in such a way that they begin to believe the truth that God isn't done with their church. More than that, they need to believe that God is just getting started with what he wants to do in and through them for his purposes!

REASON #2: THE LOST IN OUR COMMUNITIES NEED TO SEE CONGREGATIONS ALIVE AND ON MISSION.

Sadly, all too often declining churches have become "non-factors" in their communities. Where perhaps at one time this church was a central hub serving various needs in the community, they have become nothing more than an eyesore to those in the neighborhood. Sadly, I have visited with non-believers in different cities who would just as soon see dying churches in their neighborhoods disappear and become restaurants or apartment complexes than for them to remain as they are -- non-factors in the neighborhood. This must never be. How desperately neighborhoods all across our country need these declining churches to be replanted and become lighthouses for Jesus once again. Replanted churches serve as a source of true hope and encouragement, love and healing for people in their communities. The lost and the broken in these communities need the church, simply because they need Jesus.

REASON #3: WE HAVE A BIBLICAL MANDATE TO MAKE DISCIPLES WHO MAKE DISCIPLES.

As his followers, Jesus has given us a clear mission. Our mission is to make disciples who make disciples. It is that simple. This is what we're called to do both as individuals and as congregations. Jesus is speaking to his disciples in Matthew 28:18 – 20, when we read these familiar words:

> And Jesus came and said to them, "All authority in heaven and on earth has been given to me. Go therefore and make disciples of all nations, baptizing them in the name of the Father and of the Son and of the Holy Spirit, teaching them to observe all that I have commanded you. And behold I am with you always, to the end of the age."

Jesus couldn't be clearer. The mission of the church is to make disciples of all nations, baptizing them and teaching them to obey all that He's commanded. He promises to be our strength and to be with us as we seek to follow his commands. We must replant churches so the lost can be saved and discipled in the way of Jesus, that they might then go and disciple others. Simply put, more joyful, passionate disciples of Jesus will be made as we replant dying congregations.

REASON #4: GOD IS HONORED AS WE STEWARD MONEY, BUILDINGS, AND OTHER RESOURCES.

One of the great blessings of replanting a congregation is the opportunity to steward God-given resources that have been handed down throughout the history of a declining congregation. This is another reason why we need to become more serious about and passionate about replanting. Matt Schmucker is right when he writes:

> Billions of dollars, donated by faithful Christians over many decades, have been invested in land and buildings. Today, those buildings are too often underutilized or even empty—mere monuments to the past. Church planters often shun these resources and don't think twice about pursuing the potentially life-consuming "mobile church" or "church on wheels" approach to ministry.
> Why is this approach so consuming? Ask almost any planter. He'll probably tell you how much effort it takes from his best people in the church to re-set every week, let alone to relocate when a school auditorium or hotel ballroom is lost. So consider moving into an old neighborhood, revitalizing a church, and reclaiming resources that were originally given for gospel purposes.[1]

I think Matt is right on here. The Lord has been honored in the past through faithful Christians who have given generously to church building funds and other physical resources. We're called to be stewards of these generous past gifts as we seek to reach the surrounding community with the love of Christ.

REASON #5: REVITALIZED AND REPLANTED CHURCHES BRING HOPE TO OTHERS.

I hope we would all agree that when we look at the New Testament, we see a constant theme of Christian encouragement. We are to encourage one another. We are to spur one another on, to build one another up. This is true not only as individuals, but also as churches. There is nothing more encouraging to a declining congregation than to see other dying congregations be replanted, transformed and coming back to life.

What a joy it is to visit with many dying churches and to share stories of the new life the Lord has brought to other congregations just like them through replanting. To hear the stories and see pictures and meet the people of those churches helps them to see there is hope! That God is not finished with their church either.

REASON #6: OTHER DECLINING CHURCHES NEED FRESH VISION, IDEAS, AND MINISTRY STRATEGIES

Dying churches receive hope when they see other struggling churches come back to life. But they receive more than just hope. There are also all kinds of practical ideas and ministry strategies that are gained in working with and learning from former declining churches. This is yet another great joy in church replanting—it's not just for the sake of one church getting healthy, but churches helping one another to become healthy again.

The vision we must have as leaders in the Church when it comes to this conversation of replanting is not to see one or two churches become healthy again, but to see an entire *movement* of churches replanted for the glory of God. Many churches that were once close to death, coming back to health and life again. This happens as replanted churches radically cooperate with dying congregations that they might share with them fresh vision, ideas and ministry resources of various kinds. We are in this together.

REASON #7: WE DESIRE THE PRAISE AND GLORY OF GOD'S NAME THROUGHOUT THE EARTH.

This is the ultimate goal, the ultimate end in church replanting because it is the ultimate goal, the ultimate end of all creation. The reason that God's glory must be our ultimate goal is because he *alone* is worthy of glory. God desires to be glorified and he has invited us to joyfully pursue the glory of his name in our lives and ministries. This includes the replanting of churches. There's probably no text in the Bible that reveals the passion that God has for his own glory more than what we see in Isaiah 48:9 – 11. This is where we read the Lord speaking,

> For my name's sake I defer my anger, for the sake of my praise I restrain it for you, that I may not cut you off. Behold, I have refined you, but not as silver; I have tried you in the furnace of affliction. For my own sake, for my own sake, I do it, for how should my name be profaned? My glory I will not give to another.

We're reminded in this text that the Lord has allowed many churches to struggle and go through difficult seasons, ultimately for his glory. But here's the reality: God, in his love, grace, and kindness, brings churches back from near death for his glory too. He desires servants, leaders, followers, and congregations who are humble enough to say, *"Lord, this is all about you! This is not my church, this is Your church. This is the bride of Christ that Jesus died to save. Lord, be glorified in us. Be glorified in this church. For Your glory alone, Lord!"*

Matt Schmucker writes:

> For the sake of God's name being rightly represented in the world, we need to be jealous for the witness of his church. Why? So that God's glory might be spread and magnified. His name is defamed when so-called Christian churches misrepresent him with tolerance of sin, their bad marriage practices, wrong views on sexuality, and a host of heresies from salvation to the authority of Scripture.

I pray against those churches that would defame God's name. I pray they would die or at least be invisible to the neighborhood.

I positively pray for those true churches in my neighborhood that proclaim truth, that rightly gather those who have been born again, and whose ultimate purpose is God's glory. Consider revitalizing for the sake of God's name.[2]

God is about his glory. We must be about his glory as well. Mark Clifton has written extensively on this very topic of replanting churches for the sake of God's fame and God's glory. He writes:

> A dying church robs God of His Glory. The key to revitalization of a church near death is a passion for the Glory of God in all things. This alone must be the beginning and primary motivation for a Legacy replant, even over worthy objectives such as reaching the community, growing the church and meeting

needs. The purpose of all creation is the glory of God. He created everything for His own glory.[3]

As Romans 11:36 proclaims, *"For of him and through him and to him are all things, to whom be glory forever."* Clifton is right— All things are to bring glory to the Lord. This is true in church replanting. We want to see the glory of God spread to the ends of the earth as we see hopeless situations and dying churches redeemed for his fame. We want to see churches come back to life. Even ones that some have looked at and said, "It's all over - No hope there." God has always been in the business of bringing dead things back to life (namely his own Son, Jesus). In the same way, he is in the business of bringing dying churches back to life. His desire is the same in our churches today.

WHY YOUR CHURCH CAN AND SHOULD REPLANT

Ok, so perhaps you are sitting there and you are sold on this idea of church replanting. You get the sad reality that congregations in our country are sick and dying and they need radical help. They need other churches to come alongside them and help them be replanted as new congregations. The question is this: What role are you and your church going to play in this replanting movement? What would it look like for your congregation to replant a dying church? At this point you might be asking yourself, "Is this really possible for a congregation like ours? Can we do this? What if we don't have a ton of money? Isn't this the kind of thing only large churches can pull off?" Your church, regardless of its size and available resources, can and *should* replant a dying church. Let me respond to five common questions and concerns that often come from churches considering replanting.

Question #1: How can we afford to replant a church?

Many churches get intimidated when they begin thinking about how much it could potentially cost to replant a church. Sadly, the fears that arise from these types of discussions often put to death conversation and any real attempts at coming alongside a declining church to help replant it. The reality is that replanting a congregation can be done quite effectively without a huge amount of financial support. Yes of course there are expenses, but a church can get creative with how these resources come together. There is no question that financial partnership with a denomination, other churches, and individuals is incredibly helpful. But even if there is not a great deal of outside financial support, effectively replanting a church can still happen. But how?

The most effective replants are always primarily focused on and passionate *about loving God and loving people*. It is done through the faithful preaching of the Word, intentional pursuit of the lost living in the surrounding community, dependent prayer, and consistent, joyful, grace-fueled shepherding of every single life that enters the doors of that church. Effective replanting is not about smoke machines and laser light shows. It is about biblical ministry. And the truth is this: None of these things take tons of money. They take a heart for God and people, a love for his Word, a white-hot commitment to making disciples, and a lot of Spirit-powered hard work. Any size church can do this.

Question #2: Who would we send from our church to go do this?

We will be talking more about this in Chapter 5, but your church is a perfect environment to raise up and send out a replanter and his family. Your church is a perfect church to send out an entire team to help the replanter revitalize this dying congregation. Remember, replanting is not about big numbers, it is about big faith in a big God and a willingness to go wherever he leads. You may not have a lead replanting pastor at the moment in your congregation, but finding this future replanter may not be as difficult as it seems on the surface. There are several key places to look. Let me offer three.

First of all, seminaries. It would be wise for your church to begin to develop a relationship with local seminaries, or if there is not a seminary near you, seminaries that are affiliated with your denomination or theological tribe. As mentioned before, there are an increasing number of men feeling called to church replanting and revitalization. Many seminary students, once they graduate, may not be ready to jump right away into a full-time ministry position, much less be ready to lead a replant. Often it can be best for these future replanters to spend a year or two in a congregation like yours where they can be further trained and equipped to be ready in time to be sent out.

This is why developing a replanting residency program at your church is so vital.

Second, along with seminaries, it is important to form relationships with other churches and leaders in your area or around the country that are passionate about and committed to church planting and replanting. It is often through connections with these types of churches and leaders that you will come across a replanter that is a good fit for your church. In my experience, it is these relationships that have been the most helpful for finding potential replanters that our congregation can equip, train, and send out.

Third, a great resource for finding potential replanters is leaders within your denomination. Set a meeting with one of your local denominational leaders to share your church's vision of wanting to replant a dying church. Ask them to help you find a potential replanter that could be a good fit serving as an resident at your church. These denominational leaders have many connections and can be very helpful.

Question #3: How will this benefit our congregation?

That is a good question. We should remember that we don't ultimately replant other churches for our benefit, but for the benefit of others and the advancement of God's Kingdom. With that said, there actually *are* benefits to replanting a church out of your congregation.

Helping a dying church will aid in bringing fresh vision and passion to your people. Many of your people are bored—they just are. They won't tell you that, but it's likely true. This isn't just true of folks in your congregation, but in my own congregation, and in almost every other congregation I know of! So what do we do about this? How do we fight boredom in our people? We need to find ways to get congregants out of the bleachers and into the game. Replanting a dying church can create all kinds of excitement and fresh passion for people in your church. It helps them get into the game, use their gifts, and give their lives away for the purposes of God and the advancement of the gospel.

There are so many ways for your people to be actively engaged and involved when replanting a church. Whether it is through prayer, working on updating the building, or encouraging the remaining saints who are there;

when churches like yours come alongside to encourage and replant a dying church, it brings new life, energy, and joy to you, the Sending Church.

Replanter Jeff DeClue has a great analogy for this. He says that many of us have great memories of a family pet, especially a dog. Have you ever noticed when a puppy matures they really get set in their ways? Older dogs get up each day, eat, and find a good shade tree to nap under. Have you ever noticed what happens when you introduce a new puppy into your family? There's a lot of excitement, a lot of jumping around, a lot of playing because puppies are easily excited! They play so hard they trip over themselves but jump right up, ready to keep playing! And these crazy little puppies always find that old dog napping under the tree and try desperately to get him to come play. The puppy jumps over the dog, nips at its ears, and harasses that old dog until he jumps up and chases the puppy away. After a few annoyed, frustrated chases around the yard, the old dog begins to realize just how fun this playing feels. Before long, years have been shed off the dog and he soon is playing like a puppy again.

Sadly, the majority of our churches in America have settled into routines like that old dog. Church replants are much like the young puppies—they run hard into the community, make mistakes and trip at times, but are radically spreading the gospel in unique and exciting new ways. In our church, we have found that introducing partner churches of any age alongside a church replant brings energy and passion to that church. They remember how great it feels living on mission in their community. The volunteer teams that come help a church replant return to their home church taking with them new-found zeal. This very same thing can happen in your church when you replant another congregation.

Question #4: What if we've never done anything like this before?

Perhaps your church has never done anything quite this big before, but there is always a first time for everything, right? Does your church desire to be part of the mission of God on this earth to make disciples of all nations? Does your church desire to walk by faith and trust God in radical ways? Does your church long to be part of something that will make a difference in the lives of many for generations to come? I can't think of a greater next step for your church than to take a leap of faith and help replant a church. Many congregations live in that place of talking about trusting God and maybe one day taking a risk for God. But the truth is, that "someday" never comes. Now is the time. The need is greater than ever. Will your church go? That is the question.

Question #5: Isn't it better to just plant a new church instead?

There is no question that we need to be planting more and more churches throughout the world. We need to raise up and send out more and more faithful, Jesus-loving, people-shepherding, Bible-preaching, disciple-making church planters throughout North America and to the ends of the earth. However, at the same time, we must begin replanting dying churches as well. As I've said before, this is not an either/or, but rather, a both/and. We need to both plant and replant churches. If we are going to push the darkness back in our cities, we must not only begin new churches, but passionately pursue the redemption and revitalization of dying churches also. It is not a win for the community if one church is planted, while two other churches die. Yet that's what is happening in many parts of our country and world. We must plant and replant churches both. While I praise God for churches that are sending out church planters, we also need churches that are willing to raise up and send out church replanters and revitalizers.

WHAT IS GOD CALLING YOU TO DO?

My loving challenge is that your church will begin to prayerfully consider what it would look like to be a replanting church. Perhaps your church is better suited to send out and plant a new church than to come alongside a dying church that needs to be replanted. Praise God if that is the case! Do it! However, maybe you are one of the churches that is better suited to help revitalize and replant a dying congregation, simply given your history, resources, and demographics. We need churches that are committed to this ministry as well. What is God calling you to do? What role will your church play?

FOR FURTHER REFLECTION

Discussion Questions

1. How many of us have made New Year's resolutions to get healthy? How many of us actually became healthy? Why or why not? Many churches say they want to get healthy, but they don't want to do the things needed to move in a healthy direction. Why do you think that is?

2. What does it look like to live life alive and on mission? What difference does it make if outsiders/non-believers see this in a church or not?

3. Throughout history, the gospel has been spread through disciples who are making disciples. Who was one person that God used to make a big difference in your spiritual growth? How do you create this kind of disciple-reproducing culture in a church?

4. In the cycle of church replanting, the vision is for a church to go from dying to becoming healthy to being able to be a church that replants others. How does a church stay healthy during the replanting process so that it can continue to have the resources to replant?

Ways to Pray

- Pray for your church body to be a testimony as to why you should replant churches.

- Pray for God to provide people & resources so that your church can begin replanting soon and continue at a healthy pace.

Chapter 3

UNDERSTANDING GOD'S HEART FOR REPLANTING

God does his best work when things seem hopeless. He always has. This is true when it comes to working in the lives of individuals, and it is also true when it comes to working in the lives of dying churches. God's heart is *for* his church, *including* churches that are dying. When considering the topic of God's heart for replanting, there are four biblical convictions that are critical for us to hold. If these are not believed at the very core, I would question whether you are truly on board with the work of church replanting.

CONVICTION #1: GOD DESIRES TO SEE DYING AND DECLINING CHURCHES COME BACK TO LIFE FOR HIS GLORY.

If you don't believe this, replanting is not for you. But my guess is if you have read this far, you already believe this. Without a doubt, God desires to see dying and declining churches come back to life. One of the many things I love about God and Scripture is that it is so clear that in our weakness, he is strong. He's always looking for humble servants that he can use for his purposes and to bring glory to himself. We must become less so that he might become more. Here's the thing about the Lord: unlike our fallen world, he uses and loves underdogs! Everywhere in the Scriptures, whether you're talking David and Goliath, or Jesus' disciples, or the Apostle Paul, the Lord always goes after and uses the "wrong" people. He chooses players on his team that you and I would never choose. He chooses the weak, the foolish, the uncool, and uses them in mighty ways.

This is the heart of God. This is the heart of God for individuals and for churches. God loves underdog churches. He loves it when the world is saying, "That church is dead and done. That church just needs to shut the doors." That's when God says, "You watch. I'm ready to do my best work right here, right now." The Lord is like that, and He's always been that way. Let's praise him for it!

In 2 Corinthians, chapter 12, verses 9-10, the Apostle Paul writes this:

> But he said to me, "My grace is sufficient for you, for my power is made perfect in weakness." Therefore, I will boast all the more gladly of my weaknesses, so that the power of Christ may rest upon me. For the sake of Christ, then, I am content with weaknesses, insults, hardships, persecutions, and calamities. For when I am weak, then I am strong.

This is key to every one of us as believers and leaders in Christ's Church—that when we are weak, we are strong in the Lord. It's true as churches and congregations, as well. When a church recognizes it's weakness and brokenness, it is then in a place of humility where the Lord does his best work. It is in that place that God does the impossible. It is in that place that God makes a church strong again and brings it back to life for his glory.

Years ago, I came across a powerful quote from the great Baptist preacher Charles Spurgeon that I come back to often. Concerning weakness and humility in ministry, Spurgeon writes,

> A primary qualification for serving God with any amount of success, and for doing God's work well and triumphantly, is a sense of our own weakness. When God's warrior marches forth to battle, strong in his own might, when he boasts, "I know that I shall conquer, my own right arm and my conquering sword shall get unto me the victory," defeat is not far distant. God will not go forth with that man who marches in his own strength. He who reckoneth on victory thus has reckoned wrongly, for "it is not by might, nor by power, but by my Spirit, saith the Lord of hosts." They who go forth to fight, boasting of their prowess, shall return with their banners trailed in the dust, and their armour stained with disgrace.[1]

What a great, yet convicting image. How often we seek to go forth in battle by our own strength. What foolishness! What pride! Spurgeon goes on,

> Those who serve God must serve Him in His own way, and in His strength, or He will never accept their service. That which man doth, unaided by divine strength, God can never own. The mere fruits of the earth He casteth away; He will only reap that corn, the seed of which was sown from heaven, watered by grace, and ripened by the sun of divine love. God will empty out all that thou hast before He will put His own into thee; He will first clean out thy granaries before He will fill them with the finest of the wheat.[2]

In other words, until we recognize our emptiness and weakness, he can't fill us with the power of his Spirit. And if you're like me, I not only want, but know I need, his power. I need his power more than anything in my life and ministry.

And then listen to Spurgeon's final words of hope and encouragement:

> The river of God is full of water; but not one drop of it flows from earthly springs. God will have no strength used in His battles but the strength which He Himself imparts.
>
>   Are you mourning over your own weakness? Take courage, for there must be a consciousness of weakness before the Lord will give thee victory. Your emptiness is but the preparation for your being filled, and your casting down is but the making ready for your lifting up.[3]

Such wise and truth-filled words for each of us. Let me offer two simple but important points of application, the first being personal for each of us. As pastors and church leaders, we must understand and embrace this truth: Until we empty ourselves, humbling ourselves before the Lord, he will not do what he wants to do in us and through us. The Lord doesn't need us—he doesn't need anything. But, it is his delight to use us and invite us into his work of ministry and mission in the world.

A second application is for dying and declining churches. Until a congregation humbles itself, and recognizes its need, this church should not expect the Lord to pour out his Spirit and bring dead bones back to life. He is looking for a humble and dependent people who seek to make a big deal about him as they joyfully submit to his Word and his Will. Remember, both in our personal lives and in our churches, God loves to give strength to the needy. To those who are desperate for him. Will we be those kinds of people? Those kinds of churches?

In John 7:37 – 39, Jesus says this:

> On the last day of the feast, the great day, Jesus stood up and cried out, "If anyone thirsts, let him come to me and drink. Whoever believes in me, as the Scripture has said, 'Out of his heart will flow rivers of living water.'" Now this he said about the Spirit, whom those who believed in him were to receive, for as yet the Spirit had not been given, because Jesus was not yet glorified.

Jesus is pointing to the indwelling power of the Holy Spirit we need as individuals, leaders, and churches. I often pray that the church I serve will be filled with the Holy Spirit of God and that many would be saved by the Spirit. That marriages would be restored. That children, at a young age, would come to a saving faith in Christ. This is what I desire to see in our church, and the Spirit of God desires to see this far more than I do. He always has. But it begins with us, as his people, humbling ourselves in faith, asking and believing that the Lord can do these things according to his perfect will. It begins with each of us on our knees, praying with David in Psalm 51:10–12: "Create in me a clean heart, O God, and renew a right spirit within me. Cast me not away from your presence, and take not your Holy Spirit from me. Restore to me the joy of your salvation, and uphold me with a willing spirit."

May this prayer be the cry of our hearts as individuals and as churches. The hard truth is this: Any church that cannot pray the prayer, "Oh God create in us a clean heart, renew us, revive us, humble us" is too prideful, too proud, too hard-hearted. If they can't pray that prayer, that church should not expect God to do miraculous things and bring that church back to life. Our posture must always be one of humility before the Lord.

CONVICTION #2: GOD NOT ONLY HAS THE DESIRE, BUT THE POWER TO BRING DYING AND DECLINING CHURCHES BACK TO LIFE FOR HIS GLORY.

I hope you believe this. When it comes to replanting dying churches, God isn't sitting there wringing his hands and saying, "Oh boy, I sure wish that kind of thing could happen, but I really don't have the power to do anything about it." No, the Lord is the all-powerful, sovereign King of the universe. He not only has the desire but also the power to bring anything that is dead back to life, including a local church.

Ezekiel 37 is a great picture of the Lord bringing something dead back to life. At this point, both Jerusalem and the temple have been destroyed. Judgment has come. But God reveals himself in this passage as a God of revitalization; as a God of resurrection.

In Ezekiel 37:1-6 we read this,

> The hand of the LORD was upon me, and he brought me out in the Spirit of the LORD and set me down in the middle of the valley; it was full of bones. And he led me around among them, and behold, there were very many on the surface of the valley, and behold, they were very dry. And he said to me, "Son of man, can these bones live?" And I answered, "O Lord GOD, you know." Then he said to me, "Prophesy over these bones, and say to them, O dry bones, hear the word of the LORD. Thus says the Lord GOD to these bones: Behold, I will cause breath to enter you, and you shall live. And I will lay sinews upon you, and will cause flesh to come upon you, and cover you with skin, and put breath in you, and you shall live, and you shall know that I am the LORD."

Only our God can do something as powerful and miraculous as bringing dead, dry bones back to life. He does this very thing with us as individuals and he does it with churches. There are two things that I want to point out from this passage, two essential ingredients for revitalization in the church that I think we see in this passage. The first one is this:

Ingredient#1: Faithful Preaching of God's Word

In his excellent book *Can These Dry Bones Live?*, Bill Henard writes,

> The first requirement necessitates the preaching of God's Word. God tells Ezekiel, "Prophesy concerning those bones" (37:4). As Ezekiel obeys, the Scripture unveils this magnificent vision of bones taking on tendons and flesh. Note carefully that the bones described are dry bones. These soldiers who died in battle were not afforded the privilege of a proper burial. They experienced the great disgrace of open decay. Yet God intervenes, and Ezekiel speaks to the bones.[4]

What an image as we think about church replanting and revitalization. The preaching of God's Word has the power to bring dry bones, souls, and churches back to life. It is living and active as we preach, counsel with and share the Word with folks over coffee and meals. The Word of God brings dry, dead bones back to life.

Ingredient #2: The Presence and Power of the Holy Spirit

The second ingredient for revitalization that we see here in this passage is the presence and power of God's Spirit. Again Henard writes,

> In order for the church to be revived, (to be revitalized, to experience new life, new health, new growth) it will demand a mighty work of God's Spirit. Following a particular methodology or program does not guarantee success. One might greatly desire for the church to revitalize and grow, but genuine church growth calls for more than personal passion. It requires the Spirit of God.[5]

That is the truth. We can read all the books we want. We can come up with the most dynamic, exciting, fresh, and compelling strategies the world of church revitalization and church replanting has ever seen, but without the Spirit of God moving, dead bones don't come back to life. They just don't. Church revitalization and replanting begins with laying the foundation of God's Word as it is preached and the congregation empowered by a profound movement of God's Spirit.

CONVICTION #3: TRUE CHURCH REVITALIZATION WILL NOT HAPPEN UNLESS A CONGREGATION RETURNS TO THEIR FIRST LOVE: JESUS.

Dry bones won't come back to life and churches won't be revitalized unless a church returns to its first love, which is Jesus Christ. In Revelation 2:1-5, we read words that perhaps many of us in the church are familiar with. In this passage, the Lord is speaking to the church at Ephesus:

> To the angel of the church in Ephesus write: "The words of him who holds the seven stars in his right hand, who walks among the seven golden lampstands. 'I know your works, your toil and your patient endurance, and how you cannot bear with those who are evil, but have tested those who call themselves apostles and are not, and found them to be false. I know you are enduring patiently and bearing up for my name's sake, and you have not grown weary.'"

This is a great church! This is a church that is steady and faithful. This is a church that has endured much, all the while remaining steadfast in the Lord. This is a congregation that is rock solid when it comes to understanding sound doctrine. This is a church that loves the Bible. There is much to be commended in this church. But notice what Jesus says next, in verses 4 and 5,

> But I have this against you, that you have abandoned the love you had at first. Remember therefore from where you have fallen; repent, and do the works you did at first. If not, I will come to you and remove your lampstand from its place, unless you repent.

The picture here is of a church that has its doctrine right, its missions giving is probably greater than any other in its local church association, it's doing all kinds of things right, and yet when Jesus looks at the heart of this church, he sees a people that are no longer in love with him. They may say they are, but they aren't really. Their passion for Christ has dwindled. There's no zeal for the things of God. The study of God's Word has become simply an academic exercise. The Word is no longer setting the heart of this church on fire for evangelism and missions. Its head perhaps, but not its heart. And so the Lord says, "If you don't return to your first love, if you don't do those things you did at first when you had a simple, childlike faith in me and love for me, unless you repent and turn back to me, I'm going to take your lampstand away."

Mark Clifton says that in this passage, the Lord makes it clear that the pathway to new life for a dying church is repentance and remembering. Those are two key words for any church that wants to be revitalized—repent and remember. But Clifton clarifies what this type of remembering means exactly:

> …not the self-serving nostalgia of remembering the past for the sake of our own edification through control and a desire to return to a "better time", but remembering the legacy of missions and ministry that first birthed this dying church and a brokenness to see that return once again. This kind of remembering can only happen if repentance comes first. This kind of remembering can only happen when the Glory of God becomes primary rather than the glory of the past.[6]

There's one main reason why a church dies— because it loses it's first love. It is when we lose our first love that we begin to lose everything. We lose our love for the truth. We lose our love for the lost. We lose everything. When we lose our love for the Lord and the things of the Lord, we increase our love for self and our own "kingdom" rather than God's. And so we must beg God in all humility, "Oh Lord, change our hearts. Turn our hearts back toward you, that you would be the love and passion of our lives. Lord, may you be our greatest treasure in this life and forevermore!"

CONVICTION #4: WHEN A CHURCH RETURNS TO ITS FIRST LOVE, JESUS, GOD BEGINS TO BRING ABOUT REVITALIZATION THROUGH THREE TYPES OF RENEWAL.

When a church comes to the point of genuine humility, returning to Jesus and the gospel as its first love, then and only then does God begin to bring about true renewal and revitalization. He does this through three types of renewal.[7]

Type #1: Personal Renewal

When a dying congregation's leaders experience personal renewal, true congregational renewal begins. This starts with the heart of the leaders. Personal renewal means that leaders in the church recognize the need for more of the Holy Spirit. These leaders begin to grow in humility, love for people, and love for the lost. As leaders we cannot take people where we've never been. We cannot give what we do not have. This is why congregational renewal begins with personal renewal. And this is why our love for the Lord and his Word must be primary.

Type #2: Relational Renewal

In a church where leaders begin to experience personal renewal, relational renewal should naturally begin to follow. Relational renewal means that leaders are not only right with God, but now they are getting right with others. The leaders in a congregation are doing all they can to pursue peace, unity, and harmony with others in the congregation. Reconciliation marked by genuine kindness and love for other brothers and sisters in Christ should be a top priority. Rick Warren says this,

> When you have relational renewal in your church, the gossip goes down and the joy goes up. How do you know when a church has been through relational renewal? People hang around longer after the service. They want to spend time together. If people don't want to hang around after your services, you have a performance, not a church. The church is more than content; it's a community.[8]

Type #3: Missional Renewal

As leaders grow in their love for God and he begins to renew their hearts, it spreads out to others and results in relational renewal. This then begins to lead a congregation outside the walls of the church on mission. It's inevitable—if the Spirit of God renews us the Spirit of God is going to align our desires with God's desires; namely, living life on mission, seeking to reach those in the community with the good news of the gospel.

This type of missional renewal is seen not only in the leadership, but will spread through the congregation as individuals and families grow in their passion and conviction to make disciples of Jesus. When missional renewal begins to happen, a church begins to both believe they need to reach the lost and are willing to do whatever it takes to do it. It is when a church begins to experience this third type of renewal that God begins to do incredible things in a dying church. This is when replanting gets really fun! Seeing a church get back on mission, focusing no longer on itself and its survival but on the lost and the surrounding community that deeply needs Jesus. This is God's desire for dying churches. This is God's heart for replanting and revitalization.

GOD LOVES HIS CHURCH.

God loves his church. He loves his people. He loves to bring dead bones back to life. In this way, his heart is to breathe new life into dying congregations for the salvation of the lost, the joy of his people, and for the spread of his fame throughout the earth. From the world's perspective, there seems to be little hope for dying churches. However, when we see the heart of God in his

Word, we have much reason for hope. Hope that God will do what only he can do: breathe new life into the dry, dusty bones of churches all over the world for his glory.

FOR FURTHER REFLECTION

Discussion Questions

1. Read 2 Corinthians 12:9-10. Why do you think that God often seems to work more in the weak places in our lives and with the seemingly hopeless situations?

2. Until we recognize our weakness and our need to rely on God's strength, he can't fill us with his Spirit and his power. How do we help churches to name reality and become more aware of their weakness & lack of power in a way that leads to greater surrender to God?

3. What are the types of renewal that God brings about? How do they interact with each other?

Ways to Pray

- Pray for God to renew your love & devotion to him.
- Pray for God to keep himself first in both your church and the dying church.
- Pray for God to help the dying churches you serve to face reality & admit their weakness as a church.
- Pray for God to do what only he can do in the dying church.

Chapter 4

STEP#1: COUNTING THE COST & THE JOY

"There is a cost to this, boys!"

I remember these words from one of my basketball coaches when I was younger. "If you boys wanna be great basketball players. If you wanna be a great team. If you wanna win a bunch of games. If you wanna be champions, there is a cost to this, boys! *There is a cost to this!*"

Of course, my coach was right. To have success on the basketball court, as with every other area of life, it takes blood, sweat, and tears. It doesn't just happen, it takes effort, hard work, and discipline. Because of this, we always need to count the cost of anything we do: physically, spiritually, mentally, and emotionally.

When we consider all that goes into replanting a dying congregation, we have to be honest about the real challenges that will potentially come our way. As with other areas of life and ministry, Jesus calls us to count the cost.

In Luke 14:27–33, we see Jesus laying out the cost of following him, the cost of being his disciple. He says,

> Whoever does not bear his own cross and come after me cannot be my disciple. For which of you desiring to build a tower does not first sit down and count the cost whether he has enough to complete it. Otherwise when he has laid a foundation and is not able to finish all who see it begin to mock him, saying 'This man began to build and was not able to finish.' Or what king going out to encounter another king in war will not sit down first and deliberate whether he is able with 10,000 to meet him who comes against him with 20,000. And if not, while the other is yet a great far away off, he sends a delegation and asks

for terms of peace. So therefore any one of you who does not renounce all that he has cannot be my disciple.

Jesus is giving us pictures of building a tower or going to war as illustrations of the wisdom that comes through counting the cost. Specifically, he is talking about counting the cost of being his disciple. This passage is relevant not only of counting the cost in following Jesus, but in counting the cost of church replanting. Jesus is asking us if we are up for the challenges that come in helping to lead a dying or declining church back to life.

We must also be honest about the real opportunities that potentially lie ahead in replanting as well—there is great joy that comes in replanting a church! There are few things more exciting than being part of a congregation that was dying and seeing the Holy Spirit bring that church back to life. In this chapter, I want us to consider several real challenges and real opportunities that lie ahead as we consider the cost and joy of church replanting.

THERE ARE REAL CHALLENGES IN REPLANTING

Let's begin by considering several potential challenges as we begin to count the cost of church replanting.

Challenge#1: The Time-Consuming Nature of Changing Culture

One of the most exciting things for many church planters is the opportunity to help create and shape a culture from scratch. In church planting, you're creating a culture that values certain things, is passionate about certain things, has a certain way of doing things from the beginning. You're creating culture.

In replanting, you're not creating culture as much as *changing* culture. You are trying to create change in the midst of an existing culture that is not as healthy as it once was. This is a distinct difference between church planting and church replanting. The primary challenge in changing culture versus creating culture is simply this: It takes more time. It takes time to love people well enough that they trust you. It takes time to display Christ-like patience with changes you would like to make but the church isn't ready yet to make. In this regard, effective church replanting is much more like a marathon than a sprint. Changing culture is a long haul, steady run. It is a constant abiding in Jesus, loving the people of God, living on mission, preaching the Word, serving the community, praying hard for the flock and the lost, over and over again. These are means God uses to bring declining churches back to life, but it all takes time.

Challenge #2: Hidden Sacred Cows

Every existing church has sacred cows—it's just the truth. A sacred cow is an idea, custom, or tradition that is almost immune from questioning in a church, often unreasonably so. Sacred cows in churches are often above critique or criticism of any kind. More often than not, dying churches have multiple sacred cows that can be like land mines—you usually don't know that they're even there until you've already stepped on it, potentially bringing major damage to your leadership and reputation. It may be changing the music style, or putting up new artwork on the walls. It could be replacing the pews with chairs, or beginning to project song lyrics onto a screen rather than using a hymnal. Whatever it might be, stepping on these land mines can hurt the trust you're trying to build with the congregation.

So, let's not be foolish and assume there are not sacred cows in churches we are seeking to replant – there are many sacred cows. We want to be wise. When we go into a replanting context, we need to ask a lot of questions and do even more listening. Before we make changes or choose to die on a particular hill, we must lead with much wisdom and discernment.

What we are talking about here is *tactical* patience. You want to be wise and lead well. You want to shepherd well. Folks need to feel loved, and how they're going to feel loved many times is by simply being asked questions and listened to. This kind of tactical patience will help you not only recognize the hidden sacred cows that are there, but to know how to rightly lead through them or around them in a faithful, Christ-like manner.

Mark Clifton is correct when he writes,

> Dying churches tend to make their preferences paramount. Those preferences can include music, programs, preaching styles, uses of the building, resources shared with those outside the church compared to resources used for those

within the church and a host of other things. The point is this: Most members of the congregation focus on their own desires in these decisions instead of what would meet the needs of people who don't know Jesus.[1]

For every one of us, this is our tendency over time—to take our eyes off meeting the needs of *others* and to be more concerned about the needs of *ourselves*. When seeking to replant a dying church, there's an existing culture that's been created over many years, which most likely has a heavy inward focus. Sacred cows are often the fruit of this kind of heavy inward focus. It is a very real challenge we must wisely and graciously lead through in church replanting.

Challenge #3: The Sin-Laden Roots of Decline

When you look at a church that is healthy and growing and vibrant, there's a reason why it is. It's actually not a single reason, there are many reasons. Likewise, when you see a church that is on its deathbed, there are many reasons why. Often at the root of a church's decline, there is sin of one kind or another.

Every church that claims to love Jesus, love the gospel, love the Word, and love the lost, will say that they want to grow. Every church will say that they want to reach young people, children, young families, and those far from Jesus. Even dying churches will say this. The question is, in the heart of hearts of many folks in that congregation, do they really want this? Do they really want to do whatever it takes to make disciples of Christ? The hard truth is that all too often few are really willing to put preferences aside and do what it takes.

This is something we need to name as a reality. Many churches are unwilling to put preferences aside for the sake of the broken, hurting, and lost. In my experience working with dying churches, many congregations can say the right things in terms of wanting to be revitalized, wanting a fresh start to reach the lost. But when the rubber hits the road, there are often key leaders in these churches who say, "I don't actually want that. I want to reach people without having to make the changes you are talking about. If replanting means our church has to change (this or that), then we're not in."

There are always reasons a church is dying, often pertaining to individual and/or systemic sin in the congregation. Mike McKinley says this:

There's usually a good reason why a church needs to be revitalized. Churches often dwindle in size and effectiveness because of a traumatic event or years of poor leadership. As a result, church facilities and programs may be in ruins—not to mention the spiritual state of the congregation itself. In these cases, there will be much to overcome and tear down in order to move the church forward. This process is often very painful. If a church was already inclined to do the things that healthy churches do, it probably wouldn't be dying. Finding a struggling church isn't a problem. Finding a struggling church that wants to change and grow is much more difficult.[2]

Challenge #4: Warming their Love for their Community

This can be a major challenge in replanting. Helping the folks who have been a part of this church for many years fall in love with the surrounding, changing community. Many churches in need of replanting have become non-factors in their community. The reason for this is that over the years the members have taken great care and pride in the physical building, without caring just as much for the community in which the building finds itself. The building becomes an idol, which then lends itself to an inward or misguided focus. A fancy building, contrary to popular belief, will not tell the community that they are "here to stay" – a full parking lot each week and happy neighbors will tell that story. The building is a great tool – praise God! But the community doesn't care about the building. The community cares about the love that those inside that building are expressing. Whether due to fear, laziness, apathy, or lack of intentional strategy, these churches are not shining as brightly as they could for Christ and the gospel in their community.

This is one of the greatest leadership challenges in replanting—helping a dying congregation fall in love again with the surrounding community in such a way that their hearts begin to break for those who do not know Jesus.

Challenge #5: A Lack of Spiritual Health and Vibrancy

While some in the congregation may be healthy and growing in their walk with the Lord, this typically will not be the norm in declining churches. Many are stagnant. Many are dry. Many have become discouraged and it isn't necessarily their fault. It's the fact that they have not been under good shepherding. It's very likely that they have not been pastored well for a long time. They haven't eaten good spiritual food from the Word of God. As a result, they are tired and they are hungry. They need to be encouraged. They need to be fed.

But this is a challenge in replanting. You're not walking into a situation where folks are spiritually alive and fired up, ready to go live on mission. You've got folks who are tired and beat up and worn out. They need a lot of care and love. They need prayer and good food from the Word. This must be a top priority when coming into a replanting context.

Challenge #6: Shallow Growth Strategies

It is very common for a declining church to believe that all they need to do to get healthy and begin growing again is a new cutting edge program, or a new dynamic pastor, or a new magnetic youth pastor (preferably married). The mindset is this: "If we can just get that program, pastor, or youth pastor in here, we will start reaching young families again. Everything will surely get turned around!" Of course, that's not true. It's not true at all. Young families won't save a church – only Jesus. One leader cannot turn a declining church around. One program cannot do it. There's no magic bullet in church revitalization. Because of this, there often is an overabundance of purposeless programs and activities that have been tried throughout the years. Mark Clifton writes:

> Declining churches reach for programs and personalities they believe will turn the church around without embracing the changes needed to become healthy again. And it's hard to blame them for this predisposition since many past church-growth methodologies relied heavily on both. No doubt, as a dying church reflects on its heyday of growth, they recall a particular pastor or two who, by sheer force of personal charisma and leadership, moved the church to a new level. Or they recall a program or series of programs that once attracted all ages of people to become involved in the life of the church. With that history in mind, dying churches often think that applying programs and hiring personalities will be easy fixes to their problems. They quickly discover that neither fixes anything. In fact, their desire for a "silver bullet" program or personality reinforces their belief that they don't have to make major changes or repent of past mistakes or sacrifice their preferences for the needs of the unchurched, but they just have to add one more program or hire one more professional to fix the problem. In essence they are still trying to use primarily attractional methods in a community that no longer responds to those methods. It is frustrating and confusing for a dying church to accept that what worked so well in the past may in fact be hastening its demise.[3]

As painful as it might be to hear, Clifton is spot on. This magic bullet mindset of the program or personality is something we need to be aware of as we consider the leadership challenges that await us in replanting.

Challenge #7: A Large, Unmanaged Membership Roll

One mark of a healthy, growing church is that it has more visitors and attenders showing up weekly to Sunday morning worship than it does church members. There are many reasons why this is true. It communicates a lot of things. For instance, it communicates that there's a standard for membership. That church membership matters. That there are expectations for membership. That the folks that are members of this congregation are committed, they're devoted, they're all in.

In a healthy church, some of these regular visitors and attenders checking out the church may choose to pursue membership, while others may not. They realize that membership means something and there is real expectation and accountability involved. This is a good, healthy thing for a congregation. On the other hand, one of the marks of an unhealthy church is that the reverse happens—there are far more members of the congregation than there are visitors and attenders showing up in worship. It's not uncommon for churches to have three or four hundred members on the books while at the same time they only have thirty to forty in worship on a typical Sunday. This clearly is not healthy. But what should be done about it?

Simply put, what this means is that the membership rolls need to be cleaned up. There needs to be an honest evaluation considering what membership really means in this church. What are we expecting of our members? Is it clear to everyone what these expectations are? Are they following through on these expectations? How do we know? What are the distinctions between a member and a regular attender? Is this clear? Questions like these are especially important in churches where congregational members are actively involved in matters of decision making and voting. The church makes sure that members have skin in the game. A healthy church will ensure that those who have voting privileges are actively engaged in church ministry and are on board with the vision and direction of the congregation.

It is all too common to hear horror stories of churches where a major vote needs to happen to bring on a new staff member or adjust the budget only to be held hostage by "members" who are completely disengaged from the ministry and fellowship of the congregation. While there are a small, but potent number of active members in regular worship and other church activities and programs, at that congregational meeting, thirty to forty others, members who haven't been there perhaps in years, show up and sway the vote, sadly hindering the mission of that church. For this scenario, and so many like it, updating the membership rolls is absolutely critical. For an example of how to update membership rolls in an effective manner, see **Appendix J**—"How to Develop a New Church Membership Process."

REAL OPPORTUNITIES IN CHURCH REPLANTING

We have considered several potential challenges that must be considered when counting the cost of church replanting. Let's now consider some of the potential advantages and unique opportunities that await when replanting. Each of these are catalysts for great joy in this important ministry.

Opportunity #1: Exchanging a Negative Witness with a Positive One

Healthy, biblical church replanting establishes a new and fresh gospel presence in a community, while at the same time removing a bad (or at least less positive) witness. If healthy churches make a positive statement about the gospel to the surrounding community (and they do), dying churches send a negative one. What does it say to a community when a church dies? It says that this Jesus stuff, "Eh, I could take it or leave it. I mean, where's the power in this Jesus, in this gospel that they proclaim? They can't even keep their doors open."

The thought of this burdens me like no other. I hope it burdens you as well. On the flipside of this, when a community sees a dying church come back to life, that watching community sees a fresh, real, dynamic witness for Jesus where formally there was an anti-witness.

Here's what we know: Wherever that declining church is located, it is surrounded by a community filled with people who don't know Jesus. I don't care if you're talking California or Texas or Alabama or New York or

Colorado or Swaziland! Wherever that church is, I promise you, it is surrounded by people that don't know Jesus and are in desperate need of the gospel.

This is a huge opportunity that comes with church replanting. We get to see God do what only he can do: Bring a dying church back to life for his glory as the lost are saved through the person and work of Jesus Christ. In doing this, the Lord exchanges a negative church witness with a positive one in a community. The fame of Jesus spreads as a result.

Opportunity #2: A Building

You have a building! This is a huge plus in most cases for replanters. Talk to any church planter and they will share the challenges that come with not only finding a church building, but *funding* a church building. The primary reason many churches are in financial debt is due to the cost of a building. This is something you typically do not have to worry about in replanting. Moreover, when you have your own building, you can do all kinds of creative ministry. Many church planters have shared with me the ongoing challenges of having to set up and take down chairs and tables and signs week in and week out in their auditorium or school meeting area. Church planters know all too well how tiresome it can be on staff and volunteers to not have a permanent location where the space is their own.

In replanting a church, typically you've got a building. Let that sink in: You have a building! That's a really big deal. You can use that building for all kinds of purposes beyond just Sunday morning. That building can be a tool for outreach of various kinds, to kids and youth, to the homeless, to the community at large. There can be Bible studies, community groups, after school clubs. You have a building! Having a building allows a church to make a huge statement to a community that says, "We are here. We love this community. We love Jesus. We want to help and serve in his name! This building is the Lord's to be used to bless the people of this community!" There's nothing like a congregation being embedded in a particular community for the sake of the gospel. A building helps a church do this well for the long haul.

Opportunity #3: Older Christians

In a replanting context, a dying church has most likely had a very difficult time reaching younger people and younger families. What you usually find in these congregations are older saints who have been faithful for a long time, holding things together for a long time. Some might see this as a negative. I believe it is a major plus. The Church is at its healthiest when it is inter-generational. This is true and biblical. The presence of older Christians is a huge ingredient to a truly healthy, vibrant, biblical congregation. Let me share three gifts that older Christians bring to a church replant:

Maturity and Experience. They have maturity and experience in life and in following Jesus that younger people simply don't have. With that maturity and experience comes wisdom that younger folks desperately need. I get so excited when I see churches that have a vision for this, of combining and connecting older generations with the younger for the sake of mutual edification and encouragement.

Time & Availability. Younger people, younger couples, younger families are busy as can be. They just are. They're going a million miles an hour with school, sports, and all kinds of other activities and commitments. Many older saints have time and availability. Many are retired and their kids have been out of the house for a long, long time. As a result, they can serve in various ways younger people simply cannot. They have time to give and the whole congregation is blessed by them as a result.

Skills, Gifts & Passions. Older folks have skills, gifts, and passions given to them by the Lord. But sadly, so many times these individuals are underutilized and underdeveloped in our churches. Encouraging and equipping our older saints to lean into these gifts is a beautiful thing. It is a God glorifying thing. We have an opportunity through church replanting to engage and unleash older generations during their last, precious years of life. To help them finish their race strong, helping them to serve the Lord faithfully and to reach others with the gospel to the very end. What a joy this is!

Opportunity #4: Resources, Resources, Resources

Another huge plus of replanting is the resources that are often available with the existing, declining church. As Justin Deeter writes,

> The amount of resources in established churches are astounding. The amount of financial assets, facilities, and people are overwhelming. The reason most of these churches have started declining is not because they lack resources, but because they lack vision. These established churches have the resources to do incredible things for God and his mission, the problem is they may need to be reprioritized.[4]

Churches that are declining typically have resources. Even if the resources are limited, they still have something that can be used for gospel ministry. If a church has a building but doesn't have much in the way of money in the bank, that's a win. They have a building! Again, as you think about the advantages of replanting, the availability of resources for the sake of ministry is simply not a reality with most other ministry opportunities. This is a huge plus. As Mike McKinley pointedly and accurately describes this reality, he writes,

> Many dead churches are sitting on a treasure trove of resources (land, money, equipment) that can be leveraged for the spread of the gospel. Those resources are just sitting around idle, doing almost nothing for the kingdom. As a matter of good stewardship, evangelical churches interested in planting should consider revitalizing as well. And let's be honest, if we don't revitalize these churches, they will most likely fall into the hands of liberal churches, mosques, or condominium developers.[5]

Opportunity #5: A System for Financial and Legal Management

While some of their systems are probably not working great, most churches have at least *some* working systems already in place. There are most likely individuals in the congregation who take care of managing the finances as well as other administrative nuts and bolts—logistical, administrative, and legal responsibilities that are needed to keep a church going. This can potentially be hugely helpful in a replant.

Opportunity #6: History and Tradition

Some view the history and tradition of a church as solely a bad thing. And while this can be a potential negative in certain contexts, I believe it to be much more of a positive in most cases. I was with a group of pastors and denominational leaders not long ago, and as we were talking about some of the challenges involved in replanting, one of the men who was there piped up and gave a fairly brutal indictment against the whole idea of church replanting and revitalization. He looked at the group and said, "I don't get it. I really don't. This replanting thing is just crazy. I don't know how anybody could do that. It seems like a suicide mission." He went on, "You know replanting sounds to me like trying to plant a church but with a whole bunch of baggage that you've got to deal with. Why would anyone choose to do that?" He was very sincere in asking this question. He could not fathom why anyone would want to pursue a ministry like this. At that moment, a young man pursuing replanting ministry who was there, corrected this church leader and his flawed perspective. He looked at him and said, "Baggage is not what you are dealing with in replanting. *History* is what you're dealing with. A very precious history where God has been at work in major ways through the life of this congregation." What this young replanter understood is that when you have a pastor's heart and you love people well and understand that God has been at work in a declining church for many years, one begins to lean in and see the beauty of the history and the tradition of a congregation. This church has a history and tradition where God has been and still is at work. This is a history that, by God's grace, we have been invited into. It is a sacred privilege to step into this story the Lord has been writing for many years.

One of the positive things about the history and tradition of a congregation is that most likely they have been rooted in a denominational stream that has allowed this church to be part of something far bigger than just itself. One of my great concerns for many non-denominational church planting movements today is that we've created a culture where churches and pastors can be completely isolated from other pastors, leaders, and churches. This is absolutely foreign to the history of church planting within the Christian Church. The result is a lack of accountability and a lack of encouragement, among other things. It's not healthy in any way. In replanting, what you typically find is a church that has been a part of a denominational tradition. More often than not, a denominational tradition that has a solid, Christ-centered history. There's a safety and wisdom in that.

Opportunity #7: Redemption of a Church for God's Glory

The last potential advantage I want us to consider is this: ultimately the great joy of church replanting is that we get to see God glorified. We get to see God glorified as he redeems and restores a church that many people have given up on. A church that is not beautiful or powerful or influential in the eyes of the world. The Lord by his grace loves to take weakness and show off his glory and his strength in bringing dead and dying things back to life.

That's the story of the gospel! The story of the gospel is that we were dead and Christ came and made us alive. We are new creations! And this gospel story is so beautifully seen and told in the revitalization and replanting of churches. My prayer is that above all, we would be most excited about the revitalization and replanting of churches because God is glorified in it. This is the joy of joys that must fuel us as we seek to replant dying churches and see the Kingdom advance.

FOR FURTHER REFLECTION

Discussion Questions

1. What does it mean to count the cost as a church looking at replanting?

2. In the list of challenges when replanting, there are many with sensitive subjects. What do you think are the most difficult challenges to overcome from this list? What from this list are the most relative?

3. What does the author mean by "a sacred cow"? What are some of the sacred cows in many churches? How can you help a dying church deal with some of the sacred cows while still being sensitive to the history associated with these issues?)

4. What are some of the opportunities/advantages that your church situation can relate to?

Ways to Pray

- Pray for God to give dying churches church the ability to face reality & count the cost.

- Pray for the dying church to have humility to see the things that have truly led to this need to replant.

- Pray for the work that God is going to do in & through your church and the dying in the future.

Chapter 5

STEP #2: RAISING UP A REPLANTER

Leaders—we need them. Big time.

Strong, humble, visionary yet convictional leaders can be tough to find in the church these days, and yet the need for these leaders is greater than ever. This is particularly true when it comes to replanting and revitalizing dying churches. As we watch record numbers of congregations closing their doors every week all across our country, we are constantly reminded of the leadership crisis in which we find ourselves. We need pastors who can lead healthy change in a declining church with passionate vision and a shepherd's heart. The question is: Where do we find them?

Ministry leadership coach, Brian Howard, writes,

> Are you hoping that ready-made leaders will show up to help you lead the church? Are you trusting seminaries or other churches to raise up leaders for your church? If so, you will likely be waiting a long time. There are simply not enough ready-made leaders to do what we need to do in ministry.[1]

Howard is right—every church has a responsibility to strategically identify, develop, and deploy various leaders in a variety of ministry areas. This is especially true when it comes to the development of church replanters. Local churches must take seriously their call and responsibility to identify, equip and send replanters out to lead and shepherd dying churches.

For too long the church has assumed this kind of intentional leadership development is primarily the role and responsibility of our seminaries. But this is a poor assumption to make. Our seminaries serve a vital role in the *education* of those who serve in various forms of vocational ministry, however, our seminaries *do not take the place of the local church.* The local church is and always has been the primary environment for the development of pastors and church leaders. Al Mohler, President of The Southern Baptist Theological Seminary puts it well when he writes,

> The role of theological seminaries remains crucial for the education and training of Christian ministers. At its best, the seminary is an intentional gathering of Christian scholars who are dedicated to the preparation of ministers, committed to biblical truth, gifted in modeling and teaching the tasks of ministry, and passionate about the gospel... Nevertheless, count me as one seminary president who believes that the local church is even more important to the education of the pastor. The local church should see theological education as its own responsibility before it partners with a theological seminary for concentrated studies. The seminary can provide a depth and breadth of formal studies — all needed by the minister — but it cannot replace the local church as the context where ministry is learned most directly.[2]

The obvious question is, what does this look like practically? How can churches be directly involved in the development of pastors and church leaders? What does it look like for a local church to train and equip a replanter for the ministry of church revitalization? One answer to these questions is through the development of a replanting residency in your congregation.

WHAT IS A REPLANTING RESIDENCY?

When many people hear the word *residency*, they immediately think of terms like *Residency Program* or *Resident*, often associated with the medical community. Those individuals serving as medical residents are often already on a trajectory toward becoming doctors, nurses, or other types of health care providers. However, they spend their residency observing and shadowing more experienced doctors and nurses. They also are able to practice medicine in an environment where they experience honest feedback, mentoring, and learning. In a similar way, a replanting residency helps to create an environment where potential church replanters are able to learn from more seasoned pastors and leaders, get needed ministry experience in the context of a local church, and they get do it all in a safe and secure environment designed to help them grow as ministers of the gospel.

You might be wondering why your church should consider starting a replanting residency program. Perhaps you can understand the need for churches to create residencies that help equip future church replanters, but why should *your* church be one of these? That's a great question; let me give you some reasons to consider.

10 REASONS WHY YOUR CHURCH SHOULD START A RESIDENCY

Reason #1: Because It's Biblical

To be a biblical church is to be a developer of leaders. We see this throughout Scripture. Ephesians 4:12, among other places, is clear that the local church is called to "equip the saints for the work of ministry, for building up the body of Christ." We see throughout Jesus' ministry, he poured into his disciples, leading and teaching them, preparing them for ministry themselves. In Paul's relationship with Timothy, we observe the investment in a young pastor, equipping and sending him out to preach the gospel and lead God's people. If we are to be biblical churches, we must seek to be congregations that intentionally raise up pastors and deploy them into the harvest. A replanting residency can help your church do this.

Reason #2: Because Any Size Church Can Do It

I have run into pastors and church members who think only large churches can do something like this. This is simply not true. Often times the best replanting residencies happen in smaller churches. Smaller congregations are where a replanter can get an incredible amount of experience doing a variety of things, working with a wide array of people from different backgrounds and ages on a personal, relational level. Whether your church is large, medium, or small, you can do this! You have all the resources you need to train up and send out a replanter from your congregation.

Reason #3: Because Churches Help Each Other

It is such a sweet thing to see churches work together in unity. We know this is something that is close to the heart of Jesus. In John 17:21, he prays words that are true not just for individual Christians, but for congregations: "That they may all be one, just as you, Father, are in me, and I in you, that they also may be in us, so that the world may believe that you have sent me." One of the many ways we can display this type of God-honoring unity is through churches helping one another: sharing resources, giving encouragement, serving one another in tangible ways. Whatever it might look like, the Lord is honored when churches cooperate and help each other. We are always better together! When it comes to replanting, what a joy it is for a church to send their replanter out to love and lead a declining congregation in need of help. There is joy for individuals who are part of the Sending Church to come alongside the revitalizing congregation for the long haul, helping them to experience fresh life and vitality in the Lord. It is a good thing when churches help one another like this. We are all part of the same body of Christ and have the same Holy Spirit within us. We have all been given the same mission to proclaim the gospel and make disciples of all nations for the glory of God. A replanting residency allows your church to help a struggling church as you intentionally seek to prepare their future pastor to lead and serve them with the love of Christ.

Reason #4. Because Your Church Could Use Some Help

While a replanting residency is designed to equip and prepare a replanter to go out and revitalize a dying congregation, until they are sent out, your church will benefit greatly from his service in your congregation. Having another pastor in training to help teach Sunday school classes, preach during the weekend worship gatherings, help out with children's and youth ministry, and do pastoral visits is a huge blessing to the leadership and congregation.

Reason#5: Because Seeing Replanters Thrive Is a Delight

One of the great joys in church replanting is to see a replanter come alive as they use the gifts and lean into the passions God has given them for ministry. Whether it be in discovering their love for preaching God's Word, their natural wiring to care for the elderly in a congregation, or identifying administrative or leadership gifts they didn't know they had, walking alongside and developing replanters is a joy for any congregation. In fact, more than that, it is both a privilege and responsibility every congregation has, doing their part to raise up the next generation of pastors.

Reason #6: Because Your Church Needs to be Stretched

One of the great benefits in starting a replanting residency is that it stretches your congregation. Replanters may or may not have a family, but if they do, a replanting residency stretches your people to invest in, help encourage, and equip not only this replanter, but his wife and children as well. Sadly, many of our churches are stagnant and stuck in comfort zones and predictable routines. Why is this? Perhaps because our churches are not intentionally seeking to develop leaders. A replanting residency forces your people to catch a vision for leadership development and to play a role in the purposeful equipping of a future replanting pastor. This kind of stretching is a good thing for your people. They need it whether they realize it or not. This type of residency will help grow your people and give them a larger vision for the Kingdom.

Reason #7: Because the Need is Massive

Perhaps this point is obvious, but it needs to be stated again. With large numbers of churches throughout our country closing their doors for the final time every week, there has never been more of a need for trained replanters than there is today. Where are these replanters going to come from? The church down the street? The megachurches in your denomination? If we all take this attitude, very few replanters will ever be developed and sent out. If we are going to see a movement of replanting in our country and around the world, it will start with churches like yours that get into the game. To help your congregation get into the game of replanting, creating a replanting residency is a great place to start.

Reason #8: Because We Care About Reaching Those Far from God

Every one of our communities is filled with people who are far from God and do not know Jesus as their Lord and Savior. It's likely they have never heard the true gospel of grace. Who is going to proclaim this gospel to them if not

Christians in local churches within their own communities? Yes, we must plant new churches. But we must also replant dying churches. Countless neighborhoods in cities all over our country would be most effectively reached through revitalized churches in that community. If we care about reaching the lost, we will care about replanting churches, and we will further care about equipping replanting pastors who will lead those churches to reach the lost that surround them.

Reason #9: Because the Local Church is the Best Training Ground

As mentioned above, while I am so thankful for our seminaries, seminary is not designed to raise up and send out pastors and replanters. Local churches do this. Seminaries educate and sharpen, which is essential for healthy, biblical leadership in the church. However, local churches primarily coach, train and mentor. Churches observe the life of a future pastor, and can be a place where gifts are recognized, affirmed and nurtured. The local *church* is called to this, not seminary.

Reason #10: Because It's Fun!

You read that correctly. It is fun! It is fun to be part of God's work in calling, equipping, and sending a replanter and his family out to serve a dying church. It is fun to have passionate, mission-minded replanters around your church. If the replanter is married with children, it is fun to have his wife and children be part of your congregation for a season. There is much joy in doing this type of ministry together as a church, and ministry should be joyful! Starting a replanting residency in your congregation will spark fresh joy, vision, and excitement about God and what he can do in and through your church family for his glory.

THREE GUIDING QUESTIONS AS YOU DEVELOP A REPLANTING RESIDENCY

Once your church has decided to move forward in starting a replanting residency, what is next? Good question. There are three foundational questions that will guide you in this process.

1. What are we looking for in a replanting resident?
2. What do we want to develop in the replanting resident?
3. What do we do to train and prepare him to replant a church?

These three questions will help tremendously as you seek clarity on what you want the replanting residency to look like. Let's start with the first question, which gets at the heart of the kind of resident you desire to bring on.

Question #1: What Are We Looking for in a Replanting Resident?

The first step in this process is becoming crystal clear on what exactly you are looking for in a potential replanting resident. There are several non-negotiables you are looking for in this individual. Here are five to start the process:

A passion and hunger for God and his Word. We desperately need leaders in the church who are first and foremost passionate about God and his Word. A pastor cannot give to others what he does not own himself. You want to hear how he came to know Christ as Savior and Lord. You want to listen for ways in which he seeks to commune with God in worship and prayer. Is he passionate about Christ and the gospel? Does he seek to love God and honor him with his whole heart? What about his relationship with the Bible? You want to hear his view of Scripture. You want to know without a shadow of a doubt that he is absolutely committed to the inspiration, authority, and sufficiency of the Bible. More than simply his stated doctrinal convictions, you want to hear of his own personal love and hunger for God's Word. Does he love God and love God's Word? This is foundational and absolutely essential.

A deep love and care for people. Ministry is all about people. Replanting a dying church is all about loving and caring for people. There is no way to replant a dying church in a healthy, biblical, God-honoring way apart from a deep love and care for the people in that congregation. When you are looking for a replanting resident, you need to make sure that they love people well. They don't just put up with people, but that they enjoy, encourage, serve, hug, and love people! If this characteristic is not present in a potential replanting resident, keep looking until you find a man who is marked by this kind of love for others. Jesus loves people, and he calls every replanting pastor to follow his lead in sacrificially and joyfully loving others as well.

A humble, servant heart. A heart of humility is a non-negotiable when looking for a replanting resident. What does this look like? Is this individual willing and eager to do the tasks no one else wants to do? Do they prefer being unnoticed for their service and good deeds rather than being noticed and praised by others for them? This is a significant indicator of what is going on in his heart. True humility before God and people is crucial, not only when serving as a resident, but when further serving as a replanting pastor in a local church.

A hard worker. Pastoral ministry is hard work that takes sacrifice physically, spiritually, and emotionally. If a replanting resident is lazy or is constantly making excuses versus faithfully and joyfully working "as unto the Lord," not only will this create tension among other leaders, but the congregation as a whole will lose respect for him. As a result, they won't follow his leadership. A potential replanting resident must be willing to work hard for the glory of God and the good of the church. If he is unwilling to work hard as a resident in your church, there is no reason to believe he will work any harder as a replanting pastor when you send him out from your church. The last thing a declining church needs is a lazy pastor, and the last thing your church needs is a lazy resident.

A team player who encourages others. You want to find a team player. You want to find a resident who is not a loner. Is this individual aligned with the vision, mission, doctrine, and values of your church? Does he seek to humbly work alongside others? Does he encourage others or does he see them as a threat of some kind? Does he have a posture of teachability or a know-it-all mentality? Your church is a family and the leaders, including this potential resident, must work as a team and lead as a team. A humble, encouraging, team-minded lover of Jesus and people is the kind of individual you want to bring on as a replanting resident. Pray hard that God would send a man marked by these five characteristics. And continue to lift him up in prayer as he lives into this call as replanting resident.

Question #2: What do we want to develop in the resident?

Once you find a replanting resident that is marked by these characteristics, your church needs to see what you want to develop in this individual. How do you want to help him grow? What specific areas do you want to help him mature in as he prepares to replant? You must be clear on this. As the saying goes, "If you aim at nothing, you will hit it every time." Churches that have replanting residencies also must be crystal clear on what they are shooting for. There are three areas that you want to focus on:

- **The Head**
- **The Heart**
- **The Hands**

The Head. The head deals with how the resident is growing in their thinking, in their mind, in their intellect, and in their biblical and doctrinal formulation. Are they growing theologically? Are they growing in their understanding of biblical shepherding and leadership? Are they growing in their understanding of what it means and looks like to be someone who makes disciples? Are they growing in their understanding of relational and emotional intelligence? Each of these areas will focus on helping the resident grow intellectually. Another component is helping the resident mature in conviction. In their time with your church, the resident should develop greater biblical and theological conviction that will be critical once they begin serving as the replanting pastor of a local congregation.

The Heart. How are you going to help this resident grow in their heart and their character? There are three primary areas to focus on: humility, love, and integrity. Are we helping this resident grow as a humble leader who genuinely loves people? Who recognizes that this is the Lord's work and it's an honor and privilege to be a part of it? If a resident has incredible *head* knowledge but lacks a *heart* of humility, love, and integrity, he will never make it as a church replanter. You must intentionally help him honestly evaluate and intentionally grow in Christ-like humility and love. You must help him to be increasingly shaped by the daily application of the gospel to his life and ministry. This means encouraging his growth in daily, dependent, prayerful intimacy with Christ.

The Hands. The hands deal with skills and competency. This is the practical equipping of a resident which helps him grow in ministry practice. There are various areas of ministry skill residents need to grow, including leadership strategy, preaching ability, pastoral visitation, handling conflict, leading a small group, shepherding through weddings & funerals, and connecting with individuals across generations, among others. Your church is the perfect environment to help residents gain hands-on ministry experience in these areas.

As you consider what you want to develop in your replanting resident, considering the aspects of the head, heart, and hands are critical. The resident needs to grow in each of these as he prepares to replant a dying church. It is a true blessing to come alongside a resident, helping him to mature by the grace of God and the power of the Spirit. Of course, the next question that naturally arises then is, how do we train him in these different ministry areas?

Question #3: How do we train and prepare the resident?

This question gets to the nuts and bolts of what this residency is actually going to look like in your church. The replanting residency you will be creating should be designed to help replanting residents do three things: be **equipped** for effective replanting ministry, **explore** their vocational calling, and **engage** in practical ministry and leadership. Ideally, the residency should be a nine to twelve month program. While you may decide your residency will be longer or shorter in length, nine to twelve months has proven in many churches to be a duration that is appropriate and doable for the replanter. Beginning the residency in September and ending in August of the following year is in many cases a great timeframe to consider for the replanter and his family. January through December can also be an effective timeline. Let's consider the three main components of the residency in greater depth.

RESIDENCY COMPONENT #1: EQUIP

Equipping the replanter for future ministry is a key aspect to this residency. What exactly will this equipping look like? While your church may desire to include other elements, I would recommend your residency consist of three distinct learning environments: The Church Replanting Cohort, the Pastoral Cohort, and the Preaching Cohort.

The Church Replanting Cohort

This cohort will meet twice a month and will include the replanting resident, the pastoral team, other leaders in the church, and even other pastors, church leaders, replanters or potential replanters in the community that you would like to invite.[3] This learning environment is where most of the teaching designed to equip the resident specifically for leading a church replant back to health will be accomplished. There will be several books read each semester as part of this cohort experience, but the bulk of the teaching will not happen through reading books, but through 40 specific teachings related to church replanting and revitalization. These teachings are entitled, *"40 Foundations of Biblical Revitalization."* See **Appendix Q** for a full list of the 40 Foundations, but the teaching for this cohort breaks down like this:

40 Foundations of Biblical Revitalization

Part 1: Preparing for Biblical Revitalization
(September – October)

Part 2: The Heart of Biblical Revitalization
(November – December)

Part 3: The Priorities of Biblical Revitalization
(January – March)

Part 4: The Practices of Biblical Revitalization
(April-May)

Part 5: Persevering in Biblical Revitalization
(June-August)

You will have the option to have your pastor teach on the 40 Foundations, or you can use our free video curriculum that covers these teachings. All that you need for this Replant Cohort, including teacher and student notes, discussion questions, and the video and audio teachings of each lesson, are available and free for your use at *nonignorable.org* or *churchreplanters.com*.

While you may decide to follow a different format for your gathering, here is a basic meeting schedule you could use for a bi-weekly, two-hour meeting covering two foundations:

Replant Cohort Meeting Schedule
(2 hours, bi-weekly)

1. **Opening & Session Overview (5 minutes):** Welcome, housekeeping items, open in prayer.

2. **Instruction (25-30 minutes):** Watch the teaching video of the first Foundation for this session. If the cohort leader would rather teach the Foundation themselves (i.e. no video) they can use the teacher's notes during this time.

3. **Discuss & Develop (20 minutes):** Guide cohort through discussion questions and exercises to stimulate thinking and work toward application.

4. **Break (5 minutes)**

5. **Instruction (25-30 minutes):** Watch the teaching video of the second Foundation for this session. Again, if the cohort leader would rather teach the Foundation without the video, they can use the teacher's notes during this time.

6. **Discuss & Develop (20 minutes):** Guide cohort through discussion questions and exercises to stimulate thinking and work toward application.

7. **Wrap Up (10 minutes):** Review the key insights of this session and announce any assignments for the next gathering, pray and dismiss.

The Pastoral Cohort

Once a month, the replanting resident will meet with your pastor and other leaders in your church to learn about and grow in pastoral shepherding ministry. It takes place in a roundtable discussion format and will study a book of your choice each semester that focuses on pastoral shepherding ministry. The book will help facilitate in-depth discussion around matters pertaining to pastoral ministry such as knowing, leading, feeding, and protecting God's people in the local church. You can find a list of recommended book options in **Appendix U**.

The Preaching Cohort

Strong, biblical preaching is absolutely essential to the health and growth of a dying congregation. As Paul writes in Roman 10:14, "How then will they call on him in whom they have not believed? And how are they to believe in him of whom they have never heard? And how are they to hear without someone preaching?" The preaching cohort is designed to help the replanting resident grow as a preacher and communicator of God's Word. One of the key ingredients to healthy, biblical revitalization is strong preaching of the Word each and every week. God works powerfully through his Word in the hearts of his people. The Spirit uses the Word of God to bring dead churches back to life, just as he uses it to bring dead souls back to life. For this reason it is crucial that your congregation help this resident grow as a preacher.[4]

The Preaching Cohort meets once a month for an hour to an hour and a half and allows your resident to preach in a context where they will be given honest and helpful feedback from others. Along with the pastor, it is recommended to invite other leaders and members of the congregation to listen to the resident preach each month. Each observer will fill out a preaching evaluation sheet for giving critique in areas of strength and areas for growth.

The resident will preach a 25-30 minute sermon, followed by 25-30 minutes of evaluation and discussion. During this time, those present have the opportunity to offer words of encouragement and also share thoughts and observations that will help the resident identify areas for growth in their preaching. Always close this time by having those present spend time praying for him. A sample preaching cohort evaluation has been included in **Appendix T**.

Putting It All Together: The Monthly Cohort Schedule

It is recommended that these three cohorts meet at the same time on the same day each week. For example, our church's residency cohorts meet from 4-6:00 PM each Thursday afternoon at our church building. To get an idea of what the schedule for these cohorts looks like, see the sample schedule in **Appendix O**.

RESIDENCY COMPONENT #2: EXPLORE

Along with equipping the replanting resident, a second component is helping him explore his vocational calling to church replanting and revitalization. It is important to connect the resident with a mentor who can pour into his life regularly during his time at your church. This will be a key relationship for the resident and will serve as a safe person who can encourage him, pray for him, and process with him over the course of the residency. This individual may be the pastor, an elder or deacon, or another mature lay leader in the congregation.

Steve Timmis speaks to the need for pastors and those preparing for ministry (such as replanting residents) to have a mentor in their lives when he writes,

> Every shepherd in the church needs a shepherd. In the last 12 months, many pastors experienced trials and suffering. Some were health-related, others were family issues: major organ transplant, the rebellion of children, psychological damage of an adopted child, marital problems and adult children walking away from the faith. These real issues devastated many of them for several months. Some pastor friends of mine dealt with their own cancer, loss of employment, abandonment by friends and betrayal by fellow elders, and others experienced serious financial setbacks. The pain is acute and in many cases, ongoing. I'm also aware of four suicides by pastors this last year. This is four suicides too many. The devastation on their churches and their families continues to impact the body of Christ in a major way.
>
> The church leader is not exempt from problems. Quite frankly, the supernatural spiritual attack on church leaders is enormous and relentless. Who is shepherding the shepherds? Where do church leaders find their pastoral care?

For many church leaders, they have no idea where to find help. Yet, they feel lonely, abandoned, and vulnerable. They deeply desire relationships, but are not sure if they want to share their heart's deepest concerns with members of the body—even other leaders, so they suffer in silence and as a result are not able to properly shepherd the flock where they have been assigned to oversee. The whole church suffers when the leaders suffer.[5]

Timmis' wise words iterate why we want to make sure we are doing a good job of preparing this replanting resident, not only for replanting, but for a healthy physical, spiritual, emotional, and relational life. As a result, it is important to pair up each replanter with a Resident C.O.A.C.H. There are five basic purposes and functions for a C.O.A.C.H.

Five Functions of a Resident C.O.A.C.H[6]

1. Comes alongside the replanting resident as a friend, mentor, and encourager.
2. Observes the life and ministry of the replanting resident carefully, offering feedback and critique as needed.
3. Asks questions of the replanting resident, his life, his family, and his ministry, wisely and helpfully.
4. Communicates potential growth strategies, along with resources, for the life and ministry of the replanting resident.
5. Holds accountable and cares for the heart of the replanting resident.

It will be important for the C.O.A.C.H. and the resident to go over the five functions together to help set expectations for the relationship before it begins. It is recommended that the C.O.A.C.H. and resident meet every other week for 1-2 hours. The more time spent together, the easier it will be to build trust with one another, which is vital to this type of coaching relationship.

Pairing the resident with a C.O.A.C.H. who they can share their joys, fears, hopes, and concerns with will be of great benefit to their growth in life and pastoral ministry. Over the course of the year, the C.O.A.C.H. will help the resident honestly evaluate and explore their vocational calling to church replanting in a way that should bring greater conviction and clarity about God's direction for their ministry future. To help you discover more about being a mentor or coach, here are some recommended resources to check out:

Mentoring Resources

- *Gospel Coach*, Scott Thomas
- *Mentor Like Jesus*, Regi Campbell
- *As Iron Sharpens Iron*, Howard Hendricks and William Hendricks
- *Mentoring Millennials*, Daniel Egeler
- *Mentoring Leaders*, Carson Pue
- *The Heart of Mentoring*, David Stoddard

RESIDENCY COMPONENT #3: ENGAGE

Lastly, each replanting resident will spend significant time engaged in serving in various roles of ministry leadership within your church. This will help them to gain needed experience in multiple areas, which will help prepare them for future pastoral leadership in a replanting context. Your church should intentionally seek out ways the resident can be involved on some level with the following ministries of your church:

- Youth and Children's Ministry
- Counseling and Pastoral Care
- Small Groups
- Worship Service Planning and Leadership
- Weddings and Funerals
- Operations and Administration
- Local and Global Missions
- Assimilation and First Impressions
- Preaching
- Communications and Media

Providing opportunities for your resident to engage in these various ministry areas will not only be beneficial to the resident, but also to your congregation. For married residents, be intentional about ways you can involve their wife in areas of ministry as well for her own ministry growth and development. You want the couple to get the most out of their ministry experience at your church, so consider the following points of counsel.

#1: Give Your Resident Freedom to Try and Fail.

If you want your resident to grow and mature as a pastor and leader, he needs plenty of opportunity to try and fail. Create a culture where he can attempt new programs or implement a few new initiatives in your church. If they succeed, great! If they fail, extend much grace. This is a learning experience. People will come alive when they are allowed to dream without the fear of getting in trouble by leaders. Before your resident goes out on his own to lead a replant, let your church be soft ground for him to learn, grow, and fail, knowing you and the congregation are behind him 110%.

#2: Saturate Your Resident and His Family with Love and Encouragement.

In Mark 12, Jesus tells us what the most important thing in the world is: loving God with all your heart, soul, mind and strength, and loving your neighbor as yourself. Love is to be the defining mark not only of our lives, but also the defining mark of leadership development in our churches. This means we need to love and encourage our residents like crazy during this training process. Encouragement is so important. If you want to keep people fired up, encourage them! If you want your resident and his wife to be excited and energized in their time with your congregation, put a high priority on loving and encouraging them.

In Hebrews 3:13 we read, "But encourage one another daily, as long as it is called 'today' so that none of you may be hardened by sin's deceitfulness." Paul writes in 1 Thessalonians 5:11, "Therefore encourage one another and build one another up, just as you are doing." The strongest form of motivation for many pastors and leaders in the church is simply loving encouragement. Encouragement is love spoken. Your resident and his wife will need a lot of this, so saturate them.

#3: Give Personal, Specific, Grace-Filled, Continual Feedback.

Feedback is essential to one's growth in any area of life, but especially important when developing pastors in the local church. What kind of feedback is most helpful? There are four components to feedback that is both sharpening and encouraging to a resident. Feedback should be **personal, specific, grace-filled,** and **continual**.

First of all, it is personal. This means it is "in person." It is one-on-one and face-to-face. They can see you and hear you. The best feedback happens in relationship.

Secondly, it is specific. When you're giving feedback, don't be vague—be clear and use specific examples. The best encouragement and the best critique is always detailed enough to be helpful, while general feedback is typically vague and unhelpful. Don't just say, "You did a great job preaching that sermon this morning!" Instead say something like, "I loved the way you applied your sermon to our lives this morning. The challenge you gave us to intentionally share a word of encouragement with each of our children before we put them to bed each night was so helpful. I am excited to put that into practice!" Be specific in your feedback.

Thirdly, it is grace-filled. Intentional words of love and encouragement are what is going to earn you the right to have hard conversations with your resident. Grace-filled feedback creates a sense of safety and genuine care for them. Because you need to be specific, tempering that feedback with grace will protect the relationship with your resident.

Fourthly, it is continual. Don't be the church that only gives intentional encouragement or has the hard conversations with a resident at the year-end review. Do it continually. Give thoughtful feedback on a regular basis in the context of your on-going relationship. This is how your church will help your resident grow the most.

The Two Evaluations

Though feedback should be given to the resident throughout the residency process, it is recommended that the resident participate in two evaluations over the course of the nine to twelve months they are with your church. All residents will receive an evaluation at the four to six month (halfway) point. This is designed to help steer the second half of the residency. Near the end of the residency, there will be a second evaluation to help provide direction for the resident's next steps after finishing the residency. Ideally, both of these evaluations will be conducted by the pastor and a few other leaders in the church, along with a denominational leader. Particularly in the second evaluation, a denominational leader can be of help in assisting your church and this resident determine next steps for their family, whether it be replanting a congregation or getting further training or education before launching into a replanting context.

It should be made clear from the beginning of the residency that the replanting resident is not guaranteed the endorsement of your congregation to replant a church. However, pending the results of the two evaluations, the hope is that this resident will be endorsed and directed in the next steps towards becoming a Lead Church Replanter with your church serving as the Sending Church.

YOUR CHURCH CAN DO THIS!

Raising up replanters in the local church is needed, necessary, and the time is *now*. If your church truly desires to join in this movement of replanting dying churches for the glory of God, then raising up and developing replanters must become a priority and passion. I pray you and your church will trust our Sovereign God, take a leap of faith, and invest in the preparation of a replanter for a season. Your church will be blessed, the Lord will be honored, and a church that is currently nearing its death may see a day of revitalization and transformation they can only dream of at this very moment… All because you chose to raise up a replanter.

FOR FURTHER REFLECTION

Discussion Questions

1. What are some of the unique characteristics that you think a replanting pastor would need, as compared to a pastor planting a church or taking over leadership of an existing congregation?

2. Under "10 Reasons to Start a Replanting Residency", read Reason #2 again—*Because Any Size Church Can Do It.*" Why do you think that so many churches fall into the belief that they can only do things like this if they are a huge megachurch?

3. How do we help our church become a place that not only raises up replanting pastors, but also creates a culture where it is safe to learn & make mistakes in ministry?

Ways to Pray

- Pray for those who God is burdening to become a replanter.

- Pray for churches to grow in raising up leaders who will love & lead the church as pastors.

- Pray for God to use your church how He sees fit to multiply & mature leaders for his Church.

Chapter 6

STEP#3: ASSESSING THE POTENTIAL REPLANTER

Reality TV is more popular than ever these days, from shows about living in tiny houses to those focused on rating the food at America's best (and worst) restaurants. Reality TV is everywhere. And as a culture, we are obsessed with it.

Of course, there is a category of reality TV shows that is more popular than any others. Without fail, these are the shows where public, often harsh, cutting critique of an individuals' singing ability ("American Idol" or "The Voice"), entrepreneurial business idea ("Shark Tank"), or unique skill or talent ("America's Got Talent"), is on full display for all to see. As Kevin Collier rightly puts it, "Many an ego has been stroked and many a heart has been broken by the comments (or lack thereof)" that stream from these popular, yet brutal, reality shows.[1]

Honest evaluation and assessment can be a helpful thing in our lives, but as is the case so often in the world of reality TV, it can also be incredibly unhelpful and discouraging. This chapter is focused on evaluating potential replanters. Not in the way we often see on reality TV, but in the way the Lord has taught us in his Word; to come alongside potential replanters with both encouragement and critique that will help them grow as leaders, ministers of the gospel, and most importantly, men of God.

Honestly evaluating and assessing a potential replanter's readiness to go into a church and help lead it back to life is a critical step in replanting a dying church effectively. In many ways, the success or failure of a replant lies in the humility, wisdom, love, passion, and readiness of the replanter who will be pastoring and leading this congregation.

In his book, *The Salvation of Souls*, Jonathan Edwards writes about the importance of honestly evaluating one's readiness for pastoral ministry. His words apply to every replanter,

> "Those that are about to undertake this work should do it with the greatest seriousness and consideration of the vast importance of the work, how great a thing it is to have the care of precious souls committed to them, and with a suitable concern upon their minds, considering the great difficulties, dangers, and temptations that do accompany it. It is compared to going to warfare."[2]

Commenting on this quote from Edwards as it relates to church planters, Tyler Powell writes, "In preparation for this 'warfare,' assessing one's calling, character, and competency is crucial." Powell's words are just as true for church replanters as they are for planters. He goes on: "This cannot only come by one's own self-assessment, though there must be a strong conviction and confirmation internally in a church [replanter] that God is leading in this direction. Just as important as internal conviction is, there must be external confirmation in which a church [replanter] receives counsel and places himself under the honest and sometimes uncomfortable assessment by his family, peers, elders, and/or assessment centers."[3]

While your church may choose to send your potential replanter through an assessment process with your denomination or other ministry network, it is just as, if not more, vital that you, as the Sending Church, assess well throughout his time of training and service with your congregation

As a Sending Church, what exactly should you be looking for in this man you may be sending out to replant a dying congregation? What are some of the qualities? What are the characteristics?

BIBLICAL QUALIFICATIONS ARE PRIORITY #1

Before considering some of the qualities related specifically to church replanting (which your church should be watching for in your resident), we must start by looking at what the Bible says. As with all other things in life and ministry, the Lord is clear in his Word concerning the most important characteristics and qualifications for any pastor or potential church replanter. These qualifications "have been the same for almost 2,000 years. Jesus is the perfect fulfillment of these qualifications as the 'senior pastor' of the Church."[4] The following is a list of 15 biblical qualifications that must mark the life and ministry of a replanter serving as a pastor-elder in a local church context.[5] By the power and grace of God, these men are to seek to faithfully carry out this high calling of pastoral leadership and care of God's people, for the health and growth of the flock and for God's ultimate glory.

Qualification #1: Aspiration to the Office/Role

> The saying is trustworthy: If anyone aspires to the office of overseer, he desires a noble task. - 1 Timothy 3:1

The replanter truly called to serve as a pastor-elder in the local church is to be marked by both an inward consuming passion for, along with a disciplined outwardly pursuit of, the office of pastoral ministry. For him the ministry is not the best option, it is the *only* option. In fact, there may be nothing else he can imagine doing with his life that would fulfill him.[6]

Qualification #2: Above Reproach

> Therefore, an overseer must be above reproach. - 1 Timothy 3:2

> For an overseer, as God's steward, must be above reproach. - Titus 1:7

Being above reproach is the overarching, summarizing characteristic of the pastor-elder. A replanter's pastoral work, along with their relationships with those both inside and outside of the church, are to be of such moral quality that they are considered blameless to all, not bringing shame or embarrassment to the body of Christ or the name of Jesus.

Qualification #3: Devoted to His Wife; a One-Woman Man

> "…the husband of one wife". - Titus 1:6

> "Therefore, an overseer must be above reproach, the husband of one wife." - 1 Timothy 3:2

The replanter's marriage illustrates Christ's love for his church—his bride (Eph. 5:22 ff.). A pastor-elder must love his wife exclusively with his mind, will, and emotions, and not just his body. Above any ministry he might have to a congregation, a replanter must first and foremost serve, care for, and be committed to his wife. A replanter must be solely devoted to his wife, and this must be a joy and not a burden.

Qualification #4: His Children Respect & Obey Him

> He must manage his own household well, with all dignity keeping his children submissive, for if someone does not know how to manage his own household, how will he care for God's church?" 1 Timothy 3:4-5

According to the Apostle Paul, if a man does not know how to manage his own family, he will not know how to take care of God's Church. The first flock for a pastor-elder is his own family. While his children will not be perfect, a replanter's qualification for the church starts in his home management as he leads his household in the discipline and admonition of the Lord (Eph. 6:4).[7] As Warren Wiersbe writes, "If a man's own children cannot obey and respect him, then his church is not likely to respect and obey his leadership."[8]

Qualification #5: Humble - Not Arrogant

> "He must not be arrogant." - Titus 1:7

Genuine, Spirit-wrought humility must mark the life of a replanter. Arrogance and pride have no place in the life of a biblically qualified, pastor-elder. This kind of humility is fleshed out in the life of a replanter as he constantly demonstrates the gospel by readily admitting when he is wrong, assuming responsibility, and restoring relationships.[9]

Qualification #6: Gentle - Not Quick-Tempered

He must not be...quick-tempered. - Titus 1:7

...not violent but gentle. - 1 Timothy 3:3

A replanter is to be a peacemaker who is marked by gentleness and great patience. As Scott Thomas writes, "No man will be of any use in the kingdom that is quick-tempered. The difference between how Jesus demonstrated anger is that he was angry at the abuse of others in the name of religion and the dishonoring of God. We get angry at how it affects us."[10] The Apostle Paul ascribes gentleness to our Lord Jesus Christ in 2 Corinthians 10:1 when he pleads with the church at Corinth "by the meekness and gentleness of Christ." James describes the wisdom from above as first pure, then peaceable and gentle.[11] Replanters must demonstrate this kind of gentleness in all areas of their lives, by God's grace.

Qualification #7: Sober – Not Engaged in Drunkenness

He must not be...a drunkard. - Titus 1:7

...not a drunkard. - 1 Timothy 3:3

When it comes to the drinking of alcohol, there are reasons why the Apostle Paul warns against drunkenness. Pastor Steven Cole explains that church leaders, specifically pastor-elders, must be "especially careful so that they do not cause younger believers to stumble. If a younger believer, who formerly had a problem with drinking, sees me drinking, and my example causes him to fall back into his former ways, I am to some extent responsible."[12] Pastor-elders are called to be examples to the flock under their care. Drunkenness is not only unwise and unhelpful for those in the congregation, but most importantly, it is sinful in the eyes of God.

Qualification #8: Has Financial Integrity - Not Greedy for Gain

He must not be...greedy for gain. - Titus 1:7

...not a lover of money. - 1 Timothy 3:3

A replanter is to have honesty and integrity in his financial dealings, not greedy for money or worldly gain over against the blessings of God's Kingdom. A heart that is greedy and marked by an unhealthy love for money is another clear stumbling block for those in the congregation. Greed is the fruit of a heart that is failing to seek satisfaction in Christ and his gospel. Greed is the fruit of a heart that has forgotten that we serve the God who has promised to provide our every need. We don't need to be greedy out of fear of a lack of provision, for he is abundant.

Qualification #9: Hospitable

> Therefore, an overseer must be...hospitable. - 1 Timothy 3:2

> ...hospitable. - Titus. 1:8

A pastor-elder should be someone who loves people radically - including strangers. The characteristic of being hospitable should be lived out at home, church, and everywhere the pastor-elder goes, welcoming all like prodigal sons.. A replanter must be a man "who is given to being kind to newcomers and makes them feel at home - a person whose home is open for ministry and who does not shrink back from having guests, not a secretive person."[13] Alex Strauch, who has written much on hospitality in the local church, points out how many Christians are "unaware that spiritual leaders are, according to Scripture, required to be hospitable...The biblical shepherd is a shepherd of people -- God's precious, blood-bought people. And like Christ, the Chief Shepherd, the church shepherd must give himself lovingly and sacrificially for the care of God's people (1 Thes. 2:8)."[14]

Qualification #10: Self-Controlled

> Therefore an overseer must be...self-controlled. - 1 Tim. 3:2

> ...self-controlled. - Titus 1:8

Self-control is to be a characterization of every replanting pastor. The NASB translates the Greek word for "self-controlled" as "sensible" in Titus 1:8. The word is derived from the combination of sound (σως; sos) and mind (φρην; phren), resulting in the meaning of "sound mind, sane, sensible; self-controlled, sober- minded".[15] Aristotle described such a level-headed man in the *Nicomachean Ethics* as one who desired the right things in the right way at the right time.[16]

Qualification #11: Holy

> For an overseer, as God's steward, must be…holy. - Titus 1:8

The word Paul uses here for holy, ὅσιος, pertains to being without fault relative to deity, devout, pious, pleasing to God, holy. It describes a person who lives right before God and so is described as devout, dedicated or holy. ὅσιος was used to refer to that which was true to divine direction and purpose, to genuine obedience to God's will. The word describes the man who reverences the fundamental decencies of life, the things which go back beyond any man-made law. The idea in this word includes personal piety, an inner attitude of conforming to what is felt to be pleasing to God and consistent with religious practices. This man keeps himself free of anything which would "stain" him in the eyes of God.[17]

The replanter who humbly seeks to grow in holiness will wisely apply the words of Robert Murray McCheyne when he exhorts ministers of the gospel to "study universal holiness of life. Your whole usefulness depends on this, for your sermons last but an hour or two—your life preaches all the week. If Satan can only make a covetous minister a lover of praise, of pleasure, of good eating—he has ruined his ministry." [18]

Qualification #12: Able to Teach

> He must hold firm to the trustworthy word as taught, so that he may be able to give instruction in sound doctrine and also to rebuke those who contradict it. - Titus 1:9

> Therefore, an overseer must be…able to teach. - 1 Tim 3:2

The ability to teach is the only ability-based requirement of the pastor-elder in Scripture. He is to be able "to teach sound doctrine, not just be able to communicate in an excellent manner. His teaching can be to one or two, to twenty, to a hundred or to a thousand."[19] Titus 1:9 states, "He must hold firm to the sure word as taught, so that he may be able to give instruction in sound doctrine and also to confute those who contradict it." In other words, he must know biblical doctrine well and be able to explain in a clear and edifying manner. He must be astute enough theologically that he can spot errors and show a person why it is wrong and harmful.[20]

Qualification #13: Not a Recent Convert

> He must not be a recent convert, or he may become puffed up with conceit and fall into the condemnation of the devil. - 1 Timothy 3:6

Scripture is clear that leaders in the church, specifically pastor-elders, must not be new believers. John Calvin addresses this critical issue that the Apostle Paul has written about in 1 Timothy 3 when he writes,

> There being many men of distinguished ability and learning who at that time were brought to the faith, Paul forbids that such persons shall be admitted to the office of a bishop (pastor-elder), as soon as they have made profession of Christianity. And he shows how great would be the danger; for it is evident that they are commonly vain, and full of ostentation, and, in consequence of this, haughtiness and ambition will drive them headlong. What Paul says we experience; for 'novices' have not only impetuous fervor and bold daring, but are also puffed up with foolish confidence, as if they could fly beyond the clouds. Consequently, it is not without reason that they are excluded from the honor of a bishopric, till, in process of time their proud temper shall be subdued.[21]

The "condemnation of the devil" seems to be "the condemnation that the devil is under because of his being puffed up. So the new believer, given too much responsibility too soon, may easily swell with pride."[22] This implies that part of Christian seasoning is a process of humility and a growing protection against pride. There should be evidences in a pastor-elder's life that humility is a fixed virtue and not easily overturned.[23]

Qualification #14: Well Thought Of by Outsiders

> Moreover, he must be well thought of by outsiders, so that he may not fall into disgrace, into a snare of the devil. - 1 Timothy 3:7

A replanter is one who is respected and well thought of by those outside of the church. This does not mean "that everyone must like him or even appreciate him. It means that there is no credible witness by unbelievers outside of the church to an ongoing sinful behavior."[24] He is respected by those in his neighborhood and those in the community surrounding the church. Non-believers may not understand his love for Christ and the Church, but they are quick to speak positively of his character.

Qualification #15: An Example to the Flock.

> "...not domineering over those in your charge, but being examples to the flock". - 1 Peter 5:3

Replanters are to be examples of biblical purity and Godliness with regards to time management, marriage, parenting, worship, relationships and any other way. A replanter "should be someone your sons could pattern their life after and the kind of man your daughter should marry."[25] While no pastor is perfect and without sin, it should be the growing desire of every replanter to love God and others in such a way that his life is one to be exemplified by those in his congregation and beyond.

8 ESSENTIAL CHARACTERISTICS OF A REPLANTER

Along with the clear, biblical qualifications for replanting pastor-elders, when assessing the readiness of a replanter, there are eight additional characteristics that must be present. These characteristics are key indicators of whether an individual is prepared, equipped and ready to effectively lead healthy revitalization in a replanting context.[26] Again, these are characteristics specific to the ministry of church replanting and revitalization.

Characteristic #1: Visionary Shepherd

What is a visionary shepherd? A visionary shepherd has the ability to sense and see God's next steps for a congregation and the capacity to lead the church forward as a loving shepherd. He is patient, wise, strategic, and relational. What we see in a visionary shepherd is not someone who can simply dream big dreams, start new things, and get people pumped along the way. If a replanter is all visionary without a passion to shepherd souls, he will fail to win the hearts and the trust of the people. He will likely cause a big mess in his replanting efforts. He may have great ideas but is unwilling to do the hard work of doing the things needed to make those ideas become reality. Or worse, he may be unwilling to do the things he is asking others to do. The result of this kind of leadership over time is a lack of respect and trust on the part of the congregation toward this replanter. Sadly, all too often, this kind of behavior will get him fired or end up splitting the church. Being a visionary is important, but it's not enough by itself in replanting.

At the same time, it's not enough to only be a shepherd. A shepherd is someone who loves and cares for the flock. In many ways a good shepherd has the characteristics of a good chaplain - pastoral, caring, and gentle. This is an important role of a replanter. However, just as many chaplains are trained and gifted to help people process in a severe moment of crisis and spiritual need, replanters who are almost all shepherd without any real visionary leadership gifting, often end up helping congregations die due to a lack of vision rather than leading them back to life.

While each replanter is unique and will lean more toward either visionary or shepherd in their natural giftings, the most effective replanters are not exclusively one or the other. Rather, they are a combination of both: Visionary-shepherds. This is unique wiring, I realize. This is someone who is excited about the future, who can cast a vision, and can lead people toward that vision in a compelling and winsome manner. At the same time, they must love people well, shepherding folks along the way toward this vision with patience, humility, discernment, and great care.

Characteristic #2: Capacity for Suffering

The ups and downs of replanting take a toll on the replanter spiritually, physically, emotionally, relationally, and financially. The pain of replanting necessitates an ability to persevere and endure the high cost of ministry as God uses the replanter to turn a dying church around.

We just need to be honest about the fact that if a man feels called to pursue replanting and go into a church revitalization context, it must be understood from the beginning that this will not be an easy calling. This is a hard calling, which is why it is so vital for a replanter and his family to humbly and honestly count the cost before jumping in. As you assess this man to be sent from your congregation, one thing you must be looking for is a maturity that understands that suffering is going to be part of this call. An ability to wisely evaluate the potential challenges that lie ahead not only for himself personally, but for the congregation and for his family.

Yet in the midst of the challenges and suffering that can come in church replanting, there is also great joy! As we read in James 1, "Consider it pure joy when you face trials of many kinds because the testing of your faith develops perseverance." There is a very real sense in which we are called to enter into Christ's sufferings with joy for the sake of his people and the gospel, just as Christ has suffered for us.

As with *any* vocational calling within the Church or para-church – whether it's youth ministry, children's ministry, worship ministry, small group ministry, or church replanting – we need to understand that suffering is part of this calling. Because of this, we want to help potential replanters enter into the vocation of church replanting and revitlization wisely, thoughtfully, and prayerfully. As Sending Churches, we need to help them develop a solid, Biblical theology of suffering that can help them persevere through the dark times that are sure to come.

Characteristic#3: Affinity for Legacy/History

Most dying churches have bright spots in their history, seasons of health and growth that older members still look back on with great delight. Perhaps it was a time when this church was having a gospel-centered impact on children or youth or the poor in their communities. These are precious memories for remaining folks in this congregation. It is critical that a replanter not only understands and acknowledges the history and legacy of the church they want to replant, but they must also value and even enjoy that church's history. He must seek to remind the church of it and to honor it when and where possible, and then build upon the legacy of those who were there before him.

One of the ways a replanter can get into hot water quickly is by ignoring the church's history or giving the congregation the impression that he doesn't appreciate the past. This mistake is very common and can happen in a number of different ways. As one example, it is common for some replanters to give the impression that they really dislike the building. They're always talking about how old it is and how they need to change the building in this way or that way to make it more relevant and inviting. I don't doubt that most replanters have some legitimate concerns about their building needing to be updated, but they must be careful in how they communicate this with the folks who have been there for years. Remember, these are the men and women who have often sacrificed to build and paint walls in this building, replaced the windows, put in new carpet, washed the pew cushions, and sacrificially given of their finances to help pay the mortgage for the purpose of gospel ministry. They love this building—it is part of their history. Most likely, many of these folks realize that some changes need to be made to the building, however, they need to be led to help make these changes by a pastor who is careful, patient and appreciates their dedication to this building.

The most effective replanters are celebrators of a church's history. They desire to build off this history, not erase it. Where a replanter is going to get people excited and give hope to a dying church isn't simply by looking ahead to what could be. It's also in looking at what has already been—what God has already done in this congregation. It's celebrating the future and the past; dreaming and remembering together. This is why a replanter must love letting folks share stories and celebrate the wonderful things God has done through their church in the past, especially with older members. To share the story once again about that Easter back in 1968 when the neighborhood drunk finally gave church a chance, Jesus saved him, and he was baptized the next week. I mean, these are the types of stories that need to be remembered and celebrated. These are the stories that help renew hope and vision for the future. Helping people see that God's not dead and not done with their church. He's alive! God was alive back then, he's alive now, and he'll be alive in the future! This is what it looks like for a replanter to love and build off of a church's past without allowing people in the congregation to idolize it in an unhealthy way.

Characteristic #4: Multi-Generational Capacity

In replanting, it is important that the replanter is comfortable ministering to folks of all different ages. He must be able to connect fairly easily with both the young and old in his congregation so each group knows they are loved, valued and heard, and so all ages are pastored well. Again, this is a difference that is often seen between most church plants and replants—often times in a new church plant, the congregation looks a lot like the pastor and his family in terms of age, stage of life, etc. In a replanting context, however, ministry typically happens with multi-generational congregants, which is an amazing opportunity even in the face of real challenges. I truly believe the church is at its best when it's multi-generational. In replanting, there are unique challenges that accompany this type of multi-generational reality, and yet at the same time, unique joys.

Practically then, the replanter must be someone who can hang out with and encourage the nine-year-old and the ninety-year-old. Someone who feels comfortable going to the hospital when someone is dying and also showing up to watch a 3rd grader play her first soccer game. They must be an individual who is gifted and eager to float in either of these types of contexts among many others. This doesn't mean that the replanter must be off the charts gifted in ministering to every age group—it's humbly recognizing the fact that he has been called to be a pastor for the whole church. To love those of all ages and to be involved in the lives of the sheep under his care. For younger pastors who are seeking to replant and shepherd an older congregation, see **Appendix Y**—"Shepherding Older Church Members as a Younger Pastor."

Leading With Multi-Generational Capacity

One of the first things I noticed when I started to consider the possibility of marrying my church plant with a 158 year old church in our neighborhood was the drastic differences of age in the congregations. I had moved from Durham, NC to Baltimore, MD to plant a church and in our congregation I was an old guy (34 at the time). But when God opened an opportunity for us to meet in the facility of a historic church in South Baltimore I became a young guy. The existing congregation was composed of about 20 people and 90% of them were over 65 years old. Looking back over the three years since the two congregations married to form one congregation there are a few things I wish I would have known then.

Often times you will find that the senior adults in an existing church have given the better part of their life to service in the church. One of the senior adults in our church (Ray) had been a member for 62 years and he served as a deacon that cared for the facilities. When we met for the first time he asked if I wanted to take a tour of the facility. I accepted his invitation but what I didn't know was that I was honoring him by walking slowly through the building listening to stories. Sometimes we just need to slow our pace so that we can shepherd the senior adults well. Something that I was not prepared for was the expectations of what a pastor was and was not based on the past experience with other pastors. God has shaped me and gifted me in specific ways. However, that doesn't always match up to what our senior adults have experienced with former pastors. That being said, I think it is wise to not allow the praise to go to your head and don't let the criticism crush your spirit. Be a faithful shepherd to the sheep and don't try to meet expectations that are cultural but not biblical. Another aspect that I had to learn about ministering in the midst of a replant that wasn't applicable to me as a church planter is the art of hospital and home visits. Friends, I wish I could say that this comes naturally to me but it doesn't. This is something that I have to be intentional about or it won't happen. The work that Brian Croft has done with the Practical Shepherding ministry has produced some great resources that have served me well in this new season of ministry.

Ultimately I think we must see the senior adults that remain in these existing churches as blessings to celebrate and not obstacles to overcome. This doesn't mean that we acquiesce to everything that they want or expect. It does mean that we see the image of God in them and we recognize that Christ shed his blood so that they might learn to rest in the good news of the gospel. Pastors, let us serve the

elderly sheep well and in doing so demonstrate the Good Shepherd's
heart to the watching congregation.

Brad O'Brien
Lead Pastor
Jesus Our Redeemer Church

Characteristic #5: Resourceful Generalist

What does it mean to be a resourceful generalist? Scant resources, limited
budgets, small or non-existent staff and absent or out of date technology are
standard features in a dying and declining church. That's not a shock, right?
Replanters wear many hats. They know how to get things done, gather
resources and do the best with what they have in front of them. The lack of
available resources should not reduce their efforts, energy, or impact to love
and lead their people well.

A replanter is going into a situation where resources are limited on all
kinds of levels. This means the replanter must be a generalist, willing to do
whatever it takes to shepherd this church. The replanter must recognize,
"Hey, I may be the custodian, secretary, preacher, worship leader, and the
middle school Sunday School teacher all on the same Sunday! This is part of
the calling to replant!" The replanter must be willing to say, "Whatever you
need, God. Whatever this church needs, I'm willing to do." That's really
what I'm getting at when describing a resourceful generalist: A humble,
servant's heart that is willing to do whatever is needed and whatever it takes
to lovingly lead this church back to health.

This might mean serving in areas that are not your favorite places to
serve and doing things you'd rather not do. It means leading areas of ministry
outside of your comfort zone. A resourceful generalist does the best they can
with what they have. But at the same time, this doesn't mean they seek to do
everything themselves. It means equipping others in the giftings God's given
them and unleashing *them* to serve in various ways as well. A resourceful
generalist is a servant leader willing to model sacrificial, joyful service before

anyone else in the congregation. No task is beneath them. The congregation knows and sees this in the way the replanter leads this church.

A Quick Word on Plurality:
4 Reasons for Pastor-Elder Plurality in Replanting

In this chapter we are discussing the qualifications specifically related to the lead replanting pastor-elder. However, on the heels of considering the need for this replanter to be a resourceful generalist, I believe it is appropriate to briefly address the whole idea of plurality in pastoral leadership. While some may disagree, I feel it is both biblical and wise to consider the role a plurality of pastor-elders will play in the long-term health of the replant, the lead replanter, and his family. As Brian Croft writes,

Although not explicitly stated by Paul to Timothy, it is consistently implied all throughout the New Testament that there is to be more than one pastor and deacon in each local church. Other than the passages that describe the qualifications of a pastor or deacon (1 Tim. 3:1-13; Titus 1:5-9) there are numerous examples of both these offices serving with other qualified men, sharing the responsibilities (Acts 20:28; 1 Peter 5:1-4; Heb. 13:17). Not to mention, the burdens and responsibilities of these two offices are too great for one man to carry alone.[27]

While it may take some time to raise up other qualified pastor-elders in the replant, beyond the clear teaching of Scripture on this issue, let me briefly share four practical reasons it is wise to move toward this shared leadership model.

Reason #1: Helps to assure that Jesus remains the primary leader and hero of the replant. Any replant that is built on one pastor-elder is vulnerable to making that individual the hero rather than Jesus. When things are going great in the church that pastor-elder gets way too much credit and when things are going bad, he gets way too much blame. A plurality of pastor-elders helps to keep each of these in check.

Reason #2: Prepares the replant for future health. Life is short. Not one of us will be in our church forever, which is why replanters should always seek to lead with the future in mind. Building a team of pastor-elders who shepherd the flock helps to set the congregation up well for healthy pastoral leadership if the lead replanter dies or is called away to another ministry.

Reason #3: Long-haul sustainability comes as a result of shared pastoral duties. Pastoral ministry is hard work. It is taxing on a physical, mental, emotional, and spiritual level. The primary reason I believe the Apostle Paul always speaks of a plurality of pastor-elders in his letters is because one guy can't do it all alone! Shepherding takes a team to do well. If we desire to have pastor-elders who are healthy in mind, body, and soul for ministry and their families for the long-haul, a plurality of shepherds is absolutely vital.

Reason #4: The health of a diverse, yet unified, pulpit. A shared pulpit is a good thing when those sharing the pulpit are a unified group of humble, Biblically qualified pastor-elders. This shared preaching approach will allow the congregation to be fed by different pastor-elders, each with unique personalities and giftings. There is not one preacher who will connect with everyone in the same way in the same congregation. A shared preaching model helps teach those in the replant to value and experience a variety of preachers, all committed to loving and shepherding God's people through the faithful, expositional preaching of God's Word. It also can aid in getting away from a cult of personality – we want people to follow Jesus, not a personality in the pulpit.

#6: Tactical Patience

Progress and pace are different in church replanting. Some things can be addressed immediately; others have to wait—either for the congregation to be ready to move or for the resources to be present. A replanter is continually looking toward what is up ahead and is seeking to help the congregation move forward, yet they know that timing and patience are key in bringing the church along. Tactical patience understands that waiting is not wasted time.

There are two key components to this idea of tactical patience. One is timing, the other is patient wisdom. It's not one or the other that's needed to lead a replant, but both. Tactical patience comes in knowing the timing of when to change something in the church, and also when *not* to change something. Knowing when to say something, and when not to say something. What hills are hills to die on, and which aren't.

At the heart of tactical patience is wisdom and discernment that is ours only through the power and leading of the Holy Spirit. Tactical patience means knowing the right and a wrong time to make a decision or to have a conversation, being patient enough to wait on God's timing to address that issue.

Characteristic #7: Emotional Intelligence

Replanting a church, as with ministry in general, is all about people. It involves a lot of understanding, relating to, and caring for all different types of people created in the image of God. Ministry is people-work. The reason why many pastors fail in the Church is not because they don't know enough Bible and theology, it's because they aren't good with people. They may be overly awkward with people or not realize that many perceive him as being mad all the time because he seems to always carry a scowl on his face. The sad part is, they are probably not even aware of it! It's a lack of emotional intelligence.

There is no better indicator for success in relationships within our ministries than one's emotional intelligence. But what exactly is emotional intelligence? Emotional intelligence, defined by the Oxford Dictionary, is the capacity to be aware of, control, and express one's emotions, and to handle interpersonal relationships judiciously and empathetically. At its core, emotional intelligence consists of the following four leadership skills or competencies:

- **Self-Awareness:** The ability to know yourself and your emotions, not as you wish they were, but as they really are.

- **Self-Regulation:** The wisdom and ability to understand the impact you have when you take action or refrain from action.

- **Social Awareness:** The ability to read other people and understand their emotions.

- **Relationship Management:** The ability to incorporate the other three skills to navigate and build positive relationships with all types of people, in one-on-one and group settings.

At the heart of emotional intelligence are lifelong skills that allow a replanting pastor to be more empathetic and have better interpersonal relationships. Personal growth in emotional intelligence helps replanters love people well, speak in an appropriate tone that brings comfort or correction, and to practice being more patient and caring with those in our ministry that are difficult to love and lead. These are skills absolutely vital in replanting a dying congregation. Emotional intelligence is a must for a replanter to be effective in leading healthy change.

Characteristic #8: Spousal Support

A replanter isn't alone in his calling. He understands that his spouse will serve an important role in supporting him as well as the family while he is leading the church. The replanter's wife possesses a love for Jesus and the Church and is committed for the long haul, understanding the road of ministry will be full of ups and downs. Perhaps most importantly, the replanter's spouse must be emotionally and spiritually prepared for the challenges that come with replanting a dying church.

As a Sending Church, it's just as vital that you are helping the replanter's wife prepare for replanting as you are the replanter, both emotionally and spiritually. This means helping her mature in regards to her relationship with the Lord, growth in the gospel, love for the Word of God, intimacy with Jesus, and her relationships with others.

The challenges of replanting can take an emotional and spiritual toll on anybody. This can be especially true for a replanter's wife. It's hard to see your husband being beat up and criticized by church members. This is often a difficult and unfortunate reality in church replanting. The Sending Church must help prepare them emotionally and spiritually for this. Each wife is different—some might be more emotionally and spiritually mature than others. However, the Sending Church must seek to lead and prepare the couple together well for this unique and challenging ministry.

EXERCISE: MARRIAGE & MINISTRY SELF-ASSESSMENT

The following is a self-assessment to help the replanter and his wife reflect on their calling to church replanting. These ten questions are valuable to have the replanter and his wife answer, honestly evaluating their responses together as individuals and as a couple. While several of these questions are directly targeted to the replanter, it is helpful for his wife to share insight and input from her perspective as his wife and best friend. It is recommended to have one or two leadership couples sit down with the replanting couple to discuss their responses to these questions.

Marriage & Ministry Self-Assessment

1. Do I see this opportunity as a mission field?

2. Am I emotionally mature enough to take upon myself the rigors of taking the lead role in a church?

3. Am I biblically and theologically competent enough to lead this congregation?

4. Am I organizationally competent?

5. How will I respond to and love my critics?

6. Will I make a commitment for the long haul, through good and bad?

7. Will I be a continuous learner about church revitalization and pastoral leadership?

8. Am I committed to being a positive example and encourager for my family on this journey?

9. Do I have pastoral mentors who can coach and encourage me?

10. Do I have a sufficient support system of peer relationships and friends?

FOR FURTHER REFLECTION

Discussion Questions

1. Take a minute to reflect on your life & share about a pastor who had a major impact on you. What were two of the qualities that made him a great pastor? How do you think he gained those two qualities in his personality & ministry?

2. When you think about the Jonathan Edwards quote that compares going into ministry to going into warfare, how important is your role as a sending/replanting church?

3. As you look at the list of 15 biblical qualifications of a replanted, how can your church help a replanting pastor live out these qualifications and grow in them?

4. When you look over the list of the essential characteristics of a replanter (that are different than a church planter), are there any that you don't totally understand? Any that stand out to you that you may not have thought of before?

Ways to Pray

- Pray for the pastors that God will raise up under your church to be sent out as replanters.

- Pray that they will live lives true to the Biblical qualifications of a pastor.

- Pray for your church to be a place where they grow in understanding themselves & their call as replanting pastors.

Chapter 7

STEP#4: EVALUATING THE POTENTIAL REPLANT

Change is part of life, and whether we like it or not, change is inevitable. It is inevitable in our personal lives, families, communities, world, and even our churches. Being leaders in the church, we *must* deal with and lead change constantly.

Leaders are agents of change, mainly because a leader's job is to help take people and churches from where they are to where they need to be. This is much easier said than done. In fact, leading change well is one of, if not *the* most challenging aspects of serving and leading in a local church context.

Leading change well is a particular challenge when it comes to church replanting. But before we can begin to talk about how to lead change well in a replant, we first need to learn how to discern whether or not a particular church is even ready for the change that comes through being replanted. This chapter is focused on helping to ask and answer strategic questions to help you evaluate a congregation's readiness to change and move forward toward true revitalization.

IS THIS CHURCH READY TO BE REPLANTED?

How do we determine whether a church is actually ready to be replanted? Many churches recognize they are struggling and in need of help, but how do we distinguish between a church that is ready to go "all in" as a replant, and a church that is not ready for that step? Specifically, we must measure their readiness particularly as it pertains to the giving up of control and decision making. This is where doing honest, strategic evaluation of a potential replant is absolutely vital.

WHY IS IT VITAL TO ASSESS WHETHER A CHURCH IS READY FOR REVITALIZATION?

Let me offer three primary reasons why this step is so important.

Reason #1: To Name Reality

I've heard it said that the number one job of a leader is always to name reality. What we must do when we're assessing a church's readiness for replanting is to identify where the church *really* is, now. What are the real strengths? What are the real challenges? What are the potential pitfalls? What does this church need to become healthy again? These are the types of questions that must be wrestled with in order to clearly see the reality of the situation.

Reason #2: To Count the Cost (and the Joy)

Good assessment helps a potential church replanter and Sending Church to count the cost. "Hey, if I'm going to give my life to this, here are some of the challenges I am walking into. At the same time here are some of the joys and opportunities that will come in this leadership situation." We want to be wise in this. We must honestly count the cost and the joy of potentially replanting this particular congregation.

Reason#3: To Determine the Fit

It's not enough to just say, "Okay, here's the cost and the joy involved. Am I ready and willing to do this?" There are other important questions to be asked as well, like if this replanting opportunity is the right fit for the Sending Church. Can we see our church having a healthy, long-haul relationship with this congregation? Is this the right fit for the replanting pastor we are going to send out—his gifts, passions, wiring? What about his wife and family? Can we see them thriving here? It is crucial to really dig in and determine the fit of this replanting opportunity.

These are three basic reasons why it's so important to thoroughly assess a potential replant on the front end and to determine the readiness of this congregation before jumping all in. Now, the next question we must think through is *how do we do this well*. In particular, what must be our posture when assessing a church's readiness?

WHAT IS THE RIGHT POSTURE WHEN ASSESSING A CHURCH'S READINESS FOR REVITALIZATION?

As you begin to evaluate a church that is considering being replanted, you are obviously dealing with a congregation in major decline and one that is in need of serious help. It's a church that needs radical revitalization. The question is whether they see this reality or not. Whether they want to be revitalized or not. Whether they are willing to do whatever it takes to make it happen. As you begin to enter into relationship with this congregation and begin to assess their readiness for replanting, what are some of the core components to doing this well?

Let me offer four keys to effectively assessing a church's readiness:

Key #1: Having a Humble and Gracious Heart

You want to pray as you are engaging this dying congregation that God will give *you* a humble heart. You want to pray that God would help you see this congregation with his eyes, full of compassion, love, and grace. "Lord, help me to see these people as You see these people. Help me to see this church as You see this church." Humility and grace help us to fight against slipping into a critical spirit. It's easy to be overly critical when looking at the surface of a dying church and see the overwhelming amount of things that are wrong. If we're not careful we can slip into a subtle pride or skepticism that is dishonoring to this church and to the Lord who loves to bring churches just like this one back to life. God wants us to see with eyes of faith that flows from a heart of humility and grace.

Key #2: Being Willing to Honestly Evaluate

When we're assessing a church, we must be honest about the good, the bad, and the ugly. We need be realists. Hopeful and faith-filled realists, yes, but realists all the same. Many a pastor has quickly, even hastily, rushed into a church revitalization context without truly assessing the lay of the land, only to find himself in a situation he and his family are not prepared for. There may be a temptation to unwisely gloss over real issues and challenges that are present in this congregation under the guise of "God's got this! He'll take care of the tough stuff in this church." While of course God is sovereign and in control of all things and he cares for this congregation deeply, this must never be an excuse for failing to do one's due diligence in assessing the readiness of a congregation for the type of radical change that replanting brings.

Key #3: Having a Hopeful Vision of What Can Be

This is one of the most exciting aspects of replanting. We must be preaching and practicing hope in what God can do in and through this church! Leading with contagious, joyful, hope-filled vision is *crucial* in effectively leading a replant. It can be so easy to feel overwhelmed and discouraged when looking at the things that need to be fixed or changed in the church, but visionary leaders don't let this weigh them down and steal their joy in what God can do. It is vital to dream as you look at this church. What could be? What could the Lord do in and through these people? In this community? In the world?

When we lead with hopeful vision, we are leading with eyes of faith. The folks in this congregation need that type of leadership desperately. This kind of hopeful leadership is not focused on what you can do to revitalize this church, but rather on what *God* can do in and through this congregation for his glory. And so we must dream as we're assessing a dying church, with real faith, hope and trust.

Key #4: Pursuing Prayerful Wisdom Continually

Through this whole process of assessment, we want to be in heavy prayer, and often. We want to be humble and honest. We want to have vision. But most importantly, we want to be constantly praying for God to give us discernment and wisdom from above, not below. This is why having several people involved in this assessment process is so important. Different personalities, giftings, and ages is crucial in helping to best discern God's leading in this process. This is not a one-man show. It is a community effort. *Churches replant churches.* Individuals don't replant churches. Therefore, churches must work together to discern and assess the readiness of a congregation.

BEFORE ANYTHING ELSE...IS THERE THEOLOGICAL ALIGNMENT?

Before moving onto other matters of assessment and evaluation, it is critical that you do your work in discerning whether or not this dying congregation is theologically aligned with your church. Why is theological alignment so important when revitalizing a congregation? To be honest, this is actually the most important question you can ask before engaging in a replanting process. If your congregation and the declining congregation are not aligned theologically in regards to primary, core doctrinal convictions, the replant simply will not work. It's that simple. There are many reasons for this. Here are just a few to consider.

Reason #1: Biblical revitalization won't happen unless it is fueled by the authority of God's Word.

Trying to revitalize a dying congregation that no longer holds to the Bible as the inspired word of God, sufficient and authoritative in all matters of faith and practice, will be very difficult, if not impossible, to revitalize. The Lord speaks through his Word. His Word has power, not only to transform the lives of individuals, but to transform congregations. Whether it be through preaching the Word each and every week or seeking to align the ministry strategies and church leadership structures with Biblical truth, if the congregation is not committed to the Bible as the final authority, you have a big problem. If the Bible is not the final authority in the church, then something else will takes its place. A church's tradition is never the final authority. An individual or family in the church who has been there for years is never the final authority. Even a pastor or the elder or deacon board is never the final authority. *The Word of God must be the final authority.* It is always the final authority because it makes God the authority. God revitalizes churches by his Spirit and through the Word. For true revitalization to happen, the Bible must be the boss. And this is a really good thing.

Reason#2: Biblical revitalization won't happen unless the true gospel is believed by both congregations.

If the Sending Church's understanding of the gospel is different from that of the dying church, you will have real problems. A shared understanding and love for the biblical gospel is non-negotiable in replanting. For instance, if a congregation who holds to an orthodox understanding of the gospel is attempting to help revitalize a congregation that does not share the same foundational convictions concerning the gospel, it will be next to impossible to move them out on mission to reach the lost in that community. Why proclaim the good news of Christ's saving work for sinners if you don't believe people are really that sinful? The point is this: There must be clarity and unified alignment in both understanding of the gospel, as well as the implications of the gospel for life, ministry, and mission. Christ Jesus and him crucified must be preached and proclaimed from the pulpit, in small groups, in Sunday school classes, children's and youth ministry, and every other area of this church if we truly desire for God to bless it and bring it back to life.

Reason #3: Biblical revitalization won't happen unless there is clarity on both theological essentials and non-essentials.

It may be that there are secondary matters of doctrine in which you choose to agree to disagree on with this dying congregation. This is a decision that must be made with great wisdom and much prayer. Perhaps there are certain doctrines or practices that might be a little bit different from what you would prefer, but they are not reason for division or cause to prevent your church from moving forward in revitalizing this congregation. For example, does it matter if this congregation prefers pews rather than chairs? Are you ok if they want their pastor to preach in khakis rather than jeans? For a while, can you gladly live with their desire to be led by piano instead of guitar in worship? These are the types of questions only you and your church leaders can answer, but it is important to be clear on these before entering a replanting process. What is most important is that you are crystal clear on the doctrinal essentials that must be shared between the two congregations if this replant is to become reality.

TWO TYPES OF ASSESSMENTS

Once you have discerned that there is indeed theological alignment between the two congregations, you are ready to begin asking different types of questions to help you assess both the history and health of this church. There are two main categories of questions that must be asked. The first category are questions to ask *outside of this church about this church* to determine its readiness for replanting. The second category are questions to ask *inside of this church about this church* to determine its readiness.

Assessment #1: External

We want to get insight and perspective from those who are not currently a part of the dying congregation. We want to hear how this church is perceived by the community because there is much we can learn about the congregation from these voices, both for good and bad. Let's consider some specific groups of people to ask and talk with. Because again, the goal here is to learn as much as you can about the culture of this church, both past and present.

Key Groups

Other Pastors and Church Leaders. Other pastors, youth pastors, church leaders, and para-church ministry leaders in the community can bring incredible insight into the health or un-health of a congregation. These are folks you want to hear from—you will want to make some phone calls to these individuals, and potentially grab a coffee with a few of these folks. You want the insight these individuals can offer.

Community Leaders. Principals and teachers in local schools can potentially be a great source of wisdom. To sit down with them and simply say, "Tell me your thoughts on this congregation. What do you know about this church? What have you heard about this church that is positive or negative?" If they don't know anything about the church, that is something you want to know as well. You need to ask *why* this is the case. How will that be changed in the future? Along with educators, other community leaders (such as city government officials and local business owners) can also be very helpful. Former Members and Pastors. While this may not always be possible, I think it can be very helpful to hear from former members, leaders, and pastors of this congregation. What was their experience like at this church? What were things they loved about this church? What were some of the challenges they experienced? What was in their decision to leave the church?

Neighbors. Often times, the best indicator of how the community perceives this congregation comes from the immediate neighbors of the church. I can remember when I first came to Calvary and literally walking around the neighborhood and asking folks what they thought of our church. Unfortunately, most of them had *no* thoughts because there hadn't been much intentional outreach to the neighborhood for a long time. A few had very positive things to share about Calvary, while still others were skeptical of churches in general and didn't know how to answer. Regardless of the responses you get, it is a helpful exercise to talk with those who live closest to the church and get their thoughts and opinions on this congregation. It is eye-opening, and you get to love and encourage individuals that, Lord willing, you will potentially lead to Christ and welcome into this new congregation.

These are four groups that help bring important insight to this congregation. Now, to get super practical, what are some of the specific questions that should be asked to these different groups of people? What exactly do we want to know, and what information are we trying to get? Of course, we aren't seeking information in order to dig up dirt on individuals or to spread gossip, but rather to help make an informed decision on whether or not there is potential to move forward in partnership. Let me share five questions I think should be asked to get the most helpful information to aid in your assessment of this congregation.

Key Questions

Question #1: What is the reputation of this church?

What is the reputation of the church in this community? Is it positive? Is it negative? Is it forgotten? In other words, nobody really thinks much of this church because people don't know much about it. It is sort of a "non-factor" in the community. If the impressions of this church are either negative or positive, why is that the case? Try to get feedback that is as specific as possible.

Question #2: What does the community need from this church?

This is an important question. This is a question that you're going to want to ask continually to those in the community once you begin to replant the church, if you choose to go that road. It is insightful to sit with different community leaders and ask, "What does this community need from this congregation? How can this church serve the community?" You will be amazed at the responses you get from these questions.

Question #3: What can you tell me about the previous pastors?

Now again, depending on the makeup and size of the community, some, perhaps many, won't be able to answer this question. They simply won't know of any pastors who have served this church in the past. However, especially in smaller communities, some will be able to. Questions such as, "What were the strengths of this pastor, as far as you could tell? What did people love about him? What were the weaknesses in his leadership? Do you know why he left? Were there problems? What were the issues?" There is much you can learn about the culture and history of a dying congregation by the answers you receive to these questions.

Question #4: What divisive issues are you aware of in this church?

Those outside the church are likely unaware of most in-house squabbles. However, the issues may be quite serious if even the surrounding community has heard or witnessed them. Moreover, knowing how divisive issues have been handled in this congregation will help the replanting pastor prepare for leading through conflict in the future.

Question #5: What are the greatest strengths & weaknesses of this church?

Again, perhaps only a small number of folks will be able to speak to these questions in a helpful way, but it can be very helpful information to have. Remember that how the community perceives this congregation, for good or bad, will affect how you strategically lead this replant into the future.

If you are able to gain information by asking these five questions of those outside the church, you will better understand what's going on inside this church. You want perspective. This is wisdom, and wisdom in this context is asking the right questions to the right people in order to gain insight, asking God to help you rightly discern and weigh what you have heard. This leads to the second category of questions that are actually more important than the first.

Assessment #2: Internal

Now we are moving from talking with those outside the congregation to those inside the congregation. These need to be asked and discussed with the people of this church who are invested and all in. These are the people you are going to be shepherding and leading in this replant. These are the people you're going to be revitalizing this church with.

Before jumping into these questions, it's important to briefly note that my assumption is that you're already on board with this congregation theologically. With the following questions, I'm trying to drive specifically at those that are going to help you to assess the readiness of this church for replanting beyond theological matters. Let's briefly go over the specific groups of people you want to talk with inside the church.

Key Groups

Older Members & Attenders. You're going to want to ask older members a lot of questions. These are folks who have been there for a long time and who have given themselves to this church. It's very likely that they're invested and highly committed.

Newer Members & Attenders. Chances are, there aren't many of these individuals in the church. However, you might be surprised. For those who are there, those who have been attending the church for just the past 1-2 years or less, you want to get to know why they are there? What do they love about this church? Even if it's one young couple or single adult, you want to pick their brains and get their insight.

Current Leaders. This is probably the most critical group of folks in the church to talk with. These leaders are most likely the primary influencers in this congregation. The reason for this is because often what happens as a church declines is that those with the most influence in the church body rise up in power. This can be a good thing or a bad thing, depending on the heart of the individual leader. There are probably other men and women in the church who have power and influence, though they are not serving in official leadership positions. You need to figure out who these individuals are. The remaining people know who has the real influence in this church, and you also need to know. You're going to want to intentionally pursue these individuals once you figure out who they are and ask a lot of questions and do even more listening.

These are the main players that will help make the transition to a replant a healthy one or a difficult one.

Key Questions

There are three primary types of questions that need to be asked to those inside the church when assessing its readiness for replanting. The first is what I'm calling questions that lead to joyful celebration. These are the easiest questions to ask. These are questions that help these remaining folks celebrate the good of their church. The good of what God has done and is doing in their congregation. We start with these types of questions in order to encourage them and begin to build trust with them.

You want to lead them with love. Take mental notes as you listen so that you can build on this legacy.

Category #1: Joyful Celebration (Easy)

In your opinion, what are the three best things about this church?

This is a great question to get things rolling. People love to brag on their church. They love it. It is both a joy for these folks to share this and it is a joy and privilege to listen to them! It will lift their spirits. They're going to care about the fact that you care, and that you want to hear them talk about the things they love about their church.

What would the average person say is the best thing about this church?

One thing that's interesting about this question is that it will give you perspective on how well they understand and see reality. Here's what I mean—notice how the question is worded. You might find that one person says one thing and somebody else says something completely different, perhaps even conflicting. This is a good thing. This will help you accurately understand what really are the best things happening in this church. Semantics matter!

What is your dream for how the church might look ten years from now?

This is a fun question to ask. You want to ask this question in a way that is encouraging and hopeful. Let them dream. Chances are, nobody has ever asked them this question. It's likely they haven't asked themselves this question since they've been in decline. One of the things you're listening for when you ask this question is what are they focused on. For instance, if all of their focus is on the building, the cosmetics of the church, saying things like, "We'd love to paint that wall," or, "We'd really like to get rid of those old broken pews and replace them with chairs," or, "We need to polish the organ," these types of responses are big indicators on what they believe the solution is to their decline.

What you're hoping to hear is this: "We want to reach people with the gospel! I remember when this church had little kids going to VBS, coming to Jesus, and young parents coming, and the community was changing. We want to see God do that again!" If all they're concerned about is the building, or other secondary matters, you want to know that now. What you're looking for is the heart of these remaining folks. Do they want to see Jesus made famous and to see the lost saved? Do they want to see the community transformed? Do they want to see God glorified?

Who is the favorite pastor in the history of the church and why?

This is an insightful question. Be sure to really listen. Listen for what they loved about the pastor. How long did this pastor serve the church? What made him the "legend" that he is in this church? Because the truth is, every pastor since has been living in the shadow of this pastor in the eyes of some. That's just the reality. Was he loved because he was such a great preacher? Or maybe because he was a great leader? Here's my guess. This pastor was deeply loved because *he* deeply loved the people of this church. I mean think about it. Why do we have fond memories of anybody? We forget about sermons and cool ministry programs and events, but we don't forget the impression someone made on our lives because they loved us so well. Whatever it was, you want to hear the stories about this beloved pastor and why he is so adored.

What is your fondest memory of the church?

Again, people love to share stories. You want to hear as many stories as you possibly can about this church. Get them talking. Encourage them to share cherished memories about special events that have taken place in the past, Sunday School classes that once were thriving, youth camps and retreats where lives were changed, unique ways in which God worked in the life of this body in decades past. What a gift it will be to listen to these sweet memories together.

So, that's the first type of question—those that lead to joyful celebration. These are easy and they are important. Start with these, but don't stop there. Next, we're going to move on to the second category:

Category #2: Honest Reflection (Moderate)

At this point, we're beginning to push in a little bit more. With these questions, we are moving from easy to moderate in terms of comfort level for those answering. These will be a bit more difficult and uncomfortable to answer. They're not quite as hard as we'll get to in a moment, but these are questions that lovingly force individuals to reflect honestly on where they are as a church.

How are decisions made in this church (both formally & informally)?

Here's what we know. Every church is going to have a formal process by which decisions are made. Typically, this process will align with whatever by-laws are still in existence. You want to know what this process is.

However, there is also going to be an informal process by which decisions are made. This can be more difficult to identify. Often times in dying churches there are particular gateways you must proceed through to get things approved. The challenge is that sometimes these gateways are almost secretive (intentional or otherwise), known only by true insiders in the church. If you fail to go through the right gateway, you're dead meat. A landmine is ready to go off at any moment! There is an informal decision making process. You need to figure out what it is. Asking lots of good questions can help immensely.

If a big decision needs to be made, to whom do the members look for blessing & approval?

What you're trying to identify by asking this question is who the power players in this church are. Who are those individuals that everybody knows you need to run things by for approval, even if the by-laws don't mandate it. Who do you need to keep in the loop regarding specific decisions that if you don't, a potential conflict awaits. Often times the secret gateways one must go through to get things passed or approved are individuals in the church. We want to identify these men and women as soon as possible. Moving forward, these are the people you will probably need to spend extra time with to try to get on board with certain decisions and changes that are sure to come. Spending the time to find the answer to this question will be beneficial in the long run as you can invest in this person, helping them use their influence in the church for good that leads to unity, not for bad that leads to division.

What is the biggest mistake made by your previous pastors or church leaders?

In ministry, you can learn a lot by learning from the mistakes of older pastors and leaders. You want to hear about the mistakes of previous pastors and leaders. What were the mistakes? What were the things that were said or not said? What were the things done or not done that caused tension, pain, and possibly division? Dig in here. Try to hear the heart behind the hurt in those sharing.

Do the church members generally (and happily) follow their pastors and leaders?

In Hebrews 13:17 we read,

> Obey your leaders and submit to them, for they keep watch over your souls as those who will give an account, so that they can do this with joy and not with grief, for that would be unprofitable for you.

We see in this verse that pastors will give an account to God for the sheep that are under their care. But there is a second piece to this verse. The other piece says that the people of the congregation are to gladly and willingly submit to the loving leadership of their pastors and leaders. Is this church a humble congregation? Do they love to follow their pastors and leaders? Have they humbly followed them in the past, and in what ways? Or is there a history of not following their leaders? Is there a history of dishonoring or even fighting against them? We want to get to the heart of this question as many sick and dying churches do not have a great track record with pastors for one reason or another.

What are the expectations laid upon church members?

Typically, churches that are healthy are churches that have a clear membership process and clear expectations. Declining churches don't. In a dying church, chances are there's no clear process nor expectations for church members. But you still want to ask the question. This church may have thirty people coming on Sunday, but on the rolls they have two hundred members.

In a church like this, you can have a business meeting where you need to vote on an important issue and all of a sudden you get seventy people showing up to vote at the meeting who haven't been in worship for years. This is a huge problem in many declining and unhealthy churches. This is why it's so important to honestly evaluate and clean up the membership rolls continually, making sure voting members are active members in the congregation.

Category #3: Necessary Evaluation (Difficult)

This third and final group of questions are the most difficult and uncomfortable questions to both ask and answer, but they are the most important. Each of these questions will probably have follow up questions that will need to be asked to press in further. As you will see, these questions serve to shed light onto the culture of the congregation, as well as some of the sacred cows that may exist.

What might a pastor say from the pulpit that would cause many of the members to cringe?

In other words, what are some of the "hot button" issues for this congregation? These are those invisible landmines a replanter can step on without seeing. These might be doctrinal. They might be philosophical. They might be political. They might be matters of lifestyle. Whatever they are, you want to approach this one very carefully and humbly. You obviously don't want to be offensive, but you do want to know what these things might be for the sake of serving this church well in the future. No need to hit hot buttons and set people off for no reason. Each church has its own culture & it's important to recognize the context ahead of time. The hope is that the remaining members are those who want to see this potential replant be a success and because of this, they will *want* to help point these hot buttons out to you. Of course, it may be that these hot buttons shouldn't be hot buttons and need to be called out, but they must be called out in the right way at the right time. Namely, after you have earned the trust of the congregation.

What items in the current worship service are non-negotiable? What items are acceptable and have been featured in the past?

Some of the biggest sacred cows in dying churches have to do with the worship service. Not all of them, but a lot of them do. The order of service, frequency of the Lord's Supper, role of the organ or piano, the dress of the pastor. The presence or lack thereof of guitars, drums, and other instruments. If there's a choir, do they wear robes or not? This is a huge topic of conversation that you really want to push into.

What is the present financial situation of the church?

As uncomfortable as it may be, it is important and necessary to gain clarity on the present financial situation of the church. If your church is going to potentially take over this declining congregation, it is critical that you are up to speed with detailed information regarding every area of finances. Questions like these must be asked: What is the budget for the current year? How much money is the church currently bringing in on a weekly and monthly basis? How much debt does this church have? What kinds of savings does this congregation have? How much money is in the checking account at the moment? As far as givers in the church, is giving spread out fairly evenly among those left in the congregation or are there one or two big givers keeping this church afloat? These and more questions must be asked and discussed regarding the finances of this church. We are called to be good stewards of God's money, which means we must have an accurate understanding and assessment of where this church currently is financially.

What are the expectations for the pastor's wife and children (spoken & unspoken)?

This is huge. In most churches there are spoken and unspoken expectations of the pastor's wife and his children. Most folks in the church won't come right out and share these so you will have to dig a little bit. What have been the expectations in the past? Have those changed? Why are those expectations there in the first place? This is worth some honest conversation.

Would this congregation have any objection to the pastor meeting with people and working on sermons from outside the church?

For example, would they be okay with the pastor working from a coffee shop? A library? A local hang out spot? Churches are different when it comes to this issue. Some congregations are fine with allowing their pastors to work from the library or a local coffee shop. In other churches, this would be a huge point of contention. These churches say, "Look, you need to be in the church building. That's what we pay you for." You want to know where this congregation falls on this issue. The reason this is a question worth asking is because part of effective church revitalization is having a pastor who is living on mission and helping the congregation to live on mission. The traditional paradigm of forcing the pastor to stay in his office all week, expecting people to come to him, completely goes against the necessary missional work of a replanting pastor. Culture has changed. For all kinds of reasons, typically pastors now must go to the people, not the other way around. He needs to be in the community, meeting new people, hanging out with lost people. This can't happen sitting behind a desk all day inside the church building. While this may seem like a small thing on the surface, it will actually have huge ramifications for how ministry is carried out by the pastor and other additional staff in the future.

In addition to those listed above, here is a list of questions that might be asked to church insiders in the process of assessing a church's readiness for being replanted:

19 Additional Questions to Ask "Insiders"

1. In your opinion, what are the three biggest challenges in the church right now?

2. What is the policy and general understanding regarding the pastor's days off and holidays?

3. Do you think it would be relatively easy for a young family to settle into the church or the town?

4. Does this church network with other churches? Who? How?

5. What are the spoken and unspoken expectations for the pastor in this church?

6. What would the average person say is the biggest problem in the church right now?

7. How would you sum up the spiritual health of the congregation in regards to prayer, a heart for evangelism, love for one another, etc.?

8. In your opinion, what was the best quality about the former pastor? What was the most difficult or challenging quality about the former pastor?

9. Why did your previous pastor leave? How long did he serve the church?

10. What do you think he would say was the biggest difficulty in pastoring this church?

11. How long have pastors typically stayed in this congregation? Over the last thirty years of the church how long is the pastor's average tenure?

12. What are some of the "sacred cows" I need to be aware of?

13. How well does this congregation do with change?

14. Can you share some of the changes that have been made (big or small) in this congregation in the past few years? How has that been received?

15. If I was your pastor, what advice would you give me in order to lead a change of some kind most effectively for everyone? What would be the appropriate process to do so, in your opinion?

16. What has been the biggest conflict in the church in the past five, ten, twenty years? What is the biggest conflict in the history of the church? Has there ever been a church split? What were the issues involved?

17. What was the topic of your last contentious business meeting? What was the disagreement about? How was the issue settled?

18. How well does this church handle conflict? Can you share an example of a conflict and how it was handled in the past two years?

19. What is potentially the most divisive issue in the church (practical, doctrinal, personal)?

THE DISCERNMENT GRID: BEING CLEAR ON THE NON-NEGOTIABLES AND NEGOTIABLES

Once you have thoroughly examined this congregation, exploring its readiness to be replanted by your congregation, you will need to compile all of the information you have gathered for the purpose of prayer, discernment, and discussion on how best to move forward.

- *Is this a congregation that is ready to be replanted or are they still a few years out?*

- *Is this congregation one that could potentially be replanted by your church? Or, is it clear that partnership with this church cannot move forward? Why or why not?*

- *Where is there alignment in theology? Where is there not?*

- *In what ways are values and convictions shared between your congregations? In what ways are they not shared? Can you move forward if they don't change any values or convictions?*

- *Are there major, costly repairs that need to happen with the building that will prevent your church from moving forward? What are they?*

- *Are there any denominational conflicts that could hinder partnership?*

This chapter is designed to help you as the Sending Church ask and discuss questions like these. The following tool has been developed to help your leaders discern whether or not to move forward in conversation with the dying church. It is simply called, "The Discernment Grid" *(see next page)*.

The Discernment Grid

	Negotiables						Non-Negotiables								
	Existing Programs	Existing Staff	Worship Style	Finances	Building	Lord's Supper (frequency)	Baptism	Church Leadership	Day to Day Operations	Growth Strategy	Denominational Alignment	Philosophy of Ministry	Philosophy of Mission	Theology	Church Polity & Government
Red (unwillingness)															
Yellow (openness)															
Green (supportiveness)															

How the Discernment Grid Works

Negotiable vs. Non-Negotiable

As you look along the left side of the Discernment Grid, you will see the two primary categories we are working with, those things that are negotiable when considering potentially partnering with this congregation and those things that are non-negotiable. If something falls into the negotiable category, it means this is something that while important to consider and be aware of, this is not an issue that will make or break moving forward in discussion with this church. It falls into the realm of, "Let's agree to disagree agreeably." On the other hand, if something falls into the non-negotiable category, it means this is an issue that must be agreed upon and aligned with or else moving forward to explore replanting together is an impossibility.

You may choose to rearrange this list of non-negotiables vs. negotiables to better reflect the values and convictions of your church. Perhaps you will add some new ones and take out some of those I have proposed. That is fine—this is simply a tool to help you and your church in this discernment process. I have listed those areas our church has found to be helpful in our discernment process with potential replants. While our heart is to see churches be replanted, we also realize that when we don't align in these specific areas with the dying church, the trajectories of the churches are very different, and it's better to say no from the beginning. Perhaps there is another Sending Church that will be a better fit for them. After many conversations with many churches of all types, our two lists include:

Non-Negotiables

- **Church Polity & Government:** The basic leadership and authority structure of the congregation as laid out in the by-laws.

- **Theology:** The core doctrinal beliefs of the congregation.

- **Philosophy of Mission:** The congregation's understanding and practice of mission, specifically as it relates to engaging culture and the lost with the gospel.

- **Philosophy of Ministry:** The congregation's understanding and application of biblical teaching to the practice of practical ministry.

- **Denominational Alignment:** The congregation's affiliation with a particular denomination.

- **Growth Strategy:** The vision and strategy of the congregation in regards to future growth and multiplication.

- **Day to Day Operations:** The practical, day to day, leadership and decision making of the congregation.

- **Church Leadership:** The role of the lead pastor-elder and other pastor-elders within the congregation.

- **Baptism:** The congregation's theology and practice of baptism.

Negotiables

- **Lord's Supper (Frequency):** The congregation's practice of the Lord's Supper, specifically its frequency.

- **Building:** The condition of the physical building and all surrounding property belonging to the congregation.

- **Finances:** The financial situation of the church including its savings, debt, monthly expenses, and monthly income.

- **Worship Style:** The style of worship, specifically music, experienced each week in the worship service.

- **Existing Staff:** The individuals who are currently on paid staff at the church and their roles.

- **Existing Programs:** The existing, active programs of the congregation for children, youth, and adults.

Red vs. Yellow vs. Green

Once you have decided on your core list of both non-negotiables and negotiables, you will move on to the rating scale. You will notice along the top of the grid, moving from left to right, three rating colors: Red, Yellow, and Green. Simply put, you will rate the potential replant in regards to their alignment with each of your non-negotiables and negotiables (it functions like a stoplight). The ratings are:

- **Red:** The potential replant is unwilling to align with your church on this non-negotiable or negotiable issue.

- **Yellow:** The potential replant is open to alignment with your church on this non-negotiable or negotiable issue.

- **Green:** The potential replant is supportive in aligning with your church on this non-negotiable or negotiable issue.

So how exactly do you rate this declining church's readiness to be replanted in light of the data you have gathered and put into the discernment grid? The following rating scale can help you in this.

The Rating Scale

Red church: A Red Church means there is one or more red ratings in the non-negotiable areas or three or more red ratings in the negotiables category.

> *What this means: If the potential replant receives a red rating, it is unwise to move forward in pursuit of replanting this congregation. There is simply not enough alignment on major things between the two churches to make it work.*

Yellow church: A Yellow Church means there is one or more yellow ratings in the non-negotiable areas or three or more yellow ratings in the negotiables category.

> *What this means: If the potential replant receives a yellow rating, your church may choose to move forward and continue conversation with this congregation but you must do so slowly and with caution. There is alignment on most things, but there are still areas of misalignment that need to be further assessed and discussed. You may talk as a church about what it could look like to coach this dying church instead of replanting it. A more distant relationship with them to walk alongside them & point them to resources might be helpful, while not fully engaging in a replanting situation where you are fully partnered together.*

Green church: A Green Church means all non-negotiable & negotiable areas are rated in the green. There might be one or two areas from the negotiable list that are yellow and you just have to lead the congregation in those areas, helping them to understand what the goal is.

> **What this means:** *There is huge potential for your church to partner with this dying congregation and replant them as new congregation. You are aligned in all major areas and next steps forward together should be taken.*

THE BOTTOM LINE

Spend some time filling in and discussing the Discernment Grid as leaders of the potential Sending Church. Again, the hope is that this will assist you in clearly identifying the potential of pursuing partnership with this dying church. To help you get started, there is a sample Discernment Grid used by our church in **Appendix B**.

The bottom line in all of this is that you want to take seriously the step of evaluating and assessing a church's readiness to be replanted. You want to know what you are getting into, for good and bad. You want to have a good feel for the culture of the church before you and your congregation decide to move forward to replant and revitalize, and asking good questions can help you honestly evaluate the partnership potential.

FOR FURTHER REFLECTION

Discussion Questions

1. What are the dangers of not taking time to assess & evaluate a potential church replant? What do you gain by making sure that you thoroughly evaluate the potential replant?

2. Review the four keys to successfully evaluating a church. What are practical ways that you (as a team) can make sure that these are embodied in your life & work as a replanting/sending church/team?

3. What are the benefits to asking multiple & different questions to those outside the church & inside the church?

4. Of all of the questions listed, which do you think will provide the most information & insight into the current life of the church?

5. Take a minute to review the discernment grid - are there things you would change in the negotiable or non-negotiable categories to better fit your church?

Ways to Pray

- Pray for your conversations with the church & people in that community.

- Pray for God to open legacy members' eyes to the reality of their church.

- Pray for humility on all sides of this relationship.

- Pray that these conversations with those outside the church will create interest in what God is doing in this church replant.

Chapter 8

STEP#5: MARRYING SENDING & LEGACY CONGREGATIONS

There aren't many things as beautiful as witnessing a marriage ceremony between two godly people.

Two different histories.

Two different family backgrounds.

Two different worlds coming together as one.

It is absolutely beautiful and the Lord is honored in this. One man and one woman united together in Jesus Christ giving their lives to one another before God, their families, and their friends. One man and one woman committing to love one another through thick and thin, good and bad, sickness and health, rich and poor.

As beautiful and wonderful as the wedding day is for most couples, anyone who is married can tell you that marriage is hard. The wedding day may have been sheer bliss, but the day in and day out journey of life together, seeking to love and serve one another as two sinners saved by grace is hard. It's humbling. It reveals our sin and deep need for the Lord and his gospel. It forces us to our knees in dependence on Jesus, trusting in his Holy Spirit to give us the strength we don't have on our own to love our spouse well, to love sacrificially, joyfully, generously, and like Jesus.

In many ways, this picture of marriage between a man and a woman is very similar to the marriage that happens in replanting. Replanting is a marriage of sorts—the Lord brings together the Sending Congregation and the struggling congregation to become one. Two imperfect and broken, yet redeemed, congregations of Christ followers coming together to unite as one. One church, rooted in Jesus Christ.

Two different histories.

Two different cultures.

Two different worlds coming together as one.

And just like any marriage, it is absolutely beautiful and the Lord is honored in this. But how does it happen? Practically speaking, what all is involved in joining together and marrying two congregations in a replant? How do you do this well? This will be our focus in this chapter.

FOUR THINGS TO REMEMBER BEFORE INITIATING THE MARRIAGE

Principle #1: Every Church is Different.

Before two congregations can start talking about a "wedding ceremony," you must first talk about what it could mean and look like to get married. I would call this "initiating the replant conversation." But before this, before initiating the replant conversation with a dying church, it is so important to remember that every church is unique. And because of this uniqueness, the process for replanting looks a little bit different for each congregation. Congregations have unique histories, cultures, and personalities. There must be some flexibility in your approach depending on the congregation you are working with. In many ways, the whole replanting process is more of an art than a science. It takes wisdom and discernment every step of the way.

For example, there will be some churches that are excited and ready to go all in from the very first conversation you have with them. The challenge with these churches is helping them slow down a little bit so that you don't get the cart before the horse and shortcut the process. Other churches will be a bit more cautious. There could be fear over what is going to happen to them and the church they've loved and served for so many years. There could be a hesitancy to trust new leaders because of past wounds from pastors and leaders who did not lead with love and grace. There could be fear because they realize they will no longer have total control over what happens in their church. All of this can be scary for people, which is why you must lead these conversations with Christ-like love and care. The point is this—every church is different and therefore the replanting process looks a little bit different each time. As you enter into these conversations moving toward a replant, much wisdom, discernment, and prayer must accompany every step in the process.

Principle #2: It is All About Building Trust.

In order to see a healthy replant become reality, significant trust must be built between the Sending Church and the church being replanted. Trust takes time to build. Of course, one of the great challenges in all of this is that the window is fairly small in terms of the amount of time you have to build this trust. By the time a congregation recognizes the urgency of pursuing a replant option in light of its rapid decline, there is typically not a lot of time left to build trust—it needs to happen in an incubated environment, and fast. Love these people as quickly as possible, doing whatever it takes to serve them, express care for them, and build trust with them.

There are many different ways to build trust with this congregation. Here just a few:

Spend Intentional Time With Them. A good first step in building trust is by simply spending time with them—there is nothing that replaces quality time. In this time spent with them, ask good questions and listen. Listen to them share stories about their lives, their families, and their church.

I can remember with one of our first church replants, spending a day driving around town with one of the congregation's core leaders who was a police officer. I wanted him to know that we loved him and we loved their church. It was an honor as he drove me around town, gave me a tour of the police station where he worked, and told me all kinds of stories about being a cop in Denver. We talked about the Lord and his faithfulness in our lives and in the lives of those in his declining church. We laughed together and we praised God together. I will never forget it, and I'm guessing he won't either. It was such a blessing to spend this day together. The Lord united our hearts as friends in a unique way that day. Trust was built. And this trust served as the foundation for us moving forward together to replant his congregation for the sake of the gospel.

Encourage them. Encouragement is powerful. Who doesn't love to be encouraged? We are commanded all throughout Scripture to encourage one another, and for good reason. Life is hard. It is easy to become discouraged for all kinds of reasons. Many folks in dying churches are discouraged as they see the congregation they love so much decline and begin to face the prospect of death. One of the most powerful ways to build trust with a church like this is to encourage them—encourage them in the ways in which they have sought to be faithful to the Lord even in difficult times. Encourage them and help them see some of the ways that God is alive and at work in their church, even though it is struggling. Encourage them as you identify evidences of God's grace in their lives. Point those out to them. A new perspective can change a lot. Encouragement can help with this. Encouragement is love spoken. This dying church needs a lot of love and encouragement. Build trust through encouragement.

Be steady and faithful, not flaky. A great pastor friend of mine who I was blessed to serve under as a youth pastor for many years, Deral Schrom, had a saying he would share with me regularly: "Stay steady." What Deral meant by this phrase in regards to ministry was simply, be faithful. Be consistent. Be a man of my word. Be steady, not flaky. I think of Deral's words often. Throughout the process of replanting a congregation, there are many meetings, conversations, email interactions, and phone calls that must happen between the Sending Church and the potential replant. Because of this, there are many opportunities to prove either your steadiness or your flakiness to this congregation. You have an opportunity to win the trust of the people through this process as you follow through on your commitments to them. Of course, you also have the opportunity to lose their trust if you fail to follow through on commitments you have made. Be steady, not flaky by following through on commitments you make to this church. You only get one shot at this.

Principle #3: Be Clear in Your Communication.

When it comes to matters in the church, you can never over-communicate. I'm convinced that under-communication is the cause for so many divisions and unnecessary conflicts in congregations. Good, clear communication is absolutely key to growing a healthy, unified church. The same is true when it comes to replanting a dying congregation.

Assuring that your communication is clear and consistent in this replanting process takes real intentionality. It means going overboard to make sure everyone is in the loop that needs to be in the loop. Don't assume anything. Ever. Don't assume that just because you spent an hour explaining the implications of replanting to the remaining leaders of the declining congregation that they completely understand what replanting really entails for them. In fact, assume they don't completely get it and that they *won't* completely get it for a long time, after many, many conversations. And even then, they still won't fully get it. This isn't an indictment against anyone's intellect or ability to comprehend what is involved with replanting, it is simply a realistic perspective on who we are as human beings. It might also be a case of selective listening, which we can all fall into. We think we understand things when we really don't or we understand some aspects but not others. We also quickly forget things we hear. Some of us forget things very quickly! When it comes to the conversation about replanting, there will be some who understand and there will be some who don't, or at least don't fully get it. Because of this, we need to over-communicate everything all the time. To get people on board and see this replant become a reality, it will mean over-communication. You may need to utilize multiple forms of communication. Phone calls, emails, text messages, or home visits, whatever it takes, clear communication is absolutely essential. Remember, in person, face to face communication is always best. This is particularly true when working with older congregations.

Principle #4: Practice Prayerful Patience… Don't Rush the Process.

As I've mentioned several times throughout this book already: The process of replanting a congregation takes time. It does not happen overnight and cannot be rushed. To do this effectively takes many conversations, time spent together, and genuine trust that serves as the foundation for the entire process. Because of this, patience must be practiced.

Of course, just as I say that, you might be thinking to yourself, "But there *isn't* much time. This church is going to die and its doors will be shut forever. This needs to happen quickly, doesn't it?" The answer to this is both yes and no. *Yes*, there is an urgency to replant this congregation as its days are numbered and change is needed soon. At the same time, *no*, you do *not* want to sacrifice the building of trust or a thoughtful, effective transition as a result of moving forward too hastily.

The Lord is sovereign in all things. He is sovereign over our lives, over the world, and over this replanting process. This should give us great peace and cause us to practice prayerful patience as we seek to move forward with wisdom, love, and unity. We want to honor God in this process by not getting ahead of him. It takes humility and patience that can only come from him. We must ask God to guide us and lead us every step of the way. We must seek his face in prayerful dependence on his Spirit to show us the way he wants us to go, asking him to give both congregations a supernatural unity that can only come from the Spirit. We must pray that the Lord's will would be done in his perfect timing, and that we would remain prayerfully patient through it all.

THE KEY PLAYERS

Throughout this replant transition process, there will be several key players that will be involved. Who are these key players? Let me very briefly introduce you to them.

Legacy Congregation

The *Legacy Congregation** is the remaining folks in the dying congregation that will potentially be replanted. In most cases, the majority of these individuals have been part of the congregation for many years and have a deep love for this church. Depending on the particular government structure of the congregation, these members will have a say in whether or not the church is to be replanted. In congregational churches, these folks are typically the ones who will give the final vote to either move forward as a replant or not.

Legacy Congregation Leaders

The **Legacy Congregation Leaders*** look different depending on the church that is being replanted. Sometimes it is whoever remains on the current deacon or elder board. In other cases, it may be the pastor who is trying to hold the church together and recognizes the church needs to be replanted. Still other times this group of folks may be made up of men and women who serve in various roles within the church. Whoever it is that makes up this group, these are the individuals who are representing and leading the Legacy Congregation, helping to discern whether replanting is the best option for their church and what it will mean and look like if the congregation decides to move forward with it.

Sending Church

This is the congregation that will come alongside and help replant the Legacy Congregation. In a very real sense, the Sending Church serves as the sponsor or mother church for the replant. The role of this church is to pray for, encourage, and serve the Legacy Congregation, however they can. Moreover, this congregation will seek to support the replant over the long haul in various ways. The Sending Church will also train up & send out the replanting pastor.

Sending Church Leaders

This entire book is actually targeted to **Sending Church Leaders***. These are key leaders from the Sending Church who will help lead the replanting process. This is the group that is also identified as the official transition team. Often this will be the lead pastor or an associate pastor along with a handful of other elders, deacons, or key leaders who are invested in and committed to seeing this replant become a reality. While the entire congregation will be involved on some level, typically these individuals will be the ones most directly involved.

Replanter

This is the pastor who has been trained up to lead the newly replanted congregation. This is an individual who is being sent out from the Sending Church as the point leader to shepherd this new replant.

Replant Core Team Members

In most replants, there is a group of new team members who will join the replanter, along with the Legacy Congregation, as they work together to begin the new church. These individuals are called *replant core team members** and they will be long-haul committed members of this new replant. Typically, core team members come from a variety of locations including the Sending Church, the surrounding community where this new replant will be located, and from other nearby towns or communities.

Volunteer Team (or V-Team)

The *Volunteer Team** is composed of individuals from the Sending Church who will be serving the new replant in various ways, particularly at their weekend worship gathering. These folks are not permanent, core team members of the replant, but rather they are individuals who are eager to serve in various ways to help the new replant. This group may help with anything from leading music, to holding babies in the nursery, to serving on the greeting team or repairing the building. A key role this team will play is training core team members of the new replant to serve in various areas of ministry. For example, a V-Team member may be running slides for the worship service, while a new core team member of the replant is with them learning how to do it. Long term sustainability is the goal here. The same will go for the children's ministry, greeting ministry, and other areas of ministry. After you start seeing the core team members handling the various parts of the weekend worship gathering well, the V-Team can start phasing out.

Denominational Leaders

In most cases, a denominational leader will be involved on some level throughout this process. This individual can be a huge help to both the Sending Church, as well as the Legacy Congregation. Denominational leaders bring a level of experience and leadership wisdom that is needed. For many Legacy Congregations that have strong ties with their denomination, denominational leaders bring credibility and a level of trust that is beneficial in helping them navigate this replanting journey.

THE 8 MEETINGS YOU MUST HAVE FOR A HEALTHY REPLANT MARRIAGE

Now we are going to get super practical. How do we get this process started? There are several meetings that must take place between the leaders of both the Sending Church and the potential Legacy Congregation. While no doubt there will be numerous phone calls and email interactions throughout this process, discussing different questions and concerns either church may have, email and phone interaction should not take the place of these eight (in person) meetings. Now let me say this. It is not a hard and fast rule that all eight of these meetings must take place without exception. There may be scenarios in which fewer meetings are needed, or perhaps a few of the meetings are combined. It might be that you actually need to add a few more meetings. Remember what is most important in all of this—building trust. Building trust is absolutely crucial, and it is built through time spent together. The more time together, the better. Trust is also built through clear communication. The more opportunity for clear communication, and asking questions to clarify, the better. This is why I recommend that all eight of these meetings take place in person. In my experience there is a much better chance for a smooth transition between the two churches if these meetings happen.

Meeting #1 – Introductions: Getting to Know One Another

Goal: *To get the key leaders from both the Sending Church and the Legacy Congregation together for the purpose of hearing about 1) the current situation of* *the legacy/declining church, 2) the heart of the Sending Church to help this Legacy Congregation, and 3) whether there is potential enough to meet again for further conversation about replanting.*

The first meeting in the transition process is a simple introductory meeting. A basic get-to-know-you meeting. This meeting is important in that it will help you determine whether there is chemistry between the two churches that could potentially lead to a replant. There are three main topics of discussion that you want to cover in this initial meeting.

Topic #1: The current situation of the Legacy Congregation

In this meeting you will get a general overview of the Legacy Congregation, including their history, affiliations, and whether or not they are a possible candidate for replanting. You will want to ask a lot of questions and listen to the key leaders of this church as they talk about their congregation. What are some of the challenges they are experiencing currently? What is the current makeup of the congregation? Are there key events that have led to the church's decline? It is recommended that you use some of the assessment questions listed in Chapter 7 to help you get helpful information out of this meeting. The bottom line is that you want to get as much information as you can about this church.

Topic #2: The heart of the Sending Church to help dying churches

Along with learning as much as you can about the history and current status of the Legacy Congregation, this meeting is an important opportunity to share the heart behind the Sending Church's desire to come alongside and help the church experience new life and vibrancy. This is the time to communicate your passion to see God revitalize dying churches for his glory. If your own church has experienced revitalization on some level, this is a great opportunity to share what God has done in and through your congregation. I know for our church, there is no greater joy for our people than to share how we were once a dying church, but God was not done with us. By his grace, he breathed new life into our congregation for the sake of the lost, the good of our community, and ultimately his glory. Sharing what God has done in your church can inspire and bring hope to these leaders, reminding them that God is not done with their church, either. Cast vision to them of how God has now given your church a desire to come alongside other declining churches like theirs to serve them, encourage them, and replant them if God so leads.

Topic #3: Is there potential enough to meet again for further conversation?

Once you have spent time hearing about the current state of the declining church and sharing the vision of the Sending Church to come alongside and help churches like their church, it will become pretty clear whether the conversation needs to continue into a second meeting. If so, the second meeting will focus on what the process of replanting will look like.

Meeting #2 – Defining the Relationship

Goal: *To clearly define the relationship between the two churches moving forward. By the end of this meeting, it must be clear to the leaders of the Legacy Congregation what exactly a church replant is and what would need to happen to officially enter the replanting process.*

Building off the information gathered from the first meeting along with additional interactions between church leaders through email and phone (and perhaps in person), the second meeting is focused on defining the relationship between these two congregations and to discuss what exactly a church replant is, including the steps needed to be taken for the Legacy Congregation to officially enter the replanting process.

In this meeting, it is important to go through all the details of what is involved in becoming a church replant. Over-communicate everything in this meeting—be crystal clear on what it will mean and what it will not mean if they choose to become a replant. This is the meeting where you want to be humbly (and brutally) honest about everything, from the surrender of all day today decision-making to the adoption of new bylaws, and to a possible new church name. You will want to put together a proposal for what it could look like moving forward if the Legacy Congregation chooses to pursue the replant option. You can see a sample of what this proposal might look like in **Appendix E.**

It is vital in this meeting to clearly explain that if the church chooses to be replanted, there will be immediate changes made. You cannot beat around the bush with this. In fact, where churches get into the most trouble with replanting is being unclear on the front end with what the replant process will entail. This must be clearly written and explained in the proposal. Be sure to go overboard explaining the Big Five, since these are typically of most concern to the Legacy Congregation being replanted. What are the Big Five you might ask?

The Big Five

#1. All day-to-day operations and decision making will be handed over to the transition team from the Sending Church for a season until the replant is healthy enough to lead itself.

#2. The by-laws of the Sending Church will be adopted in full until new bylaws can be drafted and adopted by the newly replanted congregation with the help of the Sending Church.

#3. The building ownership does not change hands. The new replant will simply "do business as" (DBA) the new name of the replant.

#4. Money doesn't change hands. The Sending Church can help manage it by putting existing monies into a designated fund for the new replant. The Sending Church can help pay bills, salaries, and other expenses with money from a designated fund. The hope is to turn all the financials back to the replant when it is healthy enough to take it on.

#5. The ultimate goal is to help the new replant become self-governing, self-sustaining, and self-replicating. The Sending Church will do all they can to help the replant reach these three markers of maturity in a timely manner.

Again, changes like the Big Five must be clearly communicated and understood by each of the key leaders of the Legacy Congregation before leaving this meeting. Fuzziness here will come back to bite you later on. As you go over the specifics of what a replant is, and what it means for this congregation to move in that direction, you can anticipate many questions from their leaders. This is a very good thing. You want them to ask many questions at this point. Clarity is everything. Remember to be intentional about explaining the *why* behind these changes. You are not wanting to change things just for the sake of changing things, but to create healthier and more efficient processes. Processes that will enable the new replant to flourish as they seek to take the gospel to their community and become a healthy, growing, vibrant congregation.

At the same time, how you communicate in this meeting is critical. Your *tone* matters. Your *body language* matters. Yes, there are significant changes that will need to be made. But you want to communicate all of this with joyful passion, humility, love and excitement. You want to help them see that these changes, while perhaps difficult to make, are what is best for the church moving forward. It is these types of changes that will help this congregation become a lighthouse for the gospel in this community once again!

You want everything out in the open as much as possible by the conclusion of this meeting. Again, clarity is key. Take your time in this meeting. Do your very best to give these leaders an accurate picture of what is coming if they choose to be replanted as a new congregation.

Meeting #3 – Determining the Direction

Goal: *To determine which direction the two churches desire to go. Do they want to pursue a potential replant of the Legacy Congregation or is it best to lovingly part ways at this point? If replanting is the desired direction, a proposed transition timeline will be presented by the Sending Church and discussed.*

In this third face to face meeting, it should be pretty clear whether or not the leaders of each of the two churches desire to pursue the replanting option. Much conversation and interaction will have taken place by this time. Many questions have been asked and answered and concerns have been addressed. Most likely there will still need to be some further discussion about any unclear or fuzzy aspects of the transition, but this is to be expected. This meeting allows for further clarification to be given and remaining questions and concerns to be addressed.

Typically, by the time of this meeting, a church that has no interest in pursuing the replanting option has let the leaders of the Sending Church know either by phone, email, or in person. As a result, in these cases, a third meeting never actually takes place. However, it is possible that the leaders will not officially choose to pull out of this process until this third meeting takes place. It may be that through conversation in this meeting it becomes clear to the leaders of the Legacy Congregation that replanting is in fact not the best option for their church. While this decision might be disappointing for the Sending Church leaders, it is much better to lovingly part ways at this point then to keep walking down a road that has no real future. If this is the result, intentionally encourage and pray for these leaders before leaving this meeting.

More often than not, it is during this meeting that leaders of both churches determine to pursue the replanting option. This is an exciting place to be, seeing leaders from both churches dreaming about what God could do in and through this new replant! It is at this point that the Sending Church leaders will present and go over a proposed transition blueprint/timeline for the replant, which you will find discussed in Chapter 12 as well as **Appendix F**. This timeline will include key dates for such things as the congregational vote, core group gatherings, *soft launch**, outreach events, and *public launch**.[1]

Meeting #4 - The Congregational Visit

Goal: *To have the Sending Church leaders visit the Legacy Congregation for the purpose of casting vision for the replant, answering and addressing questions and concerns, and encouraging the remaining members.*

While much time has been spent between the leaders of the two churches, there has probably been very little interaction between the members of the Legacy Congregation and the leaders and members of the Sending Church. This fourth meeting and congregational visit is huge in beginning to build a bridge of love and trust between the two congregations. There are three primary purposes to this congregational visit.

Purpose #1: Casting vision for the potential replant

This is your chance to share your excitement for what God can do in and through this replant! You want to help them dream about what could be. Many of these folks have not dreamed about what God can do through their church for many, many years. Remind them of who God is and of his faithfulness to them. Remind them of God's desire to reach the nations with the gospel and his heart to save the lost in their community. Remind them that God saved *them,* and now sends them to be missionaries in their own neighborhoods. Remind them that God loves to show off his strength in the midst of our weakness and that he wants to work in a mighty way through their congregation. This is your chance to cast hope-filled, passionate vision that is desperately needed in the hearts and minds of these men and women. Go big and have fun with it because we have a big God!

Purpose #2: Answering and addressing questions and concerns

At this point it's likely that the leaders of the church have been communicating to the congregation what a replant is and what it will mean to become a replanted congregation in partnership with your church. Hopefully, these leaders have been able to answer many of the questions folks in the congregation have. But many in the congregation will want to hear directly from you as leaders of the Sending Church. They will probably want you to help bring clarification to any fuzziness that might exist in their minds about the process. This is their opportunity to speak with you directly and for you to address any questions or concerns they might have. It is a great chance to help calm any fears they might have.

Purpose #3: Encouraging the remaining members of the congregation

Many of these remaining members have been part of this church for years. They have been part of this congregation in good times and bad. They have hung in there when many others probably left for all kinds of reasons. They have been *faithful.* Use this time as an opportunity to encourage them in their faithfulness. Help them to see the legacy they will be leaving for future generations that could be part of this replant. Encourage them, because they need it. Use this as a time to reinforce your love for them as a congregation and your great desire to honor the Lord and to care for them deeply in this process.

If the Sending Church has experienced revitalization itself in the past, it is highly recommended to bring members from the Sending Church to this meeting to share their own personal experiences of walking through revitalization in their own congregation. From our own experience, it is at this fourth meeting that our church will always bring some of our faithful, long haul members to share their own experiences with revitalization. It is always helpful and encouraging for the legacy members of this potential replant to hear from others who have journeyed through the fears, uncertainties, and joys of church revitalization themselves. This time together often helps to calm many fears, while building further trust with you as the Sending Church.

Meeting #5 – The Congregational Vote of the Legacy Congregation

Goal: *To be present and available for any final questions or concerns that might pop up at the congregational vote. This is also a chance to celebrate with the congregation upon their decision to officially move forward as a replant.*

For most churches, this is *the* big meeting! This is the meeting in which the congregation will vote to either move forward officially as a replant, or they will decide to remove themselves from the process. The hope is that by the time this meeting takes place, the large majority, if not the entire congregation, is fully on board with moving forward as a replant. I have been part of a few of these meetings where the congregation is divided and ultimately decides not to move forward. Let me tell you, those were painful meetings

This meeting serves as one last opportunity for members of the Legacy Congregation to ask questions and share any concerns they might have. The Sending Church leaders are present and available to respond if needed. Upon the church officially voting to move forward as a replant, it is great to have the Sending Church leaders there to celebrate with those who are at the meeting. It is a joyful moment when that decision is made by the congregation, and a game changing decision in the history of that church. You and your leaders should encourage them and again share your excitement and hope for what God has planned for the future of this new replant.

Meeting #6 – The Congregational Vote of the Sending Church

Goal: *To update the Sending Congregation on the Legacy Congregation's vote to replant, as well as discuss existing financial matters pertaining to the Legacy Congregation, while also casting vision and setting schedule for volunteer team (V-Team) members.*

Once the Legacy Congregation has officially voted to be replanted, the Sending Church should have a member's meeting where leaders are able to share about the potential replant opportunity. Specifically, there are three main purposes for this meeting.

Purpose #1: Celebrating their Vote to Be Replanted!

Praise God for what he is doing in this church. Praise him for the humility of this congregation. Praise him for giving them a desire and unity to do whatever it takes to be revitalized for the sake of the Kingdom!

Purpose #2: Voting to Move Forward and Replant this Church

Even if your by-laws do not require it, it is wise to have members vote on officially moving forward with the replant. You want to allow for questions to be answered along with any further discussion to take place at this meeting. Voting to move forward will help bring a clear sense of unity, ownership and excitement as your church body moves forward together.

Purpose #3: Discussing any Financial Matters Related to the Replant

At this point you will have seen the Legacy Congregation's financial budget and any savings they might have. This will determine how much money should be earmarked from the Sending Church's budget to help the replant succeed. Many times, a change of your budget will require a vote from the members.

Purpose #4: Discussing Building Acquisition if Needed

The Legacy Congregation may want to transfer the deed of their building and all assets to the Sending Church. In some cases, the remaining members of the Legacy Congregation will want to be removed from any liability of a building that is not ADA compliant. The Sending Church will need to confirm with their by-laws, but most require a member vote prior to the acquisition of any property.

Purpose #5: Casting Vision and Setting Schedule for Volunteer Team (V-Team) Members

The Sending Church will start sending volunteers each Sunday to help with the replant worship services. We call these members V-Team members. Singles, couples, families, and individuals of all ages make up this team. It is a blast for them to serve the new replant in this way together! It is a good idea to have sign-up sheets ready at this meeting for people to confirm Sundays to serve for the next three months (or however long you determine), which you can find **Appendix H**. A Sunday service will often require a primary point person, worship leader, slide tech, sound tech, greeters, children's ministry workers, Sunday school teacher and possibly a preacher. You can find a sample letter for V-Team point person in **Appendix G** as well as a weekend checklist **Appendix I**.

Meeting #7 – Laying Out the Game-plan

Goal: *To revisit the replant timeline and go over specific steps that need to take place in order to effectively launch this new church. This meeting will include the leaders from both congregations who have been involved throughout the process, along with any other individuals whose presence would be helpful. This includes the presence of the replanting pastor you are sending out to shepherd and lead this new replant.*

This is what I call the *Game-Time* meeting. This is the meeting where you begin to play ball and to strategize what it will take to make this replant vision a reality. For months you have been meeting and dreaming about what could be, and now is the time to begin making things happen by the power of the Spirit.

For this meeting, it is helpful to have all of the main leaders who have been involved in the process up to this point. This meeting will also include the new replanting pastor. You might find that it is helpful to have additional folks present who can help bring wisdom and insight to the conversation. When our church is replanting a new congregation and we are at this meeting in the process, we always try to bring key lay leaders from our congregation to be part of the discussion. For example, when talking about changes that will be happening with the children's ministry in this new replant, it is always helpful for one of our children's ministry leaders to be present and help answer any questions that might arise. In the same way, we always bring a member of our finance team so that they can help address any questions or concerns regarding money or budget issues. The point is this— you're working together as one team and need the right people around the table to help make this replant the best it can be.

A Quick Word on Legalities

In Chapter 12 and *Appendix A*, we will dive further into the legal issues to be handled as you replant this church, but for now, here are a few you will want to immediately begin looking into. Remember, a replant is the Legacy Congregation voting to turn all day-to-day decisions over to the Sending Church. So the church is continuing to exist (making the legal processes a lot easier) but it's changing a lot. A few things to consider:

Are you changing the church name? Then, depending on your state, you need to file a DBA with the Secretary of State and take that official paper to the bank so that you are able to accept tithe checks under all names.

Is any of the property or bank accounts being changed over to the Sending Church during the transition process? If so, not only do you need to do the legal paperwork this involves, but also think about bills to be paid, building insurance, property taxes, etc.

The purpose of this meeting is to get everyone on the same page in regards to the new direction this replant is headed. It is an opportunity to get the key leaders on the same page, mobilizing them to lead the necessary changes. This meeting serves as an opportunity to go over changes pertaining to such things as finances, worship service music, existing staff decisions, administrative details, etc. Remember that this meeting is *not* for the purpose of getting feedback from everyone. Day-to-day decision making has already been voted on and surrendered from the Legacy Congregation to the Sending Church. This meeting is designed to lay out the game plan the Sending Church, along with the replanting pastor, has put together for launching this new replant.

Meeting #8 - Weekly Check-in & Trouble-Shoot

Goal: *To provide a weekly opportunity for the replanter and other key leaders to be coached and encouraged by leaders from the Sending Church.*

Replanting is difficult. There are many ups and downs throughout the journey of leading a church from near death back to health and vibrancy. Because of this, leaders need a lot of ongoing encouragement and coaching. This final meeting is a weekly meeting for the purpose of checking-in, trouble shooting, and talking with the replanter and his key leaders about specific challenges they are facing. It is also a great opportunity to hear about what God is doing and some of the victories they're experiencing.

Depending on the location of the replant and it's distance from the Sending Church, this meeting may not be able to happen face-to-face each week. For example, I have a weekly one hour Zoom call (a mobile app similar to Skype) with several of our lead replanters every Wednesday afternoon. This allows me to have face-to-face time with these leaders even though they may live quite a distance from our church. Of course, it is ideal to meet face-to-face whenever you can, but technology now affords us great opportunities to meet on a regular basis through other means. Whatever it looks like, this weekly touch point is huge in helping the leaders of this new replant feel loved, care for, and equipped for the ministry God has called them to.

AND NOW THE MARRIAGE BEGINS...

As mentioned at the beginning of this chapter, in replanting, the Lord brings together in marriage the Sending Congregation and the Legacy Congregation that they might become one. Two imperfect, broken, yet redeemed, congregations of Christ followers coming together to unite as one church rooted in the gospel of grace. While challenges are sure to come, the journey of marriage as a new congregation has begun. This is the beautiful, redemptive picture that is church replanting.

FOR FURTHER REFLECTION

Discussion Questions

1.   Read again the four things to remember before initiating the marriage. What would happen if you didn't remember #2? #4?

2.   Where do you (& your team) fit on the list of key players in this process? Can you summarize your role in one sentence?

3.   Which of the eight meetings are you most looking forward to? Why?

4.   What kind of conversations does your team need to have ahead of time so that you are prepared to have these eight meetings with the dying church?

Ways to Pray

-   Pray for extra grace & humility in all conversations.

-   Pray for clear communication in the meetings.

-   Pray for God to raise up people to fill each of the key player roles in this process.

-   Pray for God to be glorified in the marriage of these two churches.

Chapter 9

STEP#6: GROWING A CORE TEAM & BUILDING MOMENTUM

We have all either observed it or experienced it first-hand—momentum. Maybe it was your favorite sports team or a new business you or someone you know was once part of, or perhaps you found it as you began to bite the bullet and get back into shape after a long, cold winter hanging out on the couch and watching too much Netflix.

What exactly is it? Webster defines momentum as the "strength or force gained by motion or by a set of events." It is the opposite of stagnation. It is movement, going somewhere, gaining speed, powerful. Momentum is needed when replanting a dying congregation.

Mark Lenz is right when he says, "When a local church is energized by prayer, the power of the Holy Spirit, and momentum, it becomes a great force that the gates of hell cannot withstand."[1]

The time has come to start building momentum toward the official launch of this replant. This is the step in the process where things start to get really exciting! In this phase, all of the hard research, the tough conversations you have had, the prayers you have prayed, the nights you have laid in bed dreaming about what God could do through this replant, begins to become a *reality*. This is the step where some incredible movement begins to happen.

There are two critical components to this sixth step in the replanting process. They include:

1. The development of the core team.
2. Implementing key strategies to help build momentum toward the public launch.

We will spend time in this chapter considering each of these components in depth.

THE DEVELOPMENT OF THE CORE TEAM

When you see a pastor trying to lead a congregation on his own, it rarely ends well. We were not made to minister in the church alone, and the Bible is clear on this. This is particularly true when it comes to replanting a congregation–a replanting pastor cannot do this all on his own. It is not possible. He needs help. This is why the development of a **core team*** is absolutely essential not only to the healthy launch of this new congregation, but the ongoing health, stability, and growth of this replant into the future. If you are not familiar with what a core team is or what it does, the following section will help explain.

What Is the Core Team?

Simply put, the core team are those individuals who serve as the committed leaders and servants working together to launch this new replant. It is made up of men and women, boys and girls who are all-in with this replant. While there will be folks whose excitement and commitment may wane, the core team are those individuals who have made a commitment to be part of this new church regardless of the challenges that lie ahead. This is why we call them the core team—they serve as the core of this replant.

Who Makes Up the Core Team?

Ideally, this core team will be made up of individuals from four groups of people: Existing members of the declining congregation, the replanting pastor and his family, individuals and families from the Sending Church, and other folks from the community who desire to be part of this replant. The greater representation the core team has from these four different groups of people, the better. It is healthy to have a team made up of those with diverse giftings, passions, and backgrounds. Older folks and younger folks, those who have been part of church their whole life, and those who are brand new to this whole Christian thing. Both those who are feeling tired and discouraged, and those who have fresh passionate vision for what lies ahead have an important role to play on the core team. With Christ at the center and a commitment toward love and unity amongst the core team, God will do amazing things through this group of committed servants. One thing to note — There should not be an expectation that every remaining member of the church serves as part of the core team, as being part of this team will take much time, energy, and sacrifice. It may be that some folks from the Legacy Congregation do not desire to be part of this core team. Perhaps they are just too tired to give energy to this team. *That is okay.* Just be sure to keep the remaining members in the loop with what is going on and continue to love them like crazy as you seek to earn their trust in this process.

What Qualities Should You Look for in Core Team Members?

While there are several qualities to look for in core team members, there are four that stand out. I simply call these the four C's:

#1. Character.

What kind of character or heart posture does this potential team member have? Is this person a humble servant of others? Are they encouraging or critical? Are they honest, or do they tend to stretch the truth from time to time? Is this a man or woman of integrity? Each of these questions are helpful in determining the kind of character this person has.

#2. Competency.

Is this individual competent? Is this person gifted in ways that they can help the team accomplish its vision? Are they skilled in areas where you need specific skill? Are they knowledgeable and experienced in areas where your team needs knowledge and experience? Are they able to do the job you need them to do? Are they competent for what your team needs?

#3. Chemistry.

How well does this person click with others on your core team? Solid chemistry is a crucial component to any effective team. A team works smoothly and joyfully together, even in difficult circumstances when chemistry is present. Where it is lacking, a team struggles to accomplish its mission as peripheral issues and conflicts bring unhelpful distraction.

#4. Commitment.

Are they committed to the replant and to the core team for the long haul? There is nothing worse for a team than having some members who are all-in, while others come and go as they please. It is *vital* for the health of the core team that every person who says they want to be part of it is committed through the good and bad that is sure to come.

These four C's are a helpful place to start when thinking about the types of individuals you want as part of this core team.

What is the Commitment for Those On the Core Team?

As potential core team members begin to think and pray about their involvement, it is important to be clear on the commitment you will be asking of them. You don't want to over promise and under deliver, which is why helping these individuals count the cost and the joy of being part of this core team is critical.

There is a Cost to This

It needs to be understood what exactly is being asked of these team members, namely that they are called to serve as both a minister and as a missionary as part of this team. Let me explain.

First of all, each core team member will serve as a **minister** in various ways. This means working with the replanting pastor, the leaders of the Sending Church, and the other members of the core team to find a place to serve the body of the replant. It is going to need people to serve in a wide variety of ministry areas. These could be volunteers serving as greeters, musicians, sound technicians, slide runners, children's ministry leaders or helpers, making coffee, leading a small group or adult Sunday School, etc.

This replant needs people who are willing to step up to serve in ministry in a variety of different ways.

Secondly, each potential team member must understand they are expected to live and serve as **missionaries** to the community. You need to remind your team that the driving purpose for replanting this church is *mission*. You want to reach people who are far from God with the gospel! This means those who feel called to be part of this replant core team will be expected to go show and tell the gospel boldly to their family, friends, and neighbors. This should not be a burden but a joy for those who make up this team!

There is a Joy in This

While you need to help potential team members count the cost to being part of this team, you also want to help them consider the joy of it. There are very few greater catalysts for joy than being used by God to make Jesus known in the lives of others. It's so thrilling to see people who are far from God come to know and treasure Jesus and invite others to do the same. Your core team members will be leading the way in this.

Remember how God saved you? Remember the joy of knowing Jesus and his incredible love for you in those first days, months, perhaps years of your salvation? Someone from some church introduced you to Jesus and then you were discipled by that church. The person who introduced you to Jesus and the church that you connected to rejoiced when God saved you – the angels rejoiced, Jesus rejoiced, God the Father rejoiced, the Holy Spirit rejoiced! This is the amazing work God has called your core team to lead as they help launch this replant.

JOINING THE CORE TEAM: THREE STEPS TO TAKE

Once the core team begins to form and individuals choose to commit to this team, there are a handful of steps to take. Specifically, there are three steps that will help each person officially transition onto this core team.

Step #1: Commitment to Pray

Each team member commits to praying like crazy for Jesus to be made known in a non-ignorable way in the community. Pray that people who are far from God would hear the gospel, repent of their sin, and trust in Jesus as their Lord and Savior. Pray for unity in the replant as you move toward launch. Pray for humble and teachable hearts that recognize that this is all about Jesus and his mission, *not* our comfort.

Step #2: Assessment and Covenant

A short assessment can be beneficial in helping team members discern the specific team role God wants them to play and where they can best be used for the replant. The replanting pastor will meet with each team member to talk about this assessment for the purpose of encouragement and helping them plug into the right spot.

As part of the assessment and in helping each individual discern whether or not they are going to be part of the core team, you may choose to ask each person to express their commitment to the replant by signing a covenant together. In signing a covenant, there is built-in encouragement and accountability for each person on the team, which brings a sense of solidarity in the mission. You will be able to find a sample assessment in **Appendix C** as well as a sample covenant is provided in **Appendix D** for you to edit and use as needed.

Step #3: Commitment to Attend Weekly Core Team Meeting

After members of the core team have gone through and completed their assessment, and having met individually with the replanting pastor, they will then begin to meet together as a core team on a weekly basis. At this meeting, your team will fellowship, pray together, and spend a good chunk of time being equipped for ministry by the replanting pastor. This meeting will serve as the primary gathering for your team to get aligned on the vision, mission, and strategy of this new replant. It will also be the time for each team member to be assigned specific responsibilities in preparation for the replant's launch. This is an exciting meeting that helps generate community amongst the team while instilling fresh passion and vision for what God wants to do in and through the new congregation.

IMPORTANT REMINDER: *It is important to note that this weekly core team meeting is a great on ramp for new individuals who want to join the core team. It must be clearly understood that the core team is not intended to be a closed group but an open group. The goal is for this group to grow and even double or triple by the time of the public launch.*

IMPLEMENTING NEW STRATEGIES TO HELP BUILD MOMENTUM

As the core team begins to meet on a weekly basis throughout the soft launch phase,[2] the replanter and team will begin implementing strategies to help build momentum leading up to the public launch.[3] There are different programmatic and relational strategies that can be utilized during this phase. Let me recommend several of these that have proven to be effective in replants around the country.

I-3 Relational Evangelism

One of the great challenges in any church in our culture is helping people move from being members to being missionaries. Following Jesus' call to make disciples will be one of the biggest leadership challenges in the replant. The folks who have been part of this church for so long have most likely not been taught how to live as missionaries in the community. Additionally, the folks on the core team have probably received little instruction in this area. How do you help get this core team intentionally building relationships with people in the community? How can you strategically mobilize this team to begin reaching those far from Jesus and inviting them to be part of the new replant? One simple tool that has been effective in equipping and mobilizing core team members, as well as others in a replant context, begin living on mission is I-3 Relational Evangelism. Here's how it works.[4]

Each person on the core team is given a book mark like this that they can keep in their Bible or another spot where they can see it on a regular basis:

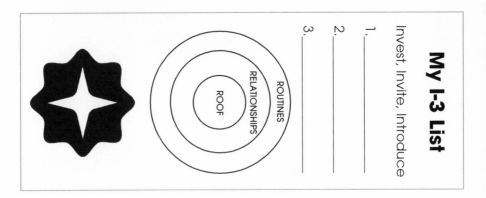

You will notice three words at the top of the bookmark: **Invest, Invite, and Introduce.** Here is what they mean.

Step #1: Invest

We want to invest in the lives of people in our community who are far from Christ. It begins with those under our **roof.** We need to help our people see that their #1 mission field is their family and/or roommates. Evangelism and mission must begin in our homes. Next, have team members think through faces of individuals they are in **relationship** with at their workplace, at school, on their street, on their sports teams, in other environments they regularly find themselves in. Finally, challenge them to think through their **routines.** Places where they shop, where they regularly get coffee or gas, the grocery store they go to the most. All of these places are filled with individuals your core team can invest in, love and serve in order to build authentic relationships with them.

Step #2: Invite

When we talk about inviting, we are talking about inviting those you are investing in to connect with your church on some level. It could be inviting them to come to a special outreach event, Sunday worship, or a Bible study at a coffee shop. For those who may say no to all three of those invitations, it may be as simple as inviting them over for a BBQ at your house just to hang out and watch a game. It is amazing how a seemingly non-church function like eating burgers and watching a game can help build a bridge of love and trust with nonbelievers. Whatever it might be, and however it might look, the core team should lead the way when it comes to inviting anyone and everyone to connect with the church family of this new replant.

Step #3: Introduce

Introducing people to Jesus is our great calling and the mission of the Church. Introducing people to Jesus that they might experience salvation and grow as his disciple for the glory of God and the advancement of his Kingdom. Introducing people to Jesus must serve as a core conviction and commitment of this new replant. If this is to happen, it must begin with the core team serving as the model of what it looks like to live this out in their daily lives, not just as part of a mission trip or formal program. There are many excellent tools you can use to help equip your team to introduce others to Jesus. Here are just a few:

Evangelism tools & apps

- *Two Ways to Live* - http://www.matthiasmedia.com.au/2wtl

- *Life On Mission: 3 Circles* - http://lifeonmissionbook.com/conversation-guide

- *The Bridge to Life* - https://www.navigators.org/Tools

- *One-Verse Evangelism* - https://www.navigators.org/Tools

- *The Story* - http://spreadtruth.com/thestory

- *Life in Six Words* - http://www.dare2share.org/mobile-app/

- *The Roman Road* - http://www.allaboutgod.com/the-roman-road.htm

- *Evangelism Explosion* - http://evangelismexplosion.org

- *The "G.O.S.P.E.L."* - http://www.dare2share.org/products-resources/free-teen-stuff/

Overall, I-3 Relational Evangelism is a great strategy to implement with your core team in the soft launch phase. It will help equip them to live on mission and help keep them focused on what this replant is all about: Making disciples for the glory of God.

A New Website

Most people today, believers and non-believers alike, will first go online to learn about a church. The days are long gone when the majority of folks based whether or not they wanted to check out your church on the look of the building, church name, or the sign out front. Those may still serve as factors for some people, but in our day, your church's web-site is the #1 place people will go to check out what your church is all about.

Designing a new website is a non-negotiable for a new replant. It gives this new church a chance to rebrand itself and allows the replanter and the core team to share their vision for the new church. It gives them a space to describe all of the exciting ways this new church desires to bless the community around it. It allows people who have lived in this town for years to see this church in a new light.

Helping to develop and pay for this new website is one of the many ways the Sending Church can bless this replant. It's likely that the Sending Church has individuals in the congregation who can help with this. If nothing else, there will be folks in the Sending Congregation who know individuals who can help. What a great ministry this could be for an individual or team of volunteers, using their gifts for new Kingdom work!

One of the great blessings of our day is that you can create new websites not only easily but also cheaply. No longer does a small congregation have to settle for a hard-to-use website due to cost. Web designing companies like Wix, Clover, and Squarespace allow anyone to create a good looking website for little money. A new, excellent looking website will benefit this replant immensely as they seek to reach their community with the gospel.

Social Media

Social media is here to stay. Over two billion people on our planet have at least one social media account. Two billion! Whether it is Twitter, Facebook, Instagram, Pinterest, or other avenues, people in our world are staying connected through social media. As Christians, we can either shun it or engage it with care and wisdom. I am of the persuasion that while I don't believe everyone should use social media, there is a place for it when it comes to engaging and connecting with others. It can be a wonderful tool to let people know about all that God is doing through the replant. Sharing pictures of outreach events or posting testimonies of how people have been impacted by your church can be used by God in powerful and encouraging ways. It is also a great avenue to let the community know about upcoming events and activities. Word spreads quickly through social media. How can your replant use it for redemptive purposes?

Local Newspaper

While it may not be very beneficial if your replant is located in a major city, in many smaller communities the local newspaper is a strategic source for advertising. In rural areas, in particular, the majority of folks still read the local paper on a daily basis. It is the best source for just that: Local news! When a church is being replanted in a smaller community, you can bet people will hear about quickly. The newspaper should be seen as an ally in getting the word out. I know several replanters who have intentionally pursued the local newspaper to write up an article on what is happening in the replant. I have yet to meet a replanter who was denied this request. My guess is that a writer for the paper will be excited to follow what is happening in your replant and will be eager to write about it not just once, but several times!

Stickers

That's right. Stickers. Stickers are great tools to help create buzz. Design a sticker to promote the new replant. Perhaps this is a sticker of a new logo you create for the church. Maybe it is as simple as the web address for the new replant that folks in the community can check out. Encourage your team and others to put the sticker on their cars, their water bottles, their backpacks, their computers, anywhere and everywhere others might see it. Stickers like this can open up conversation and opportunities to invite people to check out the church.

T-shirts

Similar to stickers, t-shirts are a great way to promote the new replant. T-shirts are also a simple and *very* effective way to create a sense of ownership among the core team. The team will be proud to wear a shirt promoting the new replant and it will be sure to spark conversation. Be sure to have your core team wear their t-shirts to each outreach event you do!

Neighborhood Networking Strategy

Building relationship is key to gathering people. Which means it is critical to be thinking of different ways you can help mobilize the core team, and others from the replant, to connect with more and more people relationally. In particular, connecting relationally with their neighbors.

Increasing numbers of people in our culture are comfortable using social media to connect with new people. This includes our neighbors. One social network site, Nextdoor, is a key way people today are connecting in your neighborhood. Let me give you a few simple ways this can be a helpful tool for your people.

- Fewer young moms feel comfortable going to the park with their kids alone these days. As a result, many will check Nextdoor to see if other young moms with kids are having a play date at the park to go join them. Young moms from your church can be intentional about setting up regular play dates at the park on Nextdoor.

- Families can use Nextdoor to advertise special picnics and other social events they want to invite other families in their neighborhood to in the local park.

- Nextdoor is a great way to advertise a garage sale folks from the replant are having. This is a great way for their neighbors to come to them to shop for treasures. Encourage them to be ready with a note pad or an app of some kind to document their neighbors' names and where they live in the community. Then they can follow up later by inviting them to dinner or other church events.

Reaching Your "Nextdoor" Neighbors

Here is an example of how one church replant, Calvary Summitview, has used Nextdoor to connect with their neighbors:

Everyone has walked by the community bulletin boards in coffee shops, local stores and city buildings. You scan the board for local news, upcoming events, stuff (for sale or FREE!) and services being offered. Often churches can take advantage of the community board by posting a flyer. Now, imagine being able to post to a community board that delivers your church's news, event or ministry directly to your neighbor's inbox. Nextdoor is a neighborhood-oriented private social media site. They offer a platform for any community member to post free stuff, news, events and concerns shared to neighbors' inboxes and community pages on their website. The Verge says about Nextdoor, "It's trying to build a local graph to complement the social graph, and it has quietly grown into one of the largest social networks in the US, with over ten million registered users spread across more than 100,000 neighborhoods." Not just pastors and replanters, but church members have an opportunity to share relevant events and news with their neighbors all across town. Calvary Summitview is a church that uses Nextdoor to help them connect with neighbors and share news from the church that would cost thousands of dollars in direct mail advertising.

So how can you use Nextdoor? A few weeks before your event, compile all the details for your event in an easy to read format. Make sure to include why the community should know about and come to your event. Clearly identify your church with your name, address and picture of your church's logo, sign or recognizable building. Tell your church members to join Nextdoor who live in the surrounding neighborhoods. When they see your event emailed to them that same day they can "THANK" you for sharing it. The more thanks clicked, the more likely people are going to see your event at the top of their newsfeed. Does it get any easier to promote your events to your community? In many ways, Nextdoor is the easiest resource to broadcast your church's events with the surrounding community.

Gabe Reed
Lead Pastor
Calvary Church Summitview

Parades and Other Community Events

A great way to let the community know that the replant is coming is to show up and serve at the popular public events in your community. The core team can have a powerful presence at events like parades, local fair and rodeo, whatever it may be. Calvary Church, a replant in La Junta, Colorado, has done this with great effectiveness. Located on the main street in downtown La Junta, Calvary has made a point to provide water both to drink and play in each year during the parade. It has allowed for great fun and connection with the La Junta community. It also serves as a wonderful opportunity to invite individuals and families to come check out their church.

BEGIN A WEEKLY PRAYER MEETING

As discussed throughout this book, true church revitalization only happens by the grace of God through the Spirit of God. If God is going to move, if there is going to be any real momentum built, if God is going to breathe life and zeal into towns and communities through this replant, then you need men and women that are going to fall on their faces in prayer. For this replant to become healthy and fruitful, it must be a church that is made up of praying people.

I often think of a story that I heard years ago about Charles Spurgeon. There was a group of American pastors who went over to London because they had heard of the great Spurgeon. They heard about this Baptist preacher; how his church was blowing up; and how they were reaching thousands upon thousands of lost people with the gospel. So this group of American pastors are over there asking, "What's the secret? We've got to see this for ourselves." They visit Spurgeon and his church. Spurgeon takes them for a walk through the church building. It's a Sunday morning, the time of morning when worship is going on. Folks are singing in the sanctuary. He takes these pastors into the depths of the church building … into the boiler room. Spurgeon opens the door and all of a sudden, in front of them is a group of four hundred people on their knees praying; Praying for the service, praying that God would move in power, praying for Spurgeon as a preacher. Spurgeon then looks as this group of men and says, "There, gentlemen, there is the secret for God's blessing his work here."

I remember the first time I heard that story and thinking, "Our church *must* have prayer like that because we *need* God to move like that!" It is through prayer that the power of God moves in and transforms the hearts of people. For this reason, one of the first things that must be prioritized in this replant is intentional, devoted, dependent, persistent prayer. Scheduling a weekly prayer meeting can help serve as a catalyst for this kind of committed prayer. Regardless of when you choose to have the prayer meeting or what particular form the meeting takes, make a weekly prayer meeting part of the DNA of the replant from the very beginning.

PRIORITIZING A SHEPHERDING MEETING

In church revitalization and replanting, pastors, with the help of other leaders, are called to shepherd the flock of God; knowing them, feeding them, leading them, and protecting them with deep love, great patience, tenderness and toughness. Shepherding must be the primary work of the replanting pastor and other spiritual leaders. Intentional shepherding is absolutely crucial to the health and growth of this congregation moving forward.

Practically, this looks like starting to create a church culture where members and visitors are shepherded well through the development and prioritization of a shepherding meeting that takes place on a regular basis. The shepherding meeting must be viewed as **non-negotiable** in helping to build momentum, not only throughout the soft launch phase of the replant, but into the public launch phase and beyond. Why? Because loving and caring for people is at the heart of biblical, Christ-centered, God-honoring ministry. It is what God wants. Shepherding God's people well is the joyful calling of the Church and its leaders. This kind of intentional shepherding work will always be more effective in creating a heathy, vibrant, mission-minded church culture than any program or event ever could.

The following is a simple game-plan for the replanter and other leaders to use in leading a weekly, bi-weekly, or monthly shepherding meeting for this new congregation. Let me explain the three meeting movements that should guide the flow of the shepherding meeting.

Meeting Movement #1: Discussing the Good Shepherd

In order for us to rightly understand our role and responsibility as shepherds of God's flock, we must first understand the pastor's primary role as an under-shepherd of the Good Shepherd. We need to remember that ultimately, all that is happening in the replant is the Good Shepherd's work. He is the Chief Shepherd and we are called to follow him first and minister to others only under his authority (1 Peter 5:4). Because of this, begin each shepherding meeting with a brief time of teaching or study and prayer, together spending time with and submitting once again to Jesus. He is the Good Shepherd over our souls and the souls of those we lead.

Meeting Movement #2: Discussing the Flock

Along with discussing the Good Shepherd, an effective shepherding meeting should focus on discussing the health of the flock, both on a macro (congregation) and micro (individual) level. There are several important discussion items concerning the flock during this movement:

1. Review new information cards and prayer requests for the flock, praying together for them.
2. Update information on individuals, including changes in address, phone, email, etc.
3. Note any drift toward inactivity among members or regular attendees.[5]
4. Identify and rejoice in the various evidences of God's grace in the lives of individuals and families.
5. Assign new members to specific pastors for intentional shepherding care.

Shepherding Tip: *At least twice a year do an annual review of your flock. During this review, celebrate what God is doing through the shepherding ministry and recommit yourselves to pursue the weak, wandering, and stray sheep. You should also evaluate where each of your sheep in the congregation are in regards to their personal, spiritual health. This will include an evaluation of worship attendance, community group commitment, and ministry involvement. To help with this, be sure to consult other leaders in the church such as an individual's community group or ministry team leader for any insight they may have.*

Meeting Movement #3: Discussing the Shepherd

Shepherding is tough work and it takes a team to do it well. To help your shepherding team follow through on their shepherding commitments, take time regularly to lovingly hold one another accountable, pray for one another, and speak intentional words of encouragement to one another. The following questions can help with this as they focus on the four essential shepherding functions: knowing, feeding, leading, and protecting the flock.

How well do you know the sheep you are overseeing and caring for?

1. Do you know their occupation?
2. Do you know their greatest concern at this time? Something for which to pray?
3. Do you know their general spiritual condition at this time?
4. Do you know the children in this family? How well?

How well are the sheep under your care being fed?

1. How well-fed would you consider your flock to be?
2. How could the diet of your flock be improved?
3. Is your flock taking advantage of the opportunities available to be fed?
4. Are *you* being an example of hungering and thirsting for God's Word?

How well are the sheep under your care being led?

1. Are *you* leading as an example of godliness to your flock?
   a. How is your family life? Your marriage?
   b. Are you following through on your church commitments?

   c. How is your prayer and devotional life?

2. Have you met with any individual sheep to help give them biblical counsel?

3. Have you met with any individual sheep to cast vision to them about your church's mission and vision?

How well protected are the sheep under your care?

1. Are you aware of any wolves (inside or outside the church) that are seeking to lead your sheep astray?

2. Have you needed to lovingly confront any wandering sheep?

3. Have you needed to give private instruction and warning from the Scriptures to any particular sheep?

The shepherding task is one of great privilege and challenge. The sheep will require our attention, but we need to make sure the attention we give is marked by loving, grace-filled, proactive shepherding, not unloving, unintentional, reactionary leadership. Prioritizing a consistent shepherding meeting for the sole purpose of flock care will help to assure that your church leadership faithfully puts into practice the kind of biblical shepherding that God expects of his church and its leaders.

TRUST GOD, HAVE FUN, AND ENJOY THE JOURNEY

As you seek the Lord in prayer, intentionally beginning to love and serve your community, and working as a team to implement some of these strategies, you are doing the things that need to be done to build momentum in this replant. Ultimately, the Spirit of God is the only One who can open eyes, change hearts, and build momentum that yields good, healthy fruit over time. But we know we have a God that loves to use people and churches like yours to accomplish his purposes for his glory. Trust him in all of this. Rest in the fact that he is good, faithful, and sovereign over his Church, which includes this replant. May it be a delight for you to help replant this church and not simply a duty you feel obligated to carry out. Have fun and enjoy this journey of replanting!

FOR FURTHER REFLECTION

Discussion Questions

1. What came to mind when the author mentions momentum & examples at the beginning of the chapter? What was it about your specific example that produced momentum?

2. How do having the right team & having the right strategies work together to build momentum?

3. How can your team help a replant build a core team? What can & should be your role in this?

4. What are the Four C's to look for in core team members? In what types of situations can you most easily recognize these?

5. As you review the strategies, in what ways can you as the sending church, be helpful so that the replanted church can live this out easier

---

Ways to Pray

-   Pray for God to bring the right people to the core team at the right time.

-   Pray for God to lead & ordain the momentum towards what he is doing in this church.

-   Pray for the events & meetings that will take place to get the word out about the church.

Chapter 10

STEP#7: DESIGNING GOSPEL-CENTERED ENVIRONMENTS

We live in a culture that loves "cool," that loves "flash." Sadly, cool and flash have crept inside the church.

While the world around us seeks to steal our attention and rob our affections from loving God with all of our heart, soul, mind, and strength, many churches are pouring tons of money, time, and energy into creating a church experience that tries to compete with the best of what the world has to offer.

The problem is that God isn't into cool or flash. Especially in his Church. As Jared Wilson writes,

> I want to suggest that it's possible to get big, exciting, and successful while actually failing substantially at what God would have us do with His church. It's possible to mistake the appearance of success for faithfulness and fruitfulness.[1]

What God loves is *faithfulness*. And what he calls his Church to is faithfulness. Faithfulness to God. Faithfulness to the Word. Faithfulness to the gospel.

The key to effectiveness and fruitfulness in replanting is not trying to be cool or flashy or extraordinary in the eyes of the world. It is in seeking to be faithful in the eyes of the Lord.

What does it look like to be faithful as you begin to move toward the launch of this new replant? Faithfulness in this stage is putting the gospel front and center in everything you do. Making sure the person and work of Jesus Christ is elevated and exalted in above anything and everything else. You must allow the gospel to shape the doctrine, the methodology, and programmatic philosophy of this replant.

Let's get super practical at this point and explore what it looks like in this stage to develop a weekend worship experience and community groups that are both saturated in the gospel. These two environments will be absolutely crucial to the health and growth, spiritually, relationally, and numerically, of the replant.

LAUNCHING A GOSPEL-CENTERED WEEKEND WORSHIP EXPERIENCE

After months of meeting together as a core team, strategizing, praying together, pursuing those in the community, and updating the building (if needed), the public launch has finally come! The website is up and running, new signage is in place, friends and neighbors have been invited. It's time to officially go public as a new church! The day is finally here. Praise God!

You need to ask yourself - What are people going to experience when they come? Not just the first Sunday worship gathering, but every week after that? Don't get me wrong, public launch Sunday is an exciting day. But the last thing you want to do is pull off some big, flashy event that misleads people into thinking your church is something it isn't. The goal for public launch Sunday is to put together a worship experience that is Bible-saturated, grace-filled, Spirit-empowered, Christ-centered, and God-glorifying. It needs to be one that can be *reproduced* each and every Sunday after public launch. This is absolutely essential to the long term health of a replant. A healthy, sustainable replant is not built on flash and coolness. It's built on faithfulness and consistency. Let's talk about what it looks like for your replant to develop a faithful, consistent, gospel-centered worship experience each week.

Three Essential Ingredients

What exactly do I mean by a gospel-centered weekend worship experience? I am talking about a worship experience that is shaped by and points to the gracious reality of what Jesus accomplished through his life, death, and resurrection for sinners. Every component of the worship experience must be guided by this ultimate aim. As you begin to put together a gospel-centered worship experience, there are three essential ingredients that must be included. These three ingredients are 1) gospel-shaped worship, 2) gospel-drenched hospitality, and 3) gospel-driven mission. These ingredients are not separate, but rather encourage and infuse one another. The center of the mark is a worship experience where the three overlap. It looks a bit like this:

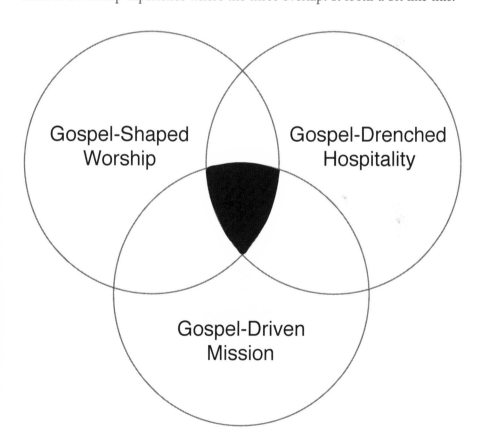

Let's consider these three ingredients on their own, specifically how they each play a vital role in pulling off a gospel-centered worship experience.

Ingredient #1: Gospel-Drenched Hospitality

Biblical hospitality is missing in many churches today. Instead of walking into a warm, encouraging, joyful environment on a Sunday morning, many people experience the opposite when walking into their local church: cold, awkward, and joyless. These are not the words you want people to use when describing your replant. The key to not being described like this is being a church that is passionate about showing gospel-drenched hospitality to every person who walks through the doors. In Romans 12:13, Paul gives this mandate to believers when he writes, "Contribute to the needs of the saints and seek to show hospitality." Just as God has shown us radical hospitality through the gospel, inviting us into his family, we must extend this same type of radical hospitality to those in our community. What does this look like practically? What will this look like in your replant week in and week out?

Cultural Characteristics of Gospel-Drenched Hospitality

Let's consider seven cultural characteristics of gospel-drenched hospitality that must mark your weekend worship gatherings.

Characteristic #1: Initiating

Gospel-drenched hospitality is initiating. In other words, it doesn't wait for people to come to it. It goes to them. On Sunday mornings, you don't wait for people to pursue you. You pursue them. Rather than being a "Here I am!" person, seek to be a "There you are!" person.

Characteristic #2: Embracing

Gospel-drenched hospitality is embracing. In other words, it reflects the heart of Christ in that no matter who walks through the doors of your replant, you run hard after them with the radical love and grace of Jesus. This means your church should be marked by hugs and high fives! Seriously. Hugs and high fives should be happening all over the place as an outflow of the grace and love of Christ. This is the gospel in action. Jesus loves prodigals, and so must your replant. Embrace prodigals like Jesus. Embrace them with your words. Embrace them with your actions.

Characteristic #3: Personal

True hospitality is experienced on a personal level. In your replant you want to extend personal hospitality to each individual who shows up. Jesus didn't die for a mass of people, he died for individuals. In the same way, our hospitality must move beyond a focus on the mass to a pursuit of individuals on a personal and more intimate level. Growing up, I can remember hearing my father and pastor, Paul, say to me, "Mark, ministry is about being present with people. It is a ministry of presence that pastors are called to. It's truly 'being there' with and for people." The older I get, the more my dad's words ring true. Gospel-drenched hospitality is shown through intentional, personal, loving presence with people.

Characteristic #4: Genuine

Genuine hospitality is real, authentic hospitality. There will be people who choose to give God one more chance by coming to your church. They don't need to be entertained. They don't need smoke machines or a rock concert. What they need is genuine, authentic, joyful love from men and women who love Jesus and love them.

Characteristic #5: Knowledgeable

It is hard to be hospitable to outsiders and new people in your church if you aren't familiar with the church you are welcoming them into. Gospel-drenched hospitality needs to be knowledgeable. It is important to equip your people to know basic information about your replant. For example, can they accurately point people to the bathrooms or specific classrooms? Can they answer basic questions about the church's history and doctrine? How about basic questions regarding the children's ministry, youth ministry, or small group ministry? Are they aware of the easiest ways to connect new people into service opportunities in the church? Think through questions like these and then equip your people to be able to answer them clearly and effortlessly. Visitors will take notice.

Characteristic #6: Prayerful

One of the differences between hospitality shown in the church and hospitality shown in a restaurant, hotel, or doctor's office, should be prayer. Gospel-drenched hospitality is prayerful. Here's what I mean. It shouldn't be strange if on Sunday mornings you look around and see members and leaders of the replant praying with and for people. Many people from the community who will be checking out your replant are hurting and broken, looking for hope. They are looking for Jesus, whether they realize it or not. In prayer, we have the privilege of taking these folks to the throne of God. Nothing brings more comfort to a hurting person showing up at your church than a hug and some prayer. So be a church that prays for one another. It's not weird to pray with and for others. It's right and it's good, not to mention that it is biblical and changes lives. Show hospitality through prayer.

Characteristic #7: Persistent

Don't give up. Be persistent in showing gospel-drenched hospitality week in and week out. You cannot do this on your own strength, but need the Holy Spirit to guide and empower you to show this kind of hospitality. Humble yourself and beg him to make you a hospitable church. Every week, pray for this. Don't give up. Don't get distracted. Stay focused on showing true hospitality to the souls God brings to your replant. You were made to love like this.

Structural Characteristics of Gospel-Drenched Hospitality

As you pursue the cultural characteristics of hospitality mentioned above, it is critical that you also develop some of the structural logistics needed to create a hospitable environment. Here are five things you will need to pull this off with excellence each week.

Characteristic #1: A prepared team

A group of people who are equipped to carry out the vision of gospel-drenched hospitality. These folks are prepared, motivated, and ready to love the heck out of people!

Characteristic #2: An inviting facility

A facility that is accessible, clean, and safe. To make sure this is the case, regularly take walks in and around the church building and look at everything through the eyes of a first time visitor. It is amazing what you will see.

Characteristic #3: Clear communication

People know where they are supposed to go and what they are supposed to do. Warm, knowledgeable greeters and clear, easy to read signage are both essential to assuring clear communication happens each week.

Characteristic #4: A "knowing" game-plan

A strategic game-plan to know, connect with, and care for people with gospel love and grace. How are you going to know who is there? Do you have a good system for taking attendance of who is there? Do you have a system for following up on visitors? What about a strategy for checking up on regulars who are absent? Work to develop a system by which you can know what is really going on in the lives of both members and visitors.

Characteristic #5: Integration strategy

A strategic plan to get people connected with the replant beyond Sunday morning. We are talking about clear, intentional assimilation that is vital for integrating people into the body of this new church.

These are five crucial components to developing a church culture marked by gospel-drenched hospitality. If you want people to feel loved and cared for in your replant, if you desire for people to experience authentic, personal relationships on Sunday mornings and beyond, work to develop each of these structural characteristics.

Ingredient #2: Gospel-Shaped Worship

The second ingredient to creating a God honoring worship experience is through intentionally designing and carrying out a gospel-shaped worship service. Much has been written in recent years on what a weekend worship service should look like and what the core elements of the worship gathering should be. You likely can find several books on this topic in your local Christian bookstore. When it comes to this conversation, there is a very wide spectrum of thoughts and opinions. There are those who believe the worship service should be geared primarily towards nonbelievers, making it as easy and comfortable for the nonbeliever as possible to hear about Jesus. Others hold firmly to the conviction that worship is primarily for believers. If nonbelievers are present, that is great, but the purpose of the worship service is for Christians to worship the Lord and bring him glory.

I would personally fall into the camp that believes the design of a Christian worship service should be primarily geared toward believers as they seek to bring glory to God through singing praises, sitting under the preached Word, praying together, giving of their tithes and offerings, and celebrating the Lord's supper together. At the same time, I believe it is vital that nonbelievers also feel welcomed and loved within this environment. This does not mean dumbing anything down, but perhaps intentionally explaining terms and transitions through the service itself. It seems to me this is simply a clear, courteous way to display Christ-like, gospel-drenched hospitality to those present who don't know Jesus.

So what are key elements that should be included in a worship service? What will the design and flow of your replant's new worship gathering look like? Should you have contemporary or traditional music? Should preaching be topical or expository? How should you do the offering? Let me propose that what must drive your response to questions like these is simply this: *the gospel*. The gospel of Jesus Christ should inform, shape, direct and guide every aspect of your worship service. To get real practical, I want to propose five essential elements to a gospel-shaped worship service for your replant. Now, perhaps you will add more, but in looking at Scripture, it seems clear that the following five elements are crucial and necessary. As you consider these five, be mindful that prayer is the thread that should weave through each and every element. In other words, each of the following worship elements must have a prayer component of some kind.

Five Essential Elements to a Gospel-Shaped Worship Service:

Element #1: Gospel Singing

We were made to sing. How can we not? In light of the love and grace and mercy our great God has shown us in Christ, how can we not sing praise to our God and King? Of course, David understood this. Throughout the Psalms we are exhorted over and over again to sing to the Lord and praise his name:

> Oh come, let us sing to the Lord; let us make a joyful noise to the rock of our salvation! Let us come into His presence with thanksgiving; let us make a joyful noise to Him with songs of praise! – Psalm 95:1-2

> Let the word of Christ dwell in you richly, teaching and admonishing one another in all wisdom, singing psalms and hymns and spiritual songs, with thankfulness in your hearts to God. – Colossians 3:16

> Praise the Lord! For it is good to sing praises to our God; for it is pleasant, and a song of praise is fitting. – Psalm 147:1

> Sing to the Lord a new song, His praise from the end of the earth, you who go down to the sea, and all that fills it, the coastlands and their inhabitants. - Isaiah 42:10

> I will sing to the Lord as long as I live; I will sing praise to my God while I have being. – Psalm 104:33

We were made to sing praise to our God! But *what* do we sing? Worship leader, Ben Haley, answers,

> For thousands of years, music has served the purpose of reminding God's people who he is and what he has done. We must sing songs worth singing: Scripturally-based, gospel-saturated, Christ-exalting songs (Ephesians 5:19). Ambiguous, weightless songs with a good melody are fun to listen to, but have no place in congregational singing.[2]

Haley is right. The singing in your worship gathering should be truth-filled, Christ-exalting praise! The gospel must be central. The first essential element then is gospel singing.

Element #2: Gospel Giving

In some circles, it has become somewhat taboo to publicly pass the offering plate in a worship service. Rather than taking time to reflect on the generosity of God and consider how we can respond to that generosity by joyfully giving of our tithes and offerings, some churches have chosen to make this an optional part of their worship gathering. Some churches put buckets in the back of the sanctuary or worship center for those who want to give something. In my opinion, this is a tragic mistake. In doing this, these churches are missing out on a major discipleship opportunity each and every week in their worship gathering.

In a gospel-centered church, which I pray your replant will be, gospel giving becomes the natural outflow of the congregation over time. If we are helping our people rightly understand and apply the good news of Jesus Christ and his life-transforming power to their lives, we should not be timid when it comes to calling people to give sacrificially to the Lord. Rather it should be our joy to call them to sacrificially give back to the One who is their greatest treasure on this earth and for eternity. While how and when a church chooses to lead this giving element in the worship service is a matter of preference, gospel giving must be a priority.

Element #3: Gospel Preaching

There is a lot of preaching going on in churches these days. There are more books on preaching being published around the world than at any other time in history. However, with this comes all sorts of ideas and opinions on what constitutes good preaching. While this is not the place for an in-depth discussion on what constitutes good preaching, let me offer that the best preaching throughout the history of the Church has always been expositional and Christ-centered preaching. Expositional means that the point of the sermon is the point of the passage being preached. It means we are not to preach our own ideas, but rather explain and apply the ideas of God as revealed in his Word. In the same way, we must also be Christ-centered in our preaching. Our sermons must be potent with the gospel, with the good news of Jesus' life, death, and resurrection for sinners. Preaching this gospel must be the ultimate aim of every sermon; to exalt Christ and to call people to worship him in spirit and in truth through the preaching of God's Word.

Pastor Dan Hallock rightly notes,

> The gospel is the main thing God wants us to know. It's the central message of all of Scripture and to miss it is not to truly preach the Bible. Moreover, understanding and believing the gospel is the way for people to be saved and sanctified. When preached correctly, the gospel is the means by which the lost are saved and the saved grow in faith and holiness.[3]

For a replant to be healthy, it must be grounded in and saturated with strong, expositional, gospel-centered preaching of the Word week in and week out. Just like any church, the folks coming to your replant don't need to be entertained. They need to be loved, pursued, welcomed, and fed the life-changing truth of God's Word through faithful, gospel-centered preaching. This is what they need: Good food from the Good Shepherd.

Element #4: Gospel Remembering and Responding

Along with gospel singing, gospel giving, and gospel preaching, the next essential element of a gospel-shaped worship service is gospel *remembering* and *responding*. The Holy Spirit uses the preaching of God's Word to bring about encouragement, challenge, and conviction. However, gospel-centered preaching, while leading us to recognize and confess our sins and failures before God, should not leave us downcast, staring at all of the ways we have fallen short. No, gospel-centered preaching leads us to repentance at the foot of the cross. It is here that through faith we experience the forgiveness and justification that is ours in Christ alone. It is here that we find hope, and peace, and joy in him, not because of anything we have done, but solely as a result of Christ's finished work on our behalf. This is the good news of the gospel!

It is in remembering this gospel that we then want to give our people a chance to respond. This response can look a lot of different ways. For some it might be a time of recommitment to their faith, or for others, surrendering to Christ for the first time. For still others it might be a time of practicing forgiveness toward someone who has hurt them. For the majority of the

Christians present, a proper response to the gospel is the celebration of the Lord's supper.

The Lord instituted this supper as a way for us to continually celebrate our hope in him. We follow the example set forth by the early church in Acts 2:42 where we read, "They were continually devoting themselves to the apostles' teaching and to fellowship, to the breaking of bread, and to prayer." As Steve Anderson explains,

> The Lord's supper is a unique ordinance of the church, a gift given to God's people by Jesus himself. The supper is an opportunity for the believer to do three things: remember the truths of the gospel in light of their own sinfulness, approach the Lord in his kindness to receive grace once again, and (as the Apostle Paul puts it) to proclaim the gospel to those present through the receiving of the elements.[4]

It is for these reasons, among others, that we remember the gospel through celebrating the Lord's supper in our worship gatherings.

Along with baptism, the Lord's supper is an ordinance that is not optional for a biblical church. How often you choose to celebrate the Lord's supper is something your pastors and elders should be very thoughtful and prayerful about. Search the Scriptures on this. Our congregation celebrates the Lord's supper each time we gather at our weekend worship services. It is a true delight to remember what Christ has done through taking the bread and the cup together each week. However you choose to practice it, do not downplay the importance of the Lord's supper in your replant. Rather, joyfully celebrate it regularly as you rejoice in the gospel and the Savior it represents!

Element #5: Gospel Going

The final element to a gospel-shaped worship service is what could be referred to as "gospel going." The culmination of the worship gathering is in being sent out as missionaries to our community to live out and proclaim this life-changing message of the gospel to the lost, the last, and the least. Let's look at this in more depth when considering the third ingredient of a gospel-centered worship experience, gospel-driven mission.

Ingredient #3: Gospel-Driven Mission

Simply put, gospel-driven mission is being sent out as missionaries to make Jesus and his gospel non-ignorable to a lost and broken world. gospel-driven mission happens as we leave the church gathered and enter the world as the church scattered, on mission for the sake of Christ's fame.

What exactly does this look like practically? It looks like your people being sent out each week on gospel-mission to do three things by the power of the Holy Spirit to:

- **Invest in others.**
- **Invite others into Biblical community.**
- **Introduce others to Jesus.**

As discussed in Chapter 9, investing, inviting, and introducing are the three core components of the I-3 relational evangelism strategy. This is the core of what it means and looks like to live on mission on a daily basis. Living on mission is a day by day commitment, by God's grace, to put into practice these three things. This is how we show and tell the good news of Jesus boldly: Invest. Invite. Introduce. This is what it looks like to be a missionary in our communities – it is what God has sent us to do!

Just like the other ingredients of a gospel-centered worship experience, being sent out from our worship gatherings on gospel-mission is dependent on the power of the Holy Spirit. We cannot do this on our own strength. In fact, for many of us, this missional component of replanting scares us to death. We must remember that we pursue the lost not by our power or might, but by the Lord's. We also do not pursue the lost out of guilt or fear, but out of love and by the grace of God. Take comfort in these words from Tim Keller, a pastor in New York City. Keller writes,

> When we truly trust and treasure Jesus, the Holy Spirit produces new traits in us…we are compelled to share the gospel out of generosity and love, not guilt. We are freed from the fear of being ridiculed or hurt by others since we have already received the favor of God by grace. Our dealings with others reflect humility because we know we are saved only by grace alone, not because of our superior insight or character. We are hopeful about everyone because of grace, even the hard cases because we were saved only by grace, not because we were people likely to become Christians. We are courteous and careful with people. We don't have to coerce them, for it is only God's grace that opens hearts, not

our eloquence or persistence, or even their openness. Together, these traits create not only an excellent neighbor, but also a winsome evangelist.[5]

LAUNCHING A GOSPEL-SATURATED COMMUNITY GROUP MINISTRY

Along with designing a gospel-centered worship experience, the time has come to also launch a second gathering for your replant. This second gathering is focused on helping to connect members, attenders, and visitors with one another in an authentic way beyond the worship service.

As those created in the image of God, we were made to do life in community with others. As Christians, we are part of a body, a family of brothers and sisters who are in Christ. The Bible paints a beautiful picture of what it looks like when a church takes seriously the call to care for one another in genuine, sacrificial, Jesus-centered community in Acts 2:42-47. Here we read,

> And they devoted themselves to the apostles' teaching and the fellowship, to the breaking of bread and the prayers. And awe came upon every soul, and many wonders and signs were being done through the apostles. And all who believed were together and had all things in common. And they were selling their possessions and belongings and distributing the proceeds to all, as any had need. And day by day, attending the temple together and breaking bread in their homes, they received their food with glad and generous hearts, praising God and having favor with all the people. And the Lord added to their number day by day those who were being saved.

This is a beautiful vision of what a church can be when we are devoted to the Lord, and serious about being who God has called us to be. This is a picture of what the gospel can do in church communities like your replant. Within the context of a local church, people are transformed by the gospel inwardly, which then has radical, God-glorifying, outward effects in how one connects to others in community. In light of this truth, once the public launch of the replant takes place, the weekly core team meeting will now morph into a new weekly community group where true, biblical fellowship and care, like we see in Acts 2, can be experienced by every individual in your congregation.

Depending on the size of the congregation at this point, the replant may choose to launch one to three different community groups. While you may choose to call these groups by another name (i.e. Life Groups, Missional Communities, Fellowship Groups, etc.), these groups will serve as the primary connecting point for your congregation beyond the weekend worship gathering in the early stages of the replant. These groups will also serve as a primary "on ramp" for visitors and new attendees desiring to become part of the church. It is recommended that community groups meet once a week in someone's home for two hours in length. They will meet for the purpose of connecting those in the congregation with one another through sharing a meal, discussing the Word, and praying with and for one another.

There are many helpful books and resources that can assist you in designing the types of community groups that fit the vision and culture of your replant. In fact, **Appendix Z** contains a list of some of these resources. Regardless of the specific model you choose to create or follow, each community group should have three primary focuses:

Focus #1: Upward

Praying for one another, for the replant, and for the world

Take time each week as a group to pray for these needs together. Be sure to write down group members' prayer requests each week and email them to the group after the meeting so they can be praying for these requests.

Learning from God's Word together

Spend time studying and discussing God's Word together. One recommended strategy is to develop sermon-based discussion questions that can help guide these discussion times. This not only allows for easy preparation for the community group leaders, but it helps reinforce the biblical teaching that is taking place through the preaching at the weekend worship service.

Sharing ways God is at work in your lives

Spend some time asking one another questions that help people recognize some of the ways God is working in, through, and around them. Celebrate the ways God is at work, together!

Focus #2: Inward

Sharing a weekly meal with one another

Food is a gift from the Lord and is to be enjoyed together! I truly believe food should be a non-negotiable component of your community group gathering, not simply because people need to eat, but because this kind of food fellowship is biblical. Meals are central to fellowship among believers throughout the Scriptures, just as they have been throughout the history of the Church. God's people are in need of the same thing today. The community group gathering allows for those in the church to experience a weekly meal like this together.

A few things to remember about the meal: 1) Be sure to make it potluck style where everyone is able to contribute something. 2) Get creative and have different themed food nights (Homemade pizza night, Taco night, Breakfast night, Bacon night, Comfort food night, Family favorite night, etc.). Your group will love this! 3) Remember that during the meal time, group leaders must be intentional to include everyone in conversation the best they can. Work to make everyone feel like they belong.

Doing life together throughout the week

The vision for each community group is that relationships between group members would flow out of the group gathering into the remainder of the week. In other words, the hope is that group members would be doing life together, sharing joys and burdens, hanging out and sharing meals together, attending sports games and going camping as families. All of these, among others, experienced with one another in an authentic way throughout the week. This is what it looks like to truly invest in one another in Christian community.

Caring for one another in tangible ways

As specific needs come up in the lives of those individuals or families in the community group, members should seek to care for one another in tangible ways. While prayer for each another should be a constant, joyful practice, other tangible ways members can care for one another include: Coordinating meals for sick families or new parents in the group, serving each other through childcare and running errands, or helping with lawn work or shoveling snow. There are many, many ways community groups can care for one another in tangible ways like these.

Focus #3: Outward

Inviting the disconnected to connect

Creating an environment that is welcoming to new people is crucial to the health of any community group. Over time, groups that are not intentionally inviting and welcoming outsiders can become stagnant and stale, missing out on the joy of seeing Jesus work in the lives of individuals and families who are desiring fellowship and connection within your replant. This priority and value must be explained and understood by everyone in the congregation; that every community group would be a safe place where new attendees, friends and neighbors of church members, as well as others in the surrounding community, would experience the love and care of your group.

Investing in the spiritually lost through missional living

The core members and attenders of the replant must have a growing understanding that they have been called to live as missionaries of the gospel to your community. We are not sent on this mission as individuals alone, but as a body of Christ-followers together. Regularly spend time in your group encouraging one another and praying for one another as you as a group move out on mission. Share some of the ways you are investing in the lives of those far from Jesus. Celebrate what God is doing in and through the individuals in your group! Be sure to also pray specifically for those men and women, boys and girls, the members of your group are seeking to introduce to Jesus.

Serving the community in practical ways together

One of the great ways to not only build intimacy and trust in your group, but to also show the gospel together in the community is through intentional outreach and service initiatives. It is a beautiful and wonderful thing to serve alongside other believers! Spend time dreaming about ways your group can serve others and then do it! Don't just talk about serving together, *schedule* it and follow through. Your group will be blessed as you seek to bless others.

Basic Community Group Schedule

For community groups to be most effective, it is very important to honor people's schedules. You will want to start and end as close to "on time" as you can. Here is how a typical community group schedule might look:

- **5:45** Chairs and tables set up, kitchen ready for food, atmosphere set, greeters ready
- **6:00** People arrive, mingling, setting up food
- **6:10** Introductions, communicate the plan for the evening, prayer, eat and visit
- **6:55** Gather for the discussion time, have small children go to their space
- **7:00** Share any announcements and begin discussion
- **7:45** Bring in the small children, take prayer requests and pray
- **8:00** Clean up and leave

A Few Tips for Leading Effective, Transformational Community Groups

What makes an effective community group gathering? Why is it that in most churches, some folks love their community group while others don't? Why is it common that in most churches some community groups grow spiritually and numerically, while others struggle to simply survive? I have been part of many different community groups over the years, and what I can tell you is that the most powerful, transformational, safe, loving, family-like, outward focused community groups I have ever experienced shared several things in common. The best community groups consistently do these eight things:

Preparation is obvious to those attending the group

The best groups are led by individuals who faithfully prepare every week. Whether it is preparing for the Bible discussion time, preparing the house to be warm and welcoming, or preparing activities for little kids to enjoy, the best groups are those groups where preparation is obvious.

Discussion is Word-driven

Community groups need to be firmly rooted in the Scriptures, which are the primary source of life and growth in the Christian life. While an element of the discussion time will be having folks share from their personal lives, too much sharing can make the group feel more like a support group. The focus can shift from God to an individual in the group. Work to keep the discussion Word-driven. The needs people share in the group need to be hedged-in and examined through the lens of Scripture. Help one another in this.

Isolation is impossible

It should be impossible for anyone to feel isolated and alone in a community group. The leaders of the group will set the tone for this. If new people show up, pursue them and stick with them throughout the meeting. Don't let them feel awkward and alone. For those who are shy in the group, make sure you go the extra mile to include them in discussion and interaction. At the same time, be careful not to put them on the spot in an uncomfortable way.

Encouragement is excessive

Encouragement is love spoken. Your group should be marked by Christ-like love, which means you should seek to love one another through intentional encouragement. Build one another up in the Lord with your words! Everyone in your group needs this every week. Your group leaders should model this kind of encouragement with those in the group before, during, and after the group meeting.

Practically seek to affirm everyone

This includes young and old, parents and kids, etc. Take note of special accomplishments at work, home, school, or on the ball field. Share "at-a-boys" whenever you can! Beyond the actual meeting, leaders should email, Facebook, and text message words of affirmation to those in the group. This will build a group of loving trust and over time allows the person receiving these words of encouragement to look back at them with delight again and again.

Invitation is ongoing

Constantly remind those in your group that this is an open group, meaning new people are always welcome to join. To help your group become invitational, leaders need to train the group to think invitationally. This simply means it would be wise to periodically spend time as a group brainstorming different types of people that could be invited to the group. Neighbors, friends, family members, acquaintances in the community, these are all folks who should be invited to check out a community group!

Atmosphere is "kid contagious"

The best community groups are groups where children are not simply put up with, but they are cherished and integrated into the life of the group. The simple truth is this: Young parents will not be actively involved in any community group where their kids are not safe, loved, and included. Work hard to make your group kid contagious. The food you eat, the games you play, the discussion you experience, work to make everything welcoming and inviting for kids as well as adults. Kids need adults in their lives and adults need kids. This is the beauty of the body of Christ.

Prayer is a priority

Both when you are together as a group, as well as throughout the week, your group should pray with and for one another. Prioritized, persistent prayer for one another is a mark of true Christian community. Spend time each meeting to take specific prayer requests. Have someone write the prayer requests down so they can be distributed to the group through email in order to pray for each other throughout the week. Always close your group meeting together by praying with and for one another. Be sure to bring the children in on this time. They need to see and experience God's people in prayer together. This is part of their spiritual training, just as it is for the adults in the group.

PURSUE FAITHFULNESS, NOT FLASHINESS

The Lord calls us to lives and ministries marked my faithfulness, not flash. As you seek to humbly lead this new replant in both a gospel-centered worship experience, along with gospel-saturated community groups, the Lord will be honored and lives will be changed. There is nothing cool about any of this. But there *is* great joy in all of this! Great joy, knowing that these simple means of preaching the Word, loving people well, connecting in community, and living on mission is pleasing to our Lord. Being a simple, gospel-centered, people loving, biblical church. This is the key to God-honoring revitalization. This is the key to replanting a church God's way.

FOR FURTHER REFLECTION

Discussion Questions

1. Read the Jared Wilson quote again, *"It's possible to mistake the appearance of success for faithfulness and fruitfulness."* How can you help a church & replanting pastor to recognize the difference here?

2. How can you help a replanted church move towards balancing the three ingredients of a gospel-centered weekend worship experience?

3. Take some time to brainstorm some practical ways that your (sending) church can be of use in a weekend worship service. Also brainstorm some people that come to mind who could go for a weekend to pour into the congregation at the replanted church.

4. One of the things to help outward focus happen is events for the community, which take manpower. Take time to brainstorm ways that an elderly, dying church can have an outward focus, even before

Ways to Pray

- Pray for God to help this church be faithful & fruitful and not to be blinded by success.

- Pray for each weekend to be a gospel-centered weekend for anyone who comes to worship at the replanted church.

- Pray for community and mission to be happening both naturally and intentionally for the church.

Chapter 11

STEP#8: CREATING A STRATEGY FOR SUPPORT

I am convinced that one of the main reasons why some church replants fail within the first few years is because they are attempting to do it all alone. Here's what I mean—just as there is no such thing as a lone ranger Christian, there is no such thing as a lone ranger church. Just as followers of Jesus need other followers of Jesus to pray for them, counsel, teach, and encourage them, so churches need these very same things from other churches. Replanted congregations desperately need continual encouragement, cooperation, and assistance from other churches. In particular, they need radical, long-haul support from their Sending Church. That means you as a Sending Church.

The best and healthiest families are all about commitment to one another. The Sending Church and the replant need to view one another as family, because you are. You are connected to one another as part of the family of God. You have a unique relationship that is similar to a parent and child in many ways. This means through good times and bad times, mountain tops and valleys, you must seek to be there for one another. Consider the following reasons why this is so vital to the ongoing health of a newly replanted congregation.

THREE REASONS WHY LONG HAUL ENCOURAGEMENT, COOPERATION, AND ASSISTANCE IS ESSENTIAL

Replanting Can be Discouraging

Replanting is not for everyone. As discussed earlier, it takes a particular gift mix and a clear calling from the Lord. And, like every other ministry, serving as a pastor of a church replant can be at times very discouraging. There are ups and downs when replanting a congregation. It can be discouraging when young families come and visit but don't stay because you can't offer the same types of children's programming that the large church down the street does. It is discouraging when it seems like the congregation is not catching your vision for living on mission and reaching the lost in the community. It can be discouraging when it feels like even the smallest change you try to implement is met with pushback for all kinds of silly reasons. This is why it is so vital that the Sending Church intentionally works to encourage, assist, and cooperate with the replanter and the replanted congregation over the long haul. This is honoring to the Lord, comforting and refreshing for the replanter, and is the best, most effective strategy for long-term health and growth. The goal should never be to simply get a replant started. The goal is stability and vibrancy that comes through linking arms together for years and years.

Replanting Can be Lonely

Many pastors are incredibly lonely in ministry. Loneliness is one of the leading factors for why a large number of pastors quit ministry altogether. This is especially true in smaller congregations in more rural areas. Many replants will take place in these types of communities. Regardless of where the replant is located, the Sending Church must pursue ongoing relationship with the pastor, his wife, and their family. The Sending Church must help them fight against this feeling of loneliness that is so common in ministry.

Replanting is Hard Work

Replanting a congregation is really hard work. No pastor can do this on his own. He needs help and resources from other churches and individuals. The primary source of help should come from the Sending Church. Whether through financial support, words of love and encouragement, the sending of teams to work on the building, sharing program ideas and ministry supplies or whatever else it looks like, the Sending Church must take ownership of helping the replant in as many ways as possible. The Sending Church needs to help lighten the load so that this replanting work is a joy and not a burden for the replanter, his family, and the newly replanted congregation. Radical, eager, selfless cooperation is needed.

In light of these three reasons, what exactly should long-haul encouragement, cooperation, and assistance look like practically? Let's consider a number of ways the Sending Church can come alongside to care for and encourage the newly replanted congregation, the replanter, and the replanter's family.

COMING ALONGSIDE THE NEWLY REPLANTED CONGREGATION

There are many different ways the Sending Church can come alongside the replant to encourage and serve them for the long haul. This long-term relationship is absolutely vital to the health and growth of this new church. However, it takes great intentionality to make it happen. Here are some of the ways this kind of intentional, radical cooperation can look:

Leadership Development

One of the greatest needs this new replant will have is the training of leaders in the church. This might include the training of deacons and new pastor-elders, or the training of a variety of ministry team leaders, such as the greeting and hospitality team. Your church has all kinds of resources and experienced leaders who can help train these individuals. Not only will it allow your people the excitement and privilege of connecting with people from the replant on a personal level, your investment in these leaders will help strengthen the replant and help assure that their leadership is solid and well-equipped for effective ministry in the future.

Finances

Typically it takes quite some time to put together an excellent finance team in a church, and a replant is no exception. This is another way the Sending Church can serve this congregation—helping the replant figure out their current financial situation, develop new systems of accountability, put together strategies for recording and depositing offerings, and design a new budget for the church are all ways the Sending Church can serve the replant in financial matters.

Volunteer Teams

A sure way to maintain close relationship while serving the new replant is by regularly sending volunteer teams from the Sending Church to help the new congregation. Again, it is a joy for folks in the Sending Church to take a Sunday to worship with and serve alongside their brothers and sisters in the replant. Likewise, it is a great blessing for the pastor and members of the replant to have groups come and serve. Maintaining close relationship with one another as churches is crucial. This intentional and ongoing sending of teams is a strategic way to assure that the new congregation feels loved and supported continually by the Sending Church.

Sharing Printed Materials

An easy way the Sending Church can help the replant out on a weekly basis is in sharing and printing weekly resources for the new congregation. For example, our church designs and prints out the weekly bulletin for each of our replants. This not only helps with cost and time, but it allows the replant to have a great looking bulletin they would otherwise not be able to produce on their own.

Website

In this day and age, the website is the first place the large majority of people look to find out about a new church. Most replants do not have the funds and resources to design and run an up-to-date website. This should be a primary way the Sending Church helps serve the replant. Do whatever it takes to help them have an excellent website. If that means designing it, paying for it, helping to run it, serve this new church through helping them with their website.

Graphic Design

Most likely, the Sending Church has access to graphics and design software that is visually appealing to those both inside and outside the church. Most replants do not have access to these same resources. Giving them free usage of any and all graphics used by the Sending Church will allow them to have a level of quality in their printed materials that most small churches are unable to afford or develop.

Marketing and Signage

As this new replant is preparing to launch, it is important for your church to help them with marketing and new signage both throughout the inside and outside of the church. Helping to pay for an updated sign for the church is a huge blessing, and the neighborhood will take notice! Help to design and pay for marketing materials that can help communicate to the community this new church will be launching. Flyers, door hangers, ads on Facebook or in the local newspaper are all effective means to help get the word out, letting folks in the community know you want them to be part of this new congregation.

Worship Music

Weekly worship music is an important component in helping the congregation create a God-honoring, edifying worship gathering. There are many ways the Sending Congregation can help in this area - sending musicians to help lead services, making connections with other local churches who might have worship leaders and musicians who can help periodically, or perhaps paying for a very part-time worship leader in the replant. The bottom line is that the Sending Church should be willing and eager to come alongside the newly replanted congregation to help them to have a quality worship experience on a weekly basis.

Youth and Children's Ministry Resources

In a small replant, there is typically a great need for a new approach and strategy in children's and youth ministry. At the same time, it can be a major challenge if there are few people to help lead these ministries. The Sending Church can help by sharing access to curriculum, teachers training resources, policy and procedure documents, VBS materials, along with volunteers who can help out on a weekend. All of these can help a small replant enjoy the same level of ministry excellence that you would typically find in a larger church. This is extremely helpful as they seek to reach new families in the community.

Finding Partner Churches

Replants, just like new church plants, need other partner churches to come alongside them for encouragement, prayer support, financial support, and other forms of help and assistance. It takes a great deal of time and energy to form relationships of trust with pastors and leaders of potential partner churches. As a result, it can be difficult for a replanting pastor and the few leaders in the replant to find these partner churches on their own. Typically, the time and energy needed to find partner churches is better spent focusing on the health and growth of this newly replanted congregation. As the Sending Church, your congregation can be a huge help in this by reaching out to denominational leaders and other pastors and churches, casting vision and inviting them to support this exciting new ministry. I believe there are many healthy churches that would love to partner with a new replant if only they were aware of the needs. Your church can help immensely with spreading the word and seeking partnership from these congregations.

Office Administrative Help

One of the most burdensome aspects of replanting for many replanters is having to oversee administrative tasks that are often carried out by an administrative assistant in a larger church. Time and energy that could be spent building relationships with those in the congregation and in the community can get drowned out by the pressing demands of producing the bulletin or making copies for Sunday School teachers. The Sending Church can help tremendously in this area by taking care of some of these needs.

Making copies or bulletins, gathering new information on members and visitors, or helping oversee the scheduling of events and building usage, there are countless ways the Sending Church can help with administrative needs. As a first step, I would highly recommend your congregation investing in a quality management software (along with training) for the new replant. This will be a huge blessing to them and is a strategic tool to help them care for people well, which in turn will help bring health and growth to this congregation.

Prayer Support

As with other ministry positions, replanters and their families need faithful prayer support. I'm reminded of Ephesians 6:18–20, where the Apostle Paul unapologetically asks the Christians in Ephesus to pray for him and his ministry:

> ...at all times in the Spirit, with all prayer and supplication. To that end keep alert with all perseverance, making supplication for all the saints, and also for me, that words may be given to me in opening my mouth boldly to proclaim the mystery of the gospel, for which I am an ambassador in chains, that I may declare it boldly, as I ought to speak.

Prayer must be a top priority in our church replanting efforts. Let me share twelve specific ways Sending Churches can pray for both the replanter and his family, as well as the replant as a congregation. It would be worthwhile to brainstorm creative ways you can equip and encourage people in the Sending Church to pray for these twelve things on a regular and consistent basis.

12 Prayers of a Sending Church

1. Pray the replant and its leaders will keep their eyes on God and not take a step apart from God's leading.

2. Pray for courage and boldness to go where the Lord leads.

3. Pray for humility before the Lord and people, prioritizing the raising up of other leaders.

4. Pray the replant and its leaders will not rely on their own strength, but trust in the Lord's strength.

5. Pray for a deep heart of love for those leading this new replant.

6. Pray for the health of marriages and families in the congregation.

7. Pray the replant and its leaders will walk worthy of the calling God has placed on their lives.

8. Pray for the replanter to preach the Word and the gospel boldly.

9. Pray for God to destroy idols in the hearts of the leaders and in the hearts of those in the congregation.

10. Pray for God-honoring unity in the congregation.

11. Pray the replant and its leaders will do whatever it takes to reach the lost.

12. Pray for the making of disciples who make disciples in and through the replant.

CARING FOR THE REPLANTER AND HIS FAMILY OVER THE LONG HAUL

One of the keys to effective church replanting over the long haul is intentionally caring for and encouraging the replanter, his wife, and his children. Replanters struggle in the ministry of church revitalization because they can often feel alone. They feel discouraged and are not surrounded by many, if any, encouragers. They are dealing with criticism from members, face the challenge of reaching new families. They have to learn a new church culture, and have likely left all of their friends. They are working long hours for little pay. Add to this we are all fighting against an enemy that seeks to kill and destroy the work of God.

Replanting is a battle and you as a Sending Church can be on the front lines by being a strong source of encouragement for the replanter and his family. Many Sending Churches fail in this area—they may do a good job on the front end sending the replanter out, but they do a poor job of walking with he and his family in a helpful and supportive manner over the course of months and years.

This is why your church needs to assemble a Replanter Care Team.

What is a Replanter Care Team?

The replanter care team is a group of individuals that work together for the purpose of caring for and encouraging the replanter and his family. At a minimum, the replanter care team should be comprised of a pastor of the Sending Church along with at least two others who have a special interest and care for the replanter and his family. These people should have the gift of encouragement, time, a heart for God, and a passion for replanting. One of the church members should be designated as the team leader and point person.

How often does the replanter care team meet?

The team should meet once a month for about an hour. This team will continue until the replant is established and the replanted church is healthy enough to care for the replanter and his family on their own. In addition to this monthly meeting, the team should also plan to meet for one extended meeting once a year, probably during the month of January, to discuss long term goals for the year. During the monthly meeting the team will: pray, plan and implement care for the replanter.

Pray

Take a few minutes to pray specifically for the replanter and his family.

Plan

Planning may consist of a long-term calendar and short-term goals for supporting and encouraging the replanter and his family. A Care Plan should be developed by the team, clearly laying out specific ways in which the Sending Church will show love and care to the replanter and his family on a month-to-month basis over the course of a year. The monthly team meeting will serve as a regular touch point to strategize for what is next in the Care

Plan and ensure that someone on the team is taking the lead on particular items of support.[1]

Implement

Each meeting should assign responsibility to team members and other Sending Church members who can be involved in the Care Plan. The purpose of the team is not to do all the work of caring and encouraging, but to mobilize the Sending Church to also help. This is a wonderful way to assist the Sending Church members, helping them to stay closely connected to the replanter and his family.

You will know you've had a successful meeting when team members leave with action items that will encourage and support the replanter and his family in the days ahead.

How Will the Team Know it's Been Successful?

There are two very simple components to success: 1) ensuring the team continues to implement the Care Plan and 2) regular communication (at least every 3 months) to receive honest feedback, directly from the replanter, about the success of the care plan (If you find the care plan is not meeting the needs of the replanter and his wife, adjust the plan as needed).

Let's now consider some specific ways the Care Team can intentionally care for the replanter and his family.

COMING ALONGSIDE THE REPLANTER

It is vital as the Sending Church to intentionally come alongside and encourage the replanting pastor in various ways and in an intentional and consistent manner. Here are some of the ways you can do just that.

Sermon Help

Many times it can be helpful for the replanting pastor to work with the pastor of the Sending Church in doing a sermon series together. This can be a great way for mentoring to happen, especially if the replanting pastor is younger in ministry. It is a blessing for the replanter to benefit from the coaching of a more experienced pastor, and it is a blessing for the Sending Church pastor to encourage the replanter however he can. Teamwork is crucial in replanting. This is also true when it comes to growing as preachers and teachers of the Word—the more cooperation and teamwork, the better it is for both congregations.

Sharing Books

Most pastors love books. In most replants, there is very little budget for pastors when it comes to getting new books and resources for their ongoing growth and development. The Sending Church can help with this by buying or sharing books with the replanter. You may want to create a budget line item specifically for the development and growth of the replanter just as you would any other staff member from the Sending Congregation. This will be a huge blessing to this pastor and will encourage him and his ongoing growth as a leader.

Conferences

Whenever possible, invite and pay for the replanting pastor to go to conferences with the staff of the Sending Church, or perhaps even on their own. Conferences are so helpful in caring for the soul of leaders. Sadly, many pastors in small churches are unable to afford to go to conferences of any kind. Help the replanter get to a conference, and even further help him by finding someone to fill the pulpit for the weekend after the conference. What a blessing this is for a replanter!

Weekly Video Call

Once a week, it is helpful to schedule a video call with the replanter.[2] A video call is preferred over a regular phone call because you are able to look at the replanter and engage with him in a more personal and intimate manner than a simple phone call. I would recommend having the lead pastor and one or two other leaders from the Sending Church be part of this call. Having this weekly time set up as a consistent touch point allows the replanter a safe place to share needs and concerns, get ideas on how to deal with difficult situations, and simply be encouraged. This kind of safe outlet for ongoing care and coaching is something the Sending Church can supply very easily.

A Monthly Face-to-Face Meeting

Depending on the distance from the Sending Church, it is ideal to schedule a monthly face-to-face meeting with key leaders from the Sending Church and the replanter. It might be helpful for a few other core leaders from the replant to join in this meeting as well. There is nothing like spending time together in person, laughing together, talking together, dreaming together, praying together. This is also a chance to hear updates on what God is doing in the replant, as well as discuss any current challenges they are dealing with. And of course, this meeting should take place over food—good food. And the Sending Church should buy!

Calls and Texts of Encouragement

Never underestimate the power of a quick, encouraging phone call or text message. Make it habit to regularly let the replanter know you are thankful for them and that you are praying for them. Any chance you get to affirm and build them up in some way, do it. It will mean the world to them and will be a joy for you.

COMING ALONGSIDE THE REPLANTER'S WIFE AND CHILDREN

While it is critical for the Sending Church to intentionally work to encourage and care for the replanter, it is just as important that they care for and support the replanter's wife and children. Ministry of any kind can be very hard on a pastor's family. Replanting a church brings unique pressures and challenges that not only affect the replanter, but affect his wife and kids as well. As the Sending Church, you must prioritize showing extra love and encouragement to the replanter's family. Here are some ideas to implement.

Bi-Weekly Video Call for the Replanter's Wife

One of the great ways you can serve the replanter's wife is through ongoing, intentional encouragement through a bi-weekly zoom call with other pastor's or leader's wives from the Sending Church. This is an opportunity to hear about challenges and struggles she may be having. It also gives her a regular outlet to laugh and pray with other godly women from the Sending Church.

It is an opportunity to befriend her and love her with the love of Jesus. Having a couple women from the Sending Church own this and schedule the meeting calls is highly recommended.

Sending Gift Cards and Flowers

Another way to regularly encourage a replanter's wife and kids is to surprise them with special gifts periodically. Gift cards to a favorite local restaurant, toy store, book store, gift store, or spa (for *mom*, of course) might be exactly what they need. Sending a bouquet of flowers from time to time is a simple, thoughtful gesture to express your care for the replanter's wife as well. Be intentional about surprising them with these types of thoughtful gifts.

Special Visits

Be intentional about scheduling the replanter and his family for regular visits to the Sending Church throughout the year. When they come, treat them like royalty. Get them a nice hotel if they are coming from out of town. Take care of all of their meals. Set the replanting pastor and his wife up with a special date night with childcare provided. Get creative and try to make these trips full of fun surprises for the couple and the kids.

Notes of Encouragement

Another way you can get the Sending Congregation involved in caring for the replanter's wife and children is by having them write and send special notes of encouragement on a regular basis. Few things are more encouraging than a kind, uplifting word from a friend. This is a great ministry that can involve all different ages of folks from the Sending Church. For example, elderly members who are not able to be part of other ministries in the church can help out with this special encouragement ministry. Perhaps your church can get into the rhythm of sending a large bundle of encouragement notes to the replanter's family once every few months, or spread them out and send a few notes each week. Whatever you decide to do, this is a great way to care for this dear family.

Books and Magazines

Select a "book of the month" or subscribe to magazines and devotional guides to send to the replanter's wife and children. This will be an ongoing source of encouragement and edification for them. Moreover, it shows the wife and children that the Sending Church cares for the spiritual health of everyone involved, and not just the replanting pastor. This communicates a lot to the family, and also to the members of the replant.

Invite the Replanter's Wife to Women's Events

Even if she is unable to come to many of the women's events happening at the Sending Church, it would be great if you can find a way for her to take part in some of the major events throughout the year. Of course, sometimes this means finding trusted and reliable childcare for her kids. Special retreats or conferences that women in the Sending Church will be attending are great events to invite her to join in on. The reality is this: chances are that in the replant there will be very few opportunities for her to focus on her own spiritual growth and fellowship with other godly women. The Sending Church can help immensely with this.

Birthday Cards

Sending personal cards to the replanter's wife and children on their birthdays is a wonderful reminder to them that the Sending Congregation cares about them and is thinking about them. Be sure to send a fun little gift on their birthday as well!

A Few More Ideas...

To encourage the whole family:

1. Zoo Day
2. Professional Baseball Game Day
3. Weekend in the Mountains or at the Beach
4. Amusement Park/Water Park Day

5. Surprise Cookie Tray/Popcorn/Cupcakes Sent to the Family
6. Family Movie Night at Home Package – (Redbox, Pizza, Popcorn)

To encourage the replanter's wife:

1. Bundle of Encouragement Notes and Texts
2. Starbucks Gift Card and a Book
3. Gift Certificate to have the House Cleaned
4. Spa Gift Card
5. Surprise Lunch with other Pastor's/Leader's Wives

IT'S ALL ABOUT THE LONG HAUL...

Similar to the relationship between a parent and child, the Sending Church has an obligation for the oversight and care of the replant until they are healthy enough to stand and function on their own. This should not be a burden to you, but an absolute privilege! The replant needs your ongoing support. The replanter needs your steady encouragement. The replanter's wife and kids need your faithful love and support, not just for a few days or weeks, but months and even years into the future. May the Lord, by his grace and power, give you all that you need to love this dear group of people with the intentional, radical, selfless, love of Jesus over the long haul.

FOR FURTHER REFLECTION

Discussion Questions

1. Replanting can be discouraging, lonely & hard work. Write down a few ways right now that your team can encourage, befriend, and ease the work of a replanting pastor. Take time to assign these to people on your team to put into action over the next eight months.

2. What are some of the strengths of your church that will make it easy to come alongside the replanted church to help? In what ways is your church going to have to sacrifice or step out in faith to come alongside to help the replanted church?

3. Who on your team is going to focus on pouring into the replanter? What are three of the ways that you will do this in the first year of the replant?

4. Who on your team is going to focus on pouring into the replanting pastor's wife? In what ways?

Ways to Pray

- See "12 Prayers of a Sending Church" on page 213-214.

Chapter 12

THE REPLANT BLUEPRINT

With any complex organism or organization, you must understand the parts before you understand how they all work together. For example, the human body—if you don't understand the different parts and systems of the body, then understanding the developmental process of puberty is going to be a challenge. The same goes for a replant—if you don't understand the difference between a seed and a stem, then you won't understand the process of planting and sprouting.

When it comes to church replanting, our thoughts might directly and naturally jump to the Sunday morning worship service or other programs and what it might take to pull these off. While the Sunday morning gathering, along with other ministry programs are essential to a healthy replant, there are a number of other pieces that must be thought through and come together first. If these pieces do not come together, that updated Sunday morning gathering and other new programs will struggle to happen, if they take off at all.

In order to replant a church well, you must have a game-plan. You must have a developed and well-thought out strategy for church transformation to implement. This chapter is focused on helping you and your church do this and do this well. The leaders on your transition team will play a vital role in helping to lead this process, serving as key mediators, communicators, and liaisons between the Sending Church and the Legacy Church. There are two primary components to this strategy your congregation needs to develop: **The anatomy of a replant and the development process of a replant.** The following Replant Blueprint includes each of these two components *(See following pages)*.

	PHASE 1: Identify (Month 0)	PHASE 2: Foundations (Month 1-2)
Leadership	- Conversation and prayer among the leaders to evaluate readiness of Legacy Congregation - Ongoing training of replanting pastor in Sending Church - Clearly identify the negotiables and non-negotiables	- Legacy team attend service at Sending Church and teachers shadow class - Calendar in place with replant pastors/residents, worship team, Sending Church volunteers loving on existing congregation - Begin identifying potential core team members
Systems	- Sending Church assesses current financial situation of Legacy Congregation	- Website up/email active/Facebook group - Pro-presenter install and training - Update the bulletin and info cards
Programs	- Assess the existing programs of the Legacy Congregation	- Weekly worship gathering as new replant - Sunday School continues - Outreach event - Vision night - Begin developing the four key ministry teams (Music, tech, hospitality, children's)
Building	- Assess the condition of the building	- Develop a game plan for signage - Sound system updated - Determine needed building renovation and their priority level
Legal	- Both churches must vote to move forward together and replant - Necessary leadership/officer changes - Decisions concerning property/banking details - Make name changes for church & register with SOS if necessary - Inform your denomination/network - Start/update corporate binder (with meeting minutes) - Determine finance plan/budget	- Finish denominational paperwork - Draft provisional budget

	PHASE 3: Soft Launch (Month 3-Public Launch)	PHASE 4: Public Launch
Leadership	- Begin weekly core team gathering - 1-3 relational evangelism strategy - Prayer walking - Revamp church membership	- Ongoing leadership meetings - Ongoing communication with the Sending Church and denomination or network - Replanting pastor develops & leads shepherding meeting
Systems	- Church management software integrated	- Improving existing systems and creating new systems
Programs	- Weekly worship service with lead replanter leading - Social media blitz to get the word out - Outreach events	- Weekly worship service - Community group launched - Outreach events
Building	- New, outside signage goes live - Create a coffee space - The Legacy Wall - Kids' space renovations including children's check-in set up	- Key spaces are ready for use
Legal	- Any remaining legal issues taken care of	- Identify any additional legal issues to be handled

THE ANATOMY OF A REPLANT

The first primary component to developing and implementing an effective strategy for church transformation is identifying the anatomy of the replant. This anatomy consists of five specific areas:

1. Leadership
2. Systems
3. Programs
4. Building
5. Legal

Let's consider each of these briefly.

Area #1: Leadership

This area relates to all things pertaining to the lead replanting pastor, his training, development, family, and assessment. The area of leadership also covers the care of the Legacy Congregation, development of the core launch team, casting and communication of the replant's vision and mission, as well as the raising up of another pastor-elder or two. The Sending Church pastor-elders and other ministry leaders are intimately involved in this area.

Area #2: Systems

Systems pertains to the framework of what makes a church work as an organization. It includes finances, administration, by-laws, website, children's and youth ministry check-ins & policies, shepherding software, and worship service technology, among others.

Area #3: Programs

Programs include everything related to creating a church culture with the core team, existing congregation, and others from the community. Programs would include the preaching/teaching ministry of the church, vision nights, outreach events, children's and youth ministry, weekly Sunday gathering, and community groups.

Area #4: Building

All things physical – from signage & sound system to any renovations that need to be made.

Area #5: Legal

These important aspects are typically one time things that must be done to be compliant with state & federal laws regarding the church as a non-profit corporation. You will want to do these with excellence to be above reproach, and often must ask for help from your supervising organizations to make sure they are done correctly.

THE DEVELOPMENTAL PROCESS OF A REPLANT

The second primary component to an effective strategy for church transformation in a replant is the development of a clear and timely implementation process. This implementation process is made up of four phases:

1. Identify
2. Foundations
3. Soft Launch
4. Public Launch

Let's consider each of these in more depth.

Phase #1: Identify (Month 0)

This first phase is when the Legacy Congregation connects with the potential Sending Church to ask for assistance and help. It is during this phase that both the Legacy Church and the potential Sending Church get to know one another, ask hard questions of each another, build trust with one another, and ultimately decide whether or not they want to move forward together and replant. This phase typically lasts anywhere from 1-3 months.

During Phase 1, there are several things happening in the following five areas.

Area #1: Leadership

Much conversation and prayer among the leaders of both churches. The pastor-elders, deacons, and other key leaders from the Sending Church are heavily involved in evaluating the readiness of the Legacy Church for potential replanting. It is during this season that many conversations take place between leaders of the Sending Church and the remaining members and leaders from the Legacy Congregation. Along with conversation, this is a time for intentional prayer among the leaders and congregations of both churches as they seek to discern whether or not to move forward together in a replanting effort. This is the phase where the 8 Key Meetings laid out in Chapter 8 will take place.

Ongoing training, equipping, and assessing of the replanting pastor/resident in the Sending Church. This pastor/resident is being positioned to be sent out from the Sending Church to help lead and shepherd a Legacy Congregation. They will also be preparing for assessment through the denomination or network of the Sending Church at this time. While it is possible that this individual has already successfully been assessed and approved as a replanting pastor by your denomination or network at this point, in many cases the assessment has not yet occurred.

Cleary identify the negotiables and non-negotiables. The replant process should never move beyond this first phase before the Sending Church has clearly articulated their negotiables and non-negotiables (see Chapter 7) and determined whether or not the Legacy Congregation aligns with these. If there is not harmony and alignment on both the negotiables and a large majority of non-negotiables, the replant process will be unable to move forward. However, if there *is* harmony and unity among the two churches, this will be a major step toward replanting together.

Area #2: Systems

Assess the current financial situation of the Legacy Church. At this point they will also begin to strategize for what it would look like to potentially open a sub-fund for the new replant out of the Sending Church.

Area #3: Programs

Assess the existing programs of the Legacy Church. What programs are healthy? What programs will potentially need to be changed? Are there programs that will need to be cut? This phase is not for making changes, but rather to begin thinking about potential changes in programming that might need to happen if the Legacy Church becomes a replant.

Area #4: Building

Assess the condition of the building. As the two churches are getting to know one another, it is wise to honestly assess the condition of the physical building. What condition is it currently in? Are any major repairs needed, and how much will they cost? While the Sending Church will not learn everything about the physical building in this first phase, try to gather as much information as you can, as it will most likely factor into the decision to replant this congregation or not.

Area #5: Legal

Legally, nothing needs to be done unless the decision is made by the end of Phase 1 to move forward together as a replant. If the decision is made to replant, then there are several legalities that must be carried out on the part of both the congregations. The following is a list of several of these.

Both churches must vote to move forward together and replant. Again, before the replanting process can move from phase 1 to phase 2, both the Sending Congregation and the Legacy Congregation must vote to move forward together in this replanting effort. It must be made very clear at this meeting what exactly is being voted on. Be clear on what replanting will mean for each of the congregations in terms of responsibility moving forward. As with other congregational meetings, minutes should be taken and votes should be counted and recorded for legal purposes.

Necessary leadership/officer changes made upon the official vote. If the churches vote to move forward together in a replanting effort, there will be necessary leadership/officer changes made as the Legacy Congregation surrenders all day-to-day decision making to the Sending Church. *This will* *involve the adoption of the Sending Church's by-laws to begin serving as the primary, governing document for the new replant.* While this needs to be communicated clearly, the congregation should be aware by this time that these changes will be made. Make sure no one is surprised by any of these leadership changes in the meeting itself. Do the work of communicating these critical leadership changes *before* the official congregational vote takes place.

Decisions are made concerning existing property/banking details. Hopefully the two congregations have been in communication concerning the needed property/banking changes that must occur as the Legacy Congregation now comes under the Sending Church. By way of reminder, this is only for a period of time until the new replant is able to stand on its own.

Consider a name change. It is often the case that the new replant will intentionally take on a new name. It will be important to begin using the new church name at this time. The church will also be registered with the Secretary of State, if necessary. See **Appendix X** for more information on effectively leading a church name change.

Inform your denomination or network. It will be important to communicate with your denominational or network leaders to let them know that the new replant will be happening. Most likely, they will have documents for you to fill out as the replanted congregation merges with that denomination or network.

Start or update a corporate binder that includes congregational meeting minutes for the Legacy Congregation. In particular, make sure to include the meeting minutes from the official vote to be replanted with the Sending Church.

Determine finance plan/budget. It is important at this point to evaluate the current finances and to make a game plan moving forward regarding the existing budget. It may need to be adjusted in light of the marriage with the

Sending Church. The official budget revisions will most likely happen in phase two.

Phase #2: Foundations (Month 1-2)

This second phase is focused on the first and second month of the replant, once both congregations have officially voted to move forward together. In this phase the basic foundations of the church replant are being laid to establish a new church culture and create an environment ready for change.

Area #1: Leadership

Legacy Congregation leaders attend service at Sending Church and shadow Sending Church leaders. It is important for the Legacy Congregation to get a feel for the culture of the Sending Church. It is recommended, if possible, that the Legacy Congregation leaders visit the Sending Church on multiple occasions for the purpose of shadowing the leaders of different ministry areas. These include the greeting ministry, tech ministry, children's ministry, and worship ministry. It will also be good for these leaders to sit in on other leadership meetings.

Sending Church volunteers and leaders begin visiting and loving on the Legacy Congregation. Relationship and trust continue to be built in this phase. This will happen as the Sending Church intentionally seeks out and pursues the remaining members of the Legacy Congregation with love, encouragement, and friendship.

Begin identifying potential core team members. The time has come to begin intentionally identifying those who might be interested in joining the core team of the new replant. Through one on one conversations and meetings where the vision can be cast to members of the Sending Congregation, individuals begin to think and pray about their potential involvement in this new replant. The Sending Church pastors and elders should help the replanting pastor in the assessment of all potential core team members.

Area #2: Systems

Website up, email active, social media launched. You want to begin getting the word out about this new replant. While you won't have much to communicate at this point regarding new programs or events, you can begin to let people know that the new church is beginning to form and encourage folks to prayerfully consider being part of it. It is time to get the word out and have a clear communication pathway for those who would like more information.

Pro-Presenter installation & training. As weekly worship gatherings continue to take place, the Sending Church will want to update the technology in the sanctuary as is appropriate. If the congregation is going to begin using a projector and screen more regularly throughout the service, it is important to get *Pro-Presenter* (or another quality program) installed to be used in the worship gatherings. This would also be a time to train individuals at the new replant to run the program.

Update the bulletin and information cards. For the sake of better and more effective communication, it is important to revise and update both the weekly bulletin and information card. These are both important first impression pieces for visitors and guests to the replant. When done well, these two documents will help you more clearly communicate what is happening in the replant and gather personal information and prayer requests easily and efficiently.

Area #3: Programs

Weekly worship gathering. The replant will *not* stop meeting together for weekly worship. Because of this, during phase two, the weekly worship service will be the primary program/gathering for the congregation. This will be the primary time to worship the Lord together, to continue to cast vision for the replant, care for the congregation, and communicate any upcoming changes that are on the horizon. You may choose to do a few after service potlucks during this phase for additional connection time as a congregation.

Sunday school. If the Legacy Congregation has a Sunday class or two meeting each week, it is wise to keep these going and have leaders and others from the Sending Church join them. This is a great opportunity to encourage and build relationships with the legacy folks. Remember, in replanting there are *very few* hills to die on. Typically, killing a Sunday school class or two is not one of these hills. This will mistakenly cause more harm than good in most cases.

Outreach event. It would be good to try and plan one outreach event during Phase 2. It does not need to be anything large or expensive. It may be as simple as offering to do free yard work for neighbors around the church or hosting a neighborhood BBQ after the worship gathering one Sunday. The point is for this event to mobilize the replant congregation to begin looking outward to the lost in their community and doing intentional outreach right away. This should be seen as a baby step, and that is a win for this new replant.

Vision night. At some point during Phase 2, you will want to host a vision night for the replant. Essentially, this is a night designed for friends, family members, and others in the community to come hear about the exciting vision of this new church. It is a chance to share the mission and direction of the replant and to inform those present on some of the different ways they can be involved. This is a night that aims to give clear on ramps for those who are interested in being part. Make it a fun evening with refreshments, pictures, and lots of warmth! Make people feel loved and at home.

Begin developing the four key ministry teams: music, tech, hospitality, children's ministry. As those in the replant begin to shadow and learn from leaders in the Sending Church, four key ministry teams should begin to be developed during Phase 2. These include the music, tech, hospitality, and children's ministry team.

Area #4: Building

Develop a game-plan for signage. New signage will be needed both on the inside and the outside of the building. While external signs will not be put up until the soft launch phase, it is during this second phase that you should begin to think through the game-plan for signage. Most likely, you will want to begin putting up new, internal signage sooner. Internal signage would include wayfinding and directional signs, signs that clearly label rooms and other important spaces and areas in the church, and signs that help communicate the vision and values of the new replant.

Sound system updated. Depending on the current state of the sound system in the sanctuary of the replant, this is a good time to make needed changes and updates. In most cases, the sound board, monitors, and speakers are fairly outdated. While it may work fine to use these as they are for a season, if the new church is going to change its worship style and begin utilizing a band or multiple musicians/singers, updates and upgrades will ideally need to happen sooner rather than later, if budget allows.

Determine needed building renovations and priority level. In this phase, there should be serious conversation about any building renovations that need to take place before the public launch. If there is a great deal of work that needs to be done, it should be determined what the priority, cost, and schedule of completion is for each project. As you talk through these projects, it's a good time to think of any partner churches that you could ask to help with manpower or financial support to help get the church ready. Churches are a lot quicker to partner if they know a *specific need*, and if that need fits the giftings of some in their church.

Area #5: Legal

Finish denominational paperwork. Be sure to finish filling out and then mailing to your denomination or network any required paperwork that they need. Often times, denominations will need to see a copy of the meeting minutes where the official vote to replant occurred. Check with your local denominational leader if you have any questions with this.

Create provisional budget. Once you have evaluated the existing budget and financial situation of the Legacy Congregation, it is vital to draft a provisional budget for the replant. This will most likely be done by designated leaders from the Sending Church, and if appropriate and helpful, with the assistance of key leaders from the Legacy Congregation.

Phase #3: Soft Launch (Month 3-Public Launch)

Month 3 brings the excitement of the soft launch phase. During this phase, the core team of the replant begins to move forward together on mission, seeking to reach the community and build the core team. This is also an intentional season for trial and error as the leaders of the replant begin attempting and implementing new ministry systems and strategies in preparation for the public launch.

Area #1: Leadership

Begin weekly core team gathering. Beyond the weekly worship service, during the soft launch phase the replant core team will be meeting on a weekly basis. This is a crucial time of relationship building, vision casting, strategic planning, and leadership development of those on the core team. This gathering will also allow time to unleash key ministry teams and their leaders as they begin to develop their ministries.

I-3 relational evangelism strategy. The core team will be trained in the I-3 relational evangelism strategy during the soft launch phase. This tool helps equip believers to live on mission in their community. This will also help the core team begin intentionally making connections with family, friends, neighbors, and co-workers who may desire to join the core team during the soft launch phase.

Prayer walking. The core team should spend intentional time prayer walking through the immediate neighborhood surrounding the church, as well as other areas in the community. Not only will this help the core team remain dependent on the Lord and his Spirit together, but it will help the core team to connect with one another on a deeper spiritual level.

Revamp church membership. Church membership is common in most churches. However, it is rare to find dying congregations that do membership really well. You want to do membership well as you launch this replant. **Appendix J** is designed to help you think through issues pertaining to membership, specifically how to update your outdated membership list, along with how to develop a new membership process for the replant.

Area #2: Systems

Church management software integrated. It is important for the replant to integrate and begin using a quality church management software during this soft launch phase. This software will be critical in helping to keep track of and shepherd this new congregation as it moves into the future. *Church Community Builder* and *Fellowship One* are two excellent options to consider and look into. It will also be important to help train an individual or team to help oversee this management software.

Area #3: Programs

Weekly worship service with lead replanter leading. The weekly worship service will continue but now with the replanting pastor leading the service. This includes regular preaching by the replanter. Even though this is still the soft launch phase, it is encouraged that friends and neighbors be invited to this worship gathering. As the core team begins to lead a gospel-centered worship experience including gospel-shaped worship, gospel-drenched hospitality, and gospel-driven mission, these worship gatherings will serve as prime environments to connect with folks interested in checking out Jesus and this new replant. You will most likely see new folks coming to this gathering on a regular basis as they are invited by core team members and as the word begins to spread in the community that the new replant is beginning to launch.

Social media blitz to get the word out. The core team will want to utilize social media to begin aggressively spreading the word about the new replant in this soft launch phase. Twitter, Facebook, and Instagram are all excellent avenues to connect with, and share information about, the replant. Let people know about the weekly worship gathering, outreach events, and other activities and events the replant is involved with. Once the public launch date is finalized, share this date regularly, inviting people to come and be part of it! You will want to pursue use of social media intentionally throughout the soft launch phase and beyond. Get the word out!

Outreach events. The core team should plan to lead 2-3 outreach events in the community during the soft launch phase. It is critical that the core team is living on mission, investing in and inviting those from the community to be part of this new church. It should always be understood that these outreach events are simply intentional environments for the core team, and others committed to the replant, to meet and build relationships with individuals and families from the community. Being effective missionaries in and through this replant is dependent on this kind of intentional, relational pursuit of people.

Area #4: Building

New exterior signage goes live. Once new signage goes up on the outside, the community will begin to take notice. It will be obvious that there is a new church in town! If the core team is doing a good job of spreading the word about the new replant, building relationships with folks in the community, and leading effective, relational outreach events, the new signage will not only serve to help build excitement and anticipation in the minds of those in the community, but also those already part of the replant.

Create a coffee space. Coffee is a bigger deal than you might think. Most people love to drink it and there is something about the smell and the sheer presence of coffee in an old church building that is just comforting! For this reason, it's recommended to create an intentional coffee space. Perhaps you can find some inexpensive but good quality chairs and tables where folks can sit, hang out, visit, and enjoy some coffee together. Maybe throw in some donuts or bagels as well. Whatever it looks like, and whatever type of coffee or pastries you want to make and serve, creating this type of intentional, welcoming, fellowship environment is worth your time, money, and effort. The goal should be to have this space finished and being used at least two weeks before the official public launch.

The Legacy Wall. The legacy wall is an idea born out of the simple desire to honor the wonderful history of churches our congregation has been blessed to replant. This is a great way to encourage and affirm the Legacy Congregation in this soft launch phase, helping them to see how much you truly value them and their history. *Here* is an example of how one *replant created a legacy* wall to honor the remaining members and history of the Legacy Congregation.

The Legacy Wall: Calvary La Junta
(Formerly First Baptist Church, La Junta, Colorado)

Although the congregation had been ready to close its doors with only a handful of people in attendance, the church had once been a powerhouse of ministry, gospel change, and Christian education in the region. Many of the still-present members had served in the church for decades, including one individual who attended for nearly a century and ministered to hundreds–perhaps thousands–of children as nursery director for the better part of her life after inheriting the ministry when her own mother retired. This church and congregation could boast of consistent and faithful ministry for decades. That is always worth honoring.

Even though we were starting fresh as a new church, we needed to feel the connection to the kingdom work that had gone before us in this place. In addition, we needed our legacy members to remember the best parts of their history, and we wanted new members and attenders to know the foundation of faithful lives upon which we are building the next chapter. The combination of deep roots and flourishing energy together are what promotes healthy growth in this kind of community, and both are vital to our ministry here.

Our first design idea was to build the legacy wall with salvaged barn wood, but we could not find enough for the project—around here everybody reuses their own barn wood until it falls to pieces.

Instead, we used corrugated galvanized sheet metal, to which we can attach picture frames with magnets. This allows us to update the wall as we move forward, adding to the first 125 years of the church's history now displayed. It was wonderful to see our legacy members find this special corner honoring their past, in the midst of a set of rapid physical updates and changes to the historic building. Their laughter and tears, shared memories and appreciation for our work in putting the space together were precious to witness.

Putting together the information was fairly easy for us, thanks to a group of ladies who endeavored over the decades to collect and scrapbook every clipping, article, and mention of the church or any church member that came through denominational newsletters and the local paper, which has been in operation for most of the life of the church. We searched through hundreds of articles and announcements, anniversary celebration bulletins and old photographs, for the foundational bits and pieces of First Baptist Church that we could build on as we moved the church forward into a fresh mission and vision for reaching our town. And in doing so, we gained a greater appreciation for the former life of this church, for the vitality and vibrancy of its community before it declined, which we hope to foster again within our replant.

Theologically, the most important of all the pieces we put together for the wall is a display of the first communion set used by the church at its inception in the late 1880's. It's a visible reminder that this church always has been and always will be about the atoning death and resurrection of Jesus Christ—a worthy legacy, indeed.

Matt Whitt
Lead Pastor
Calvary Church La Junta

Kids' space renovations & check-in. Creating a warm, welcoming, and safe children's ministry environment is critical for the health of any replant. The soft launch is the primary phase when the core team should work to make needed space renovations, including new, bright paint and posters on the walls, deep cleaning, new tables and chairs, and an easy to use children's check-in area. This will also involve the training of volunteers who can help lead and oversee the children's ministry and its classes. Volunteers will also need to be trained to lead the check-in area before, during, and after the weekly worship gathering. The Sending Church should help the replant get all of this set up and running smoothly.

Area #5: Legal

The Sending Church should help the replanting pastor and the replant core team identify any remaining legal issues that must be addressed before the public launch. It is recommended that the lead replanter and one or two other members from the core team set a meeting with a few leaders from the Sending Church to discuss this.

Phase #4 Public Launch

The public launch is the official kick-off of the replant. This is the culmination of months of prayers and meetings and outreach events and worship gatherings. At the same time, it is really only the beginning of reaching this community with the gospel! At this point, the foundational pieces of this replant should be in place and the core team is ready to lead and serve this new congregation.

Area #1: Leadership

Ongoing leadership meetings. Once the replant is officially launched, the replanting pastor along with any other pastors or deacons (depending on your leadership structure) will begin meeting regularly together as a leadership team.[1] It is recommended that this meeting happen 1-2 times each month. For a period of time, the pastors or other key leaders from the Sending Church may also be part of this meeting. The purpose of this meeting is to address and discuss the direction of the church, assess regularly how things are progressing as a newly established congregation, and deal with any ministry or leadership issues that have arisen.

Ongoing communication with the Sending Church and denomination or network. Clear, consistent communication between the replant and the Sending Church is vital. The same is true with the relationship between the replant and the denomination or network it is part of. The lead replanter should make it a point to send a progress report/update every month to each of these entities. Include praises of what the Lord is doing in the life of this church and its people, as well as any prayer requests and specific needs the replant may have.

Helping the replanting pastor develop and lead a shepherding meeting. Shepherding is the primary work of the pastor. Therefore, it is the primary work of the lead replanter in this replant. Intentional shepherding of the flock is absolutely crucial to the health and growth of this replant moving forward. This is why the pastors of the Sending Church should help the lead replanter develop and prioritize the most important meeting their spiritual leaders can be having: A regularly scheduled shepherding meeting for the sole purpose of shepherding the flock. Refer to Chapter 9 for a detailed explanation of what this shepherding meeting looks like.

Area #2: Systems

At this point, the primary systems should be in place, up and running. During this phase it is more about working to tweak and improve the new systems that are in place than creating new systems. In particular, attention should be given to maximizing the new church management software.

Area #3: Programs

Weekly worship service. The weekly worship service is rolling at this point. It should be the primary environment for the church body to worship and study the Word together. This gathering should be marked by the three gospel elements discussed in Chapter 9: gospel-shaped worship, gospel-drenched hospitality, and gospel-driven mission.

Launch community groups. Once the public launch happens, the weekly core team meeting will morph into a new weekly community group. The purpose of this community group is for ongoing fellowship, Bible study, mission, and prayer. Depending on the size of the congregation at this point and the readiness of its leaders, the replant may be ready to launch two to three different community groups. While you may choose to call these groups by another name, these community groups will serve as the primary connecting point for your congregation beyond the weekend worship gathering in the early stages of this replant. These groups will also serve as primary on ramps for visitors wanting to become part of the church. While having an upward focus, these groups are different from many traditional church Bible studies. These are medium sized groups (12-25 people) where individuals of all ages can connect, no matter if they have been part of the church for decades, or if this is their first week. As you multiply groups, you will want to make sure that those leading a group understand this missional vision.[2]

Outreach events. It is important to schedule regular, intentional outreach events during this phase and beyond. You may choose to do these outreach events as an entire congregation or perhaps encourage each community group to lead their own outreach event. However you decide to do it, it is important to plan for these events as opportunities to connect with friends and neighbors who don't know Christ.

Area #4: Building

Key spaces ready for use. By the public launch, the key spaces that will be used in the church building should be finished. These areas include, but are not limited to: the children's ministry area, coffee/fellowship area, the sanctuary, the main entrance area, parking lot, restrooms, and playground. Since each of these areas will be frequented regularly throughout the morning, it is important to do all you can to have them in welcoming and working condition.

Area #5: Legal

As with the soft launch phase, here the Sending Church should help the replanting pastor and the replant core team identify any remaining legal issues that must be addressed that have not yet been. The replanting pastor should seek out the appropriate leaders from the Sending Church to help with this.

THE LORD IS JUST GETTING STARTED...

The goal of this last chapter has been to help you see how all the pieces of this replanting process fit together. As you can see, replanting a church takes intentional, strategic preparation and planning. It takes hard work, patience, discernment, love, and much prayer.

There are numerous moving pieces and parts in this replanting process. There are many individuals involved in various ways within the phases of the journey. But at the end of the day, all of this strategic thinking, planning, and leading is pointless and powerless apart from the work of the Holy Spirit guiding and saturating each and every component along the way. When a dying church is replanted, it is a supernatural work of God. It is the result of the living, gracious, sovereign Lord of the universe doing what only he can do: Bringing dead bones back to life! May we each lean on our mighty Savior and King, believing and trusting that he not only loves dying churches, but it is his delight to make them thrive again for his glory.

He is just getting started...

FOR FURTHER REFLECTION

Discussion Questions

1. Who on your team is specifically in charge of the areas of the replanting anatomy?

2. What are ways that your church can make sure the replanted church is moving forward in the development process?

3. One of the key ways your church can help a newly replanted church is through getting their building ready to be used. Do you have the resources (people & money) to help make this happen? Can you schedule a time now to take a team of people to the replanted church to serve in whatever ways are needed to get the building ready?

4. Now that you have read the whole book, what two things do you (as an individual) need to put into action immediately to play your role in making this happen?

Ways to Pray

- Pray for God to saturate this whole process with his Holy Spirit's guidance and provision.

- Pray for eyes to see how to best serve the replanted church.

- Pray for God to continue to bring churches & leaders to you so that you can continue to replant churches for God's glory!

APPENDICES

A:

Frequently Asked Questions

The following are several frequently asked questions regarding specific aspects of replanting.

FINANCES AND PHYSICAL BUILDING(S)

How do we as the Sending Church pay for this replant? There seem to be a lot of expenses.

The Sending Church in many cases cannot be expected to absorb all the expenses in a replant, but they will be one of the funding partners. The main players in funding a replant are the Sending Church, the Legacy Congregation, the associated denomination and/or network, and other partner churches that are passionate about replanting. The Sending Church is the main catalyst in securing resources from the state and national levels of the denomination or network. This fact is to be shared with the Legacy Congregation as a motivating tool for them to vote to replant with you. They will identify that there is money available to help them, but they won't know how to get access to it. As the Sending Church, you should know the in's and out's on every grant available through your network or denomination on the local, state and national level to assist this replant. Be sure to share with the

Legacy Congregation that you know how to access the resources to help them.

In many cases, the Legacy Congregation has savings that can be tapped into to help with some replant expenses, along with a core group of tithers. They need to know that they are expected to be a key player to fund the incoming replanting pastor. Gaining visibility of their finances early in the discussion process is extremely helpful, but asking too soon in the discussions is risky. You must be wise and seek the Spirit's guidance. Many declining churches are still very strong givers to missions and to their denomination. Asking questions about their missional giving starts the ball rolling and allows you to see what funds are actually available. This opens the door for an easier discussion with them about what they feel they can contribute towards a pastor's salary. Lastly, you can ask if they have any savings or reserves that have been setting aside for emergencies or other needs. It is critical to recognize that often times the Legacy Congregation is in the position they are in because of poor financial management. When your leadership sees their budget, do not focus on what they have budgeted, but what they actually have in the budget. Once they vote to replant, you will be able to re-arrange their budget to put the finances where they are needed for immediate gospel-impact in their community.

The real work that is done by the Sending Church is securing partner churches to help fund the replant. Partner churches are vital to the success of a replant by sending prayer support, teams to help with outreach events, building maintenance or remodeling teams, and financial teams. If we are to see a real replanting movement occur, it cannot be done by a few Sending Churches, but rather an army of Sending Churches, large and small, partnering together to see declining churches coming back to life!

Financial matters can be a very sensitive and difficult topic to address in any church. How do we lovingly and effectively address financial matters with the Legacy Congregation?

Building trust with the Legacy Congregation and its leaders is particularly critical when it comes to discussing matters of money, finance, and budgeting. Because of this, you need to be mindful that everything you say and do in your interactions with these folks is giving them a glimpse of the church family into which they will potentially be adopted. You want to have your act together when discussing matters of money. If they are going to trust the Sending Church, they need to see that you know what you are doing. Go the extra mile to develop polished financial documents and always have an organized, printed agenda to pass out to everyone for your meetings with them. Giving a professional impression makes a big difference.

The Legacy Congregation also needs to know that you love them. This is why your conversational tone when discussing financial matters should be gentle, humble, and self-less, always thinking about what is best for the Legacy Congregation. It means that several meetings need to happen before the Legacy Congregation feels comfortable moving forward in financial partnership with your leaders. That is okay. The Lord is sovereign over all. his timing is perfect. Lead well with Christ-like love, kindness, and prayerfulness.

How do we help the replant set up a budget?

First, let's address costs that will be incurred leading up to the point where the Legacy Congregation votes to move forward as a replant. It is wise to set aside some room in your budget for travel expenses to and from the church considering being replanted. Four to five visits to the potential replant building and its surrounding community is not uncommon. Taking a few of their leaders to share a meal with you when you make a visit is always wise. Hang out with them! Spend time just getting to know one another. Intentionally setting aside time to talk about family and life is a great way to build friendship and trust. And remember, in church replanting, building trust is everything.

Now, let's consider the new replant's budget. The Sending Church's leaders will many times work with their internal finance team, treasurer or executive pastor, to build a basic but successful budget for the replant. Often the Legacy Congregation's budget is reorganized so that existing funds can be used in the wisest and most strategic way possible. The replant is getting back to the basics like the early church in Acts. They preach the Word, care for one another, worship together, share the gospel, they love their neighbors radically. The replant's budget must reflect this *simple, stripped down, relational approach to ministry* in the early stages so they can 1) fund the replanting pastor, 2) put on monthly outreach events in the community, and 3) have money available for the replanting pastor to take people out to coffee/lunches daily. Of course, it should be noted that many times partner churches and denominational grants can fund the monthly outreach events, mailings, etc., which is incredibly helpful from a financial perspective.

How do we care for the building?

The leaders from the Sending Church will help handle caring for the building. They will secure work teams from partner churches to help with remodel projects if they are needed. Visitors make a decision to enter your building and come back to your building not by how it looks, but how they were loved. There may be a few changes made to the building simply to make it an inviting place, but rarely do we see that a major remodel is necessary for the success of a replant.

What steps should be taken if we go down the road of a building acquisition?

During the discussions to replant a church you may find the leaders of the dying church want you to take legal ownership of their building. This is not common and many times can stop the replant discussion cold if the Sending Church brings it up, so use caution. The steps for a building acquisition are the same as the DBA but you will need to add one motion about the building being gifted to the new church and who remaining in their church has the right to sign the quitclaim deed. You will also want to check your church's by-laws to see if a member vote is needed before you make any property transactions and move forward with the deed process.

Following the vote, you will contact a title company to manage the quitclaim deed process. This is not a difficult process for a title company and should be fairly inexpensive. Shop around to find the best deal or ask a trusted mortgage lender for the name of a title person they recommend. The title company will search the title to make sure it is clean and draft up the paperwork to be filed at the local county building where the church building is located. A quitclaim deed is defined as such: A legal instrument which is used to transfer interest in real property. The entity transferring its interest is called the grantor, and when the **quitclaim deed** is properly completed and executed, it transfers any interest the grantor has in the property to a recipient, called the grantee.

It is highly recommended that you add a reverse clause to the quitclaim deed when it is filed. This ensures that the building can never be sold but will always be used as a church. You can state your local denomination as the grantee if the church ever ceases to exist.

How do we handle a church with CDs and various types of financial investments?

Refer to the steps for a DBA where the motion is written to add a leader from your church as a signer to their bank account. Extend this motion to state that this leader is also the approved signer for the church's CDs and other financial investments. This will allow you to gain access to the funds in a CD which in many cases will have matured but are still tied up with the bank or institution through which they were secured.

How do we make sure a parsonage or other buildings the church owns is insured?

I know this seems like a silly question but you would be shocked what real estate churches acquire over the years and forget to mention. During the various discussions with the church considering replanting, some of the last meetings will be with the leaders who oversee the finances. This is an easy time to ask if there is any other property that the church owns in addition to the main church building. A good time to ask is when you are going through the budget and you see the building insurance line. Ask who the provider is and what the policy covers. This is crucial when you go to negotiate a new insurance policy for the replant because you need to know exactly what you are insuring. It's possible to finding thousands of dollars in the church's budget that can be redirected into outreach ministry for the replant. We have found that the most common insurance provider among declining churches is, sadly, the most expensive.

LEADING AND SHEPHERDING THE LEGACY CONGREGATION

What will the relationship between the Sending Church and the replant look like over the long haul? How much oversight does the Sending Church have over the replant, and for how long?

Churches that are considering being replanted are typically, small, tired, discouraged, and feel alone. In many ways, they feel like an orphan. As the ending church, you are the parent coming in to adopt them into your family, taking them home and giving them nourishment, rest, and love. Everything you have been blessed with is now theirs. When the leaders of our church communicate this analogy to Legacy Congregations, we talk about replanting as similar to how we might parent one of our kids going away to college. We have spent a great deal of time loving and raising our kids to be ready to move away to college. Our children are making decisions on their own, but they are still sharing many expenses with their parents, such as insurance, cell phone, and their checking account. When major decisions come up, they call home to mom and dad and ask for advice. Over time, our college student becomes more and more independent, but they never leave the family—mom and dad are still always there for them. We still get together for special occasions. We love each other and love sharing the highs and lows of life together. This is how we treat the replanting relationship between the Sending Church and the replanting church.

How do we deal with Legacy Congregation members who were on board with moving forward as a replant at the time of the official vote, but have since reverted to a place of opposition, refusing to get on board with the needed changes?

Change is hard and many people are afraid of the unknown. This is especially true when it comes to church replanting. As mentioned time and again throughout this book, the Legacy Congregation must know that you love them and you love their church. They need to hear you say that you don't want their building or their money, but you want to see their church be a gospel presence in the community, making a kingdom impact once again.

The average person cannot comprehend why one person would help another person for no gain on their part. Sadly, this is often true with Christians in the church as well. A Legacy Congregation member that is not on board with the replant process may be having a difficult time understanding why any church would want to help them. They think you are just out to take their building. While this is not true and it may be hurtful, this is how some folks will probably feel. Often these feelings of mistrust are rooted in past hurts and wounded-ness at the hands of previous pastors, church leaders, or fellow church members.

We have to recognize that many people like being in smaller churches because they have a voice and they have power. Any decision that will take power away from someone who desires it will typically result in their opposition. Consider that some in the Legacy Congregation are so tired they will be more than willing and even *joyful* to hand over certain duties and responsibilities to replant team members. This can be a freeing decision. However, for others, the very mention of having replant team members step in to help serve and carry the load of the legacy folks will be perceived as the Sending Church trying to steal their power.

In these cases, what do you do? Well, it is never easy and there is not a one-size-fits-all way to respond. I wish there was! In some cases, extra time spent loving, listening and building trust is the wise thing to do. In others, practicing patience and longsuffering with these individuals, trusting the Lord to work in their hearts over time is the most strategic thing to do. In still other cases, biblical correction is absolutely appropriate. Whichever direction you feel led to pursue, your leadership in these difficult situations must be marked by grace, and intentional, relational pursuit of these individuals, with a commitment to persistent prayer for all involved. One final note, these are situations where the Sending Church's leaders should seek wisdom and counsel from other pastors and leaders who have experienced similar challenges in their own churches.

What do we do with existing staff...like a secretary or organist?

This is a great question that needs to be answered directly and with love. We value everyone who has been serving so tirelessly to keep the church alive and moving forward. We don't want to see anyone lose their job in a replant. At the same time, we do need to be good stewards of the finances that God has entrusted to us. Many times in this discussion the leaders of the Legacy Congregation will open up and say that a person has needed to be let go for some time, but no one had the heart to do it. In these cases, it is not uncommon for these leaders to ask if you, the leaders of the Sending Church, would do it for them.

If this is the case, you must decide, if in fact, the best course of action is to let this employee go or if there is a way to salvage the situation and keep this individual on staff as a productive member of the replant team. Whichever direction you choose, you must approach this with much love, wisdom and professionalism. Seek out legal counsel if needed to help bring clarity to your options, and to learn how best to move forward in a wise and God-honoring manner.

What do we do with the remaining leadership? Deacons? Elders?

We want everyone in the Legacy Congregation who desires to continue serving in the church to do so. They are desperately needed, and that must be communicated clearly. The key to determining leadership roles for a deacon or elder is to evaluate if the person is biblically qualified and is joyfully eager to move in the new direction of the replant. If they are biblically qualified, have a humble and teachable heart, are a team player, and align with the vision and mission of this replant, then the Sending Church's leadership team may decide to have them continue serving in this role.

This being said, I would highly encourage you to have these leaders from the Legacy Congregation go through the same training and preparation process as the deacons, elders, and other leaders of your church. They not only need to be familiar with what you expect in the leaders of your congregation, but they need this extra time with your leaders to help them catch the DNA of your church.

When the Legacy Congregation officially votes to be replanted, they will be voting to turn all day-to-day decision making over to the Sending Church and adopting their by-laws as their own. As a result, their leadership structure will change. Because of this, you as leaders must work to help them become familiar with the new by-laws and how decisions are made under the new structure.

It should be noted that until the replant has officially voted in their first members and is self-governed (led by their own pastors/elders), the pastors/elders of the Sending Church will serve as the interim overseers and primary decision makers of the replant. Of course, they will be leading in conjunction with the input and guidance of the replanting pastor. Once everything is running smoothly and the leaders at the Sending Church are comfortable, the leaders at the replant can start making decisions on their own with the replant pastor.

How do we navigate the challenge of one or two folks in the Legacy Congregation who simply refuse to join the majority of their church family in voting to be replanted?

These one or two people need to be loved but they also need to hear the truth. This church is going to die if something drastic doesn't happen. Think of it like a person that has been diagnosed with cancer. The doctor is prescribing chemo immediately. It is going to be hard, but it must happen if this person's life is to be saved. These one or two hold-outs are refusing to listen to the doctor and as a result, death from the cancerous tumor is all but guaranteed. The rest of the church has to confront them in love, seeking to persuade them to express their deep love for this church by listening to the doctor and following the chemo prescription with the rest of the church body. It is the only hope they have to escape imminent death.

I would recommend sharing some statistics of the reality of churches dying in America. For example, the denomination our church is part of, the Southern Baptist Convention, experiences the closing of 17 churches each and every Sunday. The last thing we want to see is this dying church become yet another one of these statistics. Hopefully, they will agree.

The truth of the matter is that the local church is too precious to let a handful of people proliferating this statistic. Find the key influencer or influencers in this Legacy Congregation and plead with them. Plead with them to stand up to the contrarians for the sake of the future of this church. It will be hard and painful, but the gospel is worth it! The salvation of souls is worth it. The glory of God shining in and through this potential replanted congregation is absolutely worth it! Pray that the Lord will give these leaders that kind of burden and that kind of vision, and that the Legacy Congregation will ultimately move forward with or without them in love.

Do all the remaining members have to be part of the core team?

No. We recognize that there are a lot of people in the Legacy Congregation that are tired and just want a season to rest. That is fine and expected. Let these individuals know that you would love to have them take a break from serving and spend a season simply attending and being spiritually fed and encouraged.

The goal is that the core team will be comprised of 1/3 legacy folks and Sending Church families, 1/3 individuals and families from the community who love Jesus, and 1/3 non-believers who have either recently accepted Christ or are desiring to learn more about Jesus.

What do we do about music in the replant? What should we make style decisions?

You should want this replant to be marked by joyful, doctrinally rich, gospel singing! While there are indeed many new worship songs being written that share these ingredients, it is hard to argue that a very large number of traditional hymns are doctrinally rich and gospel saturated. The beauty of this is that most likely the Legacy Congregation is used to singing these hymns on a week to week basis, and my guess is that the Sending Church most likely sings many of these same hymns as well, only in a current musical style.

Singing hymns in a style that is contemporary, yet not "over the top," is often a great middle ground for a new replant, especially in its early stages. You don't need electric guitars and a huge drum set. Simple is always better. An acoustic guitar with some accompanying piano and djembe works perfectly fine. The important thing is not the style, but the hearts of the worshippers in the congregation. The Lord desires to be worshipped in spirit and truth. This should be the aim of this new congregation each Sunday.

Hear this: The health and growth of a replant is not dependent on "cool." It is not dependent on loud music with smoke machines and a light show. It is dependent on the Holy Spirit using the ordinary means God has always used to grow and mature his Church: The faithful preaching of the

Word, shepherding of the flock, evangelism of the lost and discipleship of the newly converted. These convictions must serve as the foundation of everything you do in this replant. God loves to bless and use churches that are passionate about and committed to these things because these are the things that are his passion and commitment.

How is the new replanter/pastor called?

This will most likely be a foreign concept for the Legacy Congregation. They will be expecting a pastor to come and preach in view of a call and then they vote. When the Legacy Congregation votes to turn all day to day decision making over to the Sending Church, they do not get to make the decision on the new pastor. They have also voted to adopt your bylaws as their own. When dealing with bylaws, members will need to vote on certain items within the church.

The Sending Church's leadership team needs to prayerfully select the right replant pastor for this church. Hopefully your church has established a system for raising up replanters and you have a replanting resident or two you are developing to send out. If this is the case then you are prayerfully determining the right replant pastor's personality and leadership style in relation to the people in this particular Legacy Church. Many factors need to be considered when determining the right man to lead, including the size of the Legacy Congregation (remember the analogy that the larger the ship, the longer it takes to turn), how strong the remaining leaders are in the Legacy Congregation, the replanter's expectations, and if they are urban or rural (See **Appendix W**—"Replanting in a Rural vs. an Urban Context").

How do we handle membership with the remaining legacy members?

This is a unique situation with a replant since many times the polity will change from a congregation-led church to a pastor/elder led church. In the church where I pastor, we define our church polity as Jesus-led, Elder-guided and Congregation-affirmed. In order to help the Legacy Congregation to fully understand this polity shift, we want them to experience it first. As a result, we typically choose not to pursue a new membership process for at least the first three months of the replant process. However, interest and/or concerns about membership is an issue that differs with each Legacy

Congregation. For instance, while some churches may not care much about how membership is going to work in the new replant, some churches will ask about membership from day one. Membership means a great deal to these folks and they want to be considered members of this new church from the very beginning. In this case, we would recommend developing a 'charter membership' document for all of the legacy members, along with any new core team members, having them all sign one document together. This document could then be framed and celebrated as a new day in this church's history.

While it is not the ideal, and is happening in reverse, I would at this point encourage you to take all of your charter members through your new membership process as a way of making sure everyone is aligned and on board moving forward together as a church. Of course, if the Legacy Congregation is open to it, better to have everyone go through the new membership process *first* and then welcome your "charter members." I believe this is one of those areas where there must be some flexibility on the Sending Church's part when replanting a Legacy Congregation. See **Appendix J** to learn more about how to develop a new membership process for the replant once they are ready for it.

Membership and business meetings can be a difficult situation to navigate for some replants. Our practice is to hold a 'family meeting' or 'vision meeting' once a month to celebrate all that God is doing and for the replant to hear from the replanter and other leaders. Voting is held to a minimum in this meeting, vision and celebration is the highest value and our time together reflects this. When voting in these family meetings, we work to keep it to a few major items. After casting vision and celebrating all that God is doing, near the end of the meeting time, we will transition into the official business portion of the gathering and call the meeting to order by following *Robert's Rules of Order*. We will vote on such items as the following: previous meeting minutes, treasurer's report, major budget changes, membership, ordinations, and any possible real estate sale or acquisition. This portion of the meeting many times will only last 5-10 minutes, but is important and necessary to show what is happening to stay in good standing with the State. We make sure a pastor-elder from the Sending Church is present at the first few of these meetings to assist and support the replanting pastor in whatever ways are helpful.

THE REPLANT RESIDENCY

Where do we find a resident?

While at first it may seem daunting to find a replanting resident to come and serve in your church, it is not nearly as difficult as you might think. First of all, contact your area denominational leaders. Many times these leaders are connected to all types of teachers, pastors and leaders around the country. If nothing else, they can probably give you some contacts of other denominational leaders who might be connected with men desiring to pursue church replanting. Secondly, reach out to your denominational seminaries. Increasingly, there are more and more theological students studying church revitalization. For example, in my own denomination (SBC), several of our seminaries have entire masters and doctoral programs devoted to church revitalization. These seminaries can be a gold mine when it comes to finding a potential replanting resident. Thirdly, contact other pastors and churches that are passionate about revitalization and replanting. Many times these congregations have men who are considering going into replanting. This can be a way for your churches to partner if they are willing to send your church a resident to be trained under your care.

How much do we need to pay a resident? What about housing?

As far as payment, the spectrum is very wide. It depends on the church and their financial situation. There are some congregations that bring residents on as full-time staff for the year they are with them. These congregations provide housing and a full-time salary for the resident and his family. Other churches are able to provide housing for the resident, but are unable to offer any salary. Still other congregations can offer in the ball park of $500-$1000 a month, but cannot help pay for housing. However, the majority of churches that choose to pursue this type of residency are unable to provide any money or housing. Let me say that again: *most churches are unable to provide any money or housing for a resident.* I share this to show you that pursuing a replanting residency is not dependent on the financial package your church can put together. Most churches are just trying to pay their bills and make sure their pastor gets a pay check each month. They don't have extra cash to pay for a resident. *That is okay.* Money should not be the factor that prevents your church's pursuit of a resident. Keep in mind the resident is needing and desiring experience and mentoring in a local church. That is the greatest payment you can give them. Churches that are unable to pay a resident can be generous in other ways such as helping the resident and his wife find a job, keeping a lookout for reasonably priced housing, or providing free babysitting for the family. There are all kinds of ways your church can serve this family without additional expenses.

Should the resident be affiliated with our denomination?

Not necessarily. However, the reality is that when it comes to replanting dying churches, those dying churches most likely belong to a denomination and will be seeking a replanting pastor from that particular denomination. As a result, it typically makes the most sense for your church to find a resident that is part of your denomination or could become part of your denomination. This will allow for more doors to open when the time comes to seek out a church you want to help replant.

How much schooling must the resident have before coming to our church?

There is no hard and fast rule here. I personally think it is helpful if the resident has finished or is finishing their formal theological training. A resident who has graduated from seminary and can now spend a year as a resident at your church before moving on to lead a church replant is ideal. Of course, there are situations where a resident has not yet been to seminary, but because of life and ministry experience is seasoned and ready to pursue replanting. Again, there is not a hard line on this issue. The key is making sure, as best you can, that the resident you bring on has the spiritual and emotional maturity to potentially replant a dying congregation once they finish their residency with you.

Do we need to create a job description for the resident?

Yes. It is very important to be as clear as possible with the resident regarding expectations and responsibilities.

PRE-LAUNCH
RESOURCES

B:

Sample Discernment Grid

(The Calvary Family of Churches)

NON-NEGOTIABLES	Red (unwillingness)	Yellow (openness)	Green (supportiveness)
Church Polity & Government	Not autonomous denominationally governed	Congregational/ Autonomous (can make decisions on its own regarding future decisions)	Baptistic
Theology	Do not affirm major tenets of the Baptist faith & message	Evangelical theology agreeing with Baptist faith & message	SBC that align with the Baptist faith & message and hold to a Reformed understanding of the gospel
Philosophy of Mission	Anti-culture and isolating themselves from the lost; fundamentalist mindset (not interested in reaching the lost culture around them)	Recognizing & affirming the call on them as a church to reach lost people	Actively pursuing lost people as a church body; passion for missions (locally & globally)
Philosophy of Ministry	Unwillingness to align with the essential aspects of membership within the CFC	Openness to see the church live out the essential aspects of CFC membership	Approving & supporting all aspects of CFC membership document (vision, mission, core commitments of Calvary)

NON-NEGOTIABLES	Red (unwillingness)	Yellow (openness)	Green (supportiveness)
SBC Alignment	Unwilling to join the SBC	Willing to become SBC	Southern Baptist Church
Growth Strategy	Wanting to become a big church with no efforts towards multiplication	Open to plant & replant churches	Planting & replanting churches
Day-to-Day Operations	Unwilling to give up decision making on day to day/operational matters	Willing to talk through outside group leading in day to day operations	Surrendering all ongoing leadership & decisions to an outside group to lead the church through the replant
Church Leadership	Choosing to be led by solo pastor without a team of elders	Open to being led by a plurality of male pastor/elders	Already led by a plurality of male pastor/elders
Baptism	Infant Baptism		Believer Baptism

NEGOTIABLES

	Red (unwillingness)	Yellow (openness)	Green (supportiveness)
Lord's Supper (frequency)	No communion	Regular communion	Weekly communion
Building	In need of major repairs	Minor repairs needed	In good working condition
Finances	Major debt, low giving	No debt, low giving	No debt, high giving
Worship Style	Unwilling to change from what they have been doing	Open to conversations about moving in a direction that will better serve the mission of making disciples	Willing to embrace whatever will best serve the replant & community
Existing Staff	Congregation is unwilling to make any staff changes for the sake of the replant	Congregation is open to talk about potential staff changes to help serve the replanting vision	Congregation are humbly open to changing staff positions to whatever is going to best serve the replanting vision (changing job descriptions, hours, etc.)
Existing Programs	Congregation wants to maintain all existing programs as they are without evaluating how they fit into the replant vision	Congregation willing to talk about any program changes that could improve the alignment with the replanting vision	Congregation humbly willing to change or eliminate existing programs in order to better align with the replanting vision

RATING SCALE

Red Church - 1 or more red rating in any of the non-negotiable areas or 3 or more red rating in the negotiables.

> **Action:** *Pointing them to revitalization resources with no ongoing commitment moving forward.*

Yellow Church - 1 or more yellow ratings in the non-negotiable areas or 3 or more yellow rating in the negotiables.

> **Action:** *Open to conversation & coaching with no commitment to replanting.*

Green Church - All non-negotiable & negotiables areas are rated in the green.

> **Action:** *Willing to engage in conversation about replanting.*

C:

Sample Core Team Assessment

(The Calvary Family of Churches)

A WORD ON THE ASSESSMENT

Helping to launch a replant is one of the most significant ways one can invest their life in the mission of God. We think it's a fantastic way to give your life for Jesus. At the same time, it's important to recognize that this is also one of the hardest commitments someone could make.

This is why we believe in an application and assessment – the most loving thing we can do for anyone giving their life to this mission is to be honest about the difficulty ahead and what we expect of them. We desire to shepherd you well, even before actually joining the team.

The application and assessment process has three steps:

1. Fill out this application (please, write neatly or type responses) and return/ e-mail it to office@thecalvary.org.
2. Have an in-person interview with some of Calvary's leadership.
3. If all goes well, sign the team covenant and get ready for one amazing adventure.

If you have any questions about the process, e-mail **office@thecalvary.org.**

We're thankful for your desire to give your life to the mission of God and hope to have you be a part of planting and growing Calvary Church in Littleton.

BACKGROUND INFO:

Name _____

Date of Application _____

Preferred Address _____

_____

Preferred Phone _____

Email address _____

Marital Status: Single/Married

Name of spouse _____

Job and/or Ministry Experience:

THEOLOGY

1. What is the gospel (i.e. theologically speaking, not how you would explain the gospel message to a non-Christian)?

2. What is your view of the Bible?

3. What is your view of the church?

PERSONAL

1. Share how you met Jesus including what your life was like prior, the key factors that led you to Jesus, and how your life changed after meeting Jesus.

2. What role does evangelism and discipleship have in your life right now? How are you seeking to show and tell the good news of Jesus in your daily life?

3. Describe your spiritual disciplines and how you walk, hear and learn from God.

4. What do you feel like your gifts are?

5. Why do you feel called to help replant a church with Calvary?

6. Are there any major issues (i.e. areas of unrepentant sexual sin, addiction, finances, relationships, family, etc.) in your life that are negatively affecting your relationship with Christ and may impact your ministry that we should be aware of?

7. Is there anything else you think we should know or want to say?

D:

Sample Core Team Covenant

(The Calvary Family of Churches)

Helping to launch a replant is one of the most significant ways one can invest their life in the mission of God. It is a commitment that must not be taken lightly. The team's leadership desires that everyone who commits to our efforts fully understands what is expected of them.

We are asking for a one-year commitment, excluding extenuating circumstances that must be discussed with the team's leadership before any decisions are made. This covenant details the nature of this commitment, as well as the responsibilities of every member of the core team for this replant of Calvary Church.

LOVE GOD

Our foundation is the gospel - it is the principle doctrine of the faith that both reconciles us to God and helps us to grow in our relationship with him. Therefore:

We are committed to the true, biblical gospel (1 Cor. 15, Jude 3, 2 Tim. 3:16).

We are committed to knowing the gospel with excellence, and living out its implications in everyday life (1 Pet. 3:15, Gal. 2:14).

- *I affirm my responsibility to grow in Christ and his gospel through the consistent practice of spiritual disciplines.*

LOVE EACH OTHER

The gospel creates community – we are committed to living life together, challenging one another to grow in Christ. Therefore:

We are committed to a disciplined, regenerate team (Rom. 12:5, 1 Pet. 2:4-5, Matt. 18:15-20)

- *I affirm my new birth in Christ, and my responsibility to live consistently with this through obedience to his commands.*

We are committed to a unified team (Phil 2:1-11, Rom. 12:3-8, Heb. 10:24-25).

- *I affirm that I will protect the team's unity, and will not undermine the mission with my actions or words.*

- *I affirm that because we are members of one body, we will share life together in a way that models and contextualizes the implications of the gospel.*

- *I affirm that I agree with the essential doctrines of the faith as laid out by our elders. For the sake of unity, I will submit my personal beliefs in non-essential doctrines to the beliefs of the church where they differ.*

We are committed to a biblically ordered team (1 Tim. 3:1-13).

- *I affirm that I will follow the leadership and vision of the team's leadership, as well as our Sending Church, Calvary Church.*

- *I affirm that my role is exclusively to be a team member. I deny any expectation that I will receive pay or a staff position from the church now or anytime in the future, unless the Lord leads otherwise, through the leadership of Calvary Church.*

LOVE THOSE WHO ARE FAR FROM GOD

We are replanting this church to reach people who are far from God with the gospel and to make Jesus non-ignorable in this community – we exist not for ourselves but rather for the joy of others, as we strive to be a well-equipped community of missionaries that reaches our city and world with the gospel. Therefore:

We are committed to God's glory as our chief end (1 Cor. 10:31).

- *I affirm that my preferences, needs, and desires are secondary to the mission and vision of the church.*

- *I affirm that we are God's church and not our own. Therefore, my priority is not building a monolithic, self-serving church, but rather a church that prioritizes evangelism, mission, discipleship, and reproduction.*

We are committed to giving generously to the mission, and living sacrificially for its progress (2 Cor. 8:9).

- *I affirm that I will give my time, resources, and money in a sacrificial manner consistent with the gospel.*

We are committed to every member as a missionary (2 Cor. 5:20, 2 Tim. 2:2).

- *I affirm my responsibility to evangelize and make disciples who can make disciples. This is as much my responsibility as it is the church's leaders.*

- *I affirm I will pray regularly for the community and for the launch and establishment of this new replant.*

Before God, I affirm by signing this covenant that I agree with everything stated above. I have communicated concerns and reservations to the team's leaders. Also, I understand that failure to live consistently and in line with this covenant will require evaluation by the team's leadership and Calvary Church.

Team Member Signature: _____

Date: _____

Leadership Signature: _____

Date: _____

Sample Replant Proposal

(Calvary Church La Junta)

First Baptist Church La Junta

Calvary Church Replant Proposal

CALVARY Englewood   2

Dear First Baptist Church La Junta Friends,

After ministering in the Denver-metro area for many years, I am convinced our city, and the entire state of Colorado, is in great need of vibrant, dynamic, local churches to reach the tens of thousands of people that call this area their home.

Like Englewood, but perhaps for different reasons, La Junta is not an easy place to minister. Many churches end up closing their doors because of the unique difficulties they face. I believe that when a church desires to do what it takes to live and flourish, and is marked by a spirit of humility, a desire to glorify God and reach the lost above all things, the right resources, along with the right people helping and working together, genuine revitalization and turn-around can become a reality! By God's grace, this has been the story of *Calvary Church* over the past several years as the Lord has taken a declining, "near death" congregation, and brought it back to life for His glory!

Please know that along with the other leaders at *Calvary*, I am passionate to see First Baptist Church – La Junta thrive with renewed vision, passion, growth, and transformation where individuals, families, and neighborhoods are transformed for the glory of God, the salvation of the lost, and the good of La Junta and the surrounding communities. The following material is an overview and introduction to what we, in partnership with the North American Mission Board, would love to potentially see happen if *Calvary Church* and *First Baptist Church – La Junta* were to work together in replanting this congregation. The following information is humbly provided for you to consider what this type of Legacy Replant could look like, building off the wonderful history and legacy of *First Baptist Church – La Junta*, while moving forward into a new and exciting future together!

I am overjoyed at the possibility of working together for the glory of Jesus!

For His Fame,
Mark Hallock
Lead Pastor
Calvary Church-Englewood

CALVARY CHURCH | 4881 S ACOMA ST | ENGLEWOOD, CO 80110 | 303-789-3616

CALVARY Englewood   3

CALVARY LEGACY REPLANTING

The purpose of this document is to aid Calvary Legacy Replants in helping them to become a healthy, growing congregation that seeks to make Jesus non-ignorable through the making of joyful, passionate disciples of Christ!

With a passion for God's Glory to be revealed in the local church, Calvary Legacy Replanting is a comprehensive approach that brings strategic resources to a declining or dying church. This results in the replanting and re-appropriation of its resources with a passion for God's Glory to be revealed in the local church.

A dying church robs God of His Glory. The key to revitalization of a church near death is a passion for the Glory of God in all things. This alone must be the beginning and primary motivation for a Legacy replant, even over worthy objectives such as reaching the community, growing the church and meeting needs. The purpose of all creation is the glory of God. He created everything for His own glory. Romans 11:36 proclaims, "For of Him and through Him and to Him are all things, to whom be glory forever." We believe God LOVES to bring declining churches back to life and vibrancy for His glory and He calls us to be part of it!

Definition of a Calvary Legacy Replant: What it Is & Isn't

Legacy Replant: *A church determines to replant itself as a new congregation upon the legacy of ministry and missions that once existed with a new vision, a new name, and a new strategy for reaching the community with the Gospel.*

Does this mean that the existing church dissolves?

No. In an effort to honor the legacy and affirm the history of existing congregations, replanting is a merger. This means that Calvary Church and the existing congregation merge together and keep the existing history of the congregation both spiritually and legally alive.

CALVARY CHURCH | 4881 S ACOMA ST | ENGLEWOOD, CO 80110 | 303-789-3616

CALVARY Englewood

4

As a Calvary Legacy Replant, we will become part of the Calvary Family of Churches. What does that mean exactly?

The vision for the Calvary Family of Churches is to make Jesus non-ignorable in Denver and to the ends of the earth.

Our mission is to glorify God by making joyful, passionate disciples of Jesus.

- In pursuit of our vision and in faithfulness to our mission, we believe that God has called us to plant Calvary Churches that plant Calvary Churches and make disciples who make disciples.

- Calvary Church is made up of an interdependent family of self-sustaining, self- governing, self-replicating churches that share a common family name (Calvary Church), common family doctrine, a common family vision and mission, a common family philosophy of ministry, and a common set of family traits and core commitments.

What Calvary Churches Share

Common Family Name

Calvary Church

Common Family Vision

To make Jesus non-ignorable in Denver and to the ends of the earth.

Common Family Mission

To glorify God, by making joyful, passionate, disciples of Jesus

Common Family Core Commitments

- Worship God passionately
- Connect with one another authentically
- Grow to know God deeply
- Go to show and tell the gospel boldly

CALVARY Englewood   5

> **NOTE:** *Many of these commonalities are formally adopted to through a common set of by-laws that govern Calvary Churches. Also, for the clearest communication to our Calvary congregations of our shared vision, mission, and core commitments, we use the same language and visual identity or branding.*

- *This may include, but is not limited to: "The Point Student Ministries", "Calvary Kids", "Community Groups", "DNA Discipleship Groups", "All-In", etc.*

- *Every congregation will be called "Calvary (geographical reference)" to keep uniformity and branding consistency.*

- *Each congregation needs to be allowed to maintain a personality of its own while remaining aligned with the core DNA and convictions of the Calvary Family of Churches (CFC).*

Common Family Doctrine

The Baptist Faith and Message (2000)

Calvary Church Common Family Traits

These 9 common family traits serve as 9 of the "constants" that give shape to the vision, mission, and ministry philosophy of each Calvary congregation. These represent and help produce the type of culture and "DNA" we desire to instill within each of our churches and their leadership.

1. Biblical Theology

We are committed to proclaiming, embracing, and living out the full counsel of God's redemptive message as revealed to us in the Scriptures. While we are intentional about reaching the immediate culture in a relevant way, we are committed to the biblical doctrines of the Christian faith. We do not believe that effective cultural engagement must lead to doctrinal compromise, rather we believe that faithful Gospel contextualization is what is needed to bring temporal and eternal transformation to individuals, families, churches, and communities.

2. Shepherd Leadership

CALVARY CHURCH | 4881 S ACOMA ST | ENGLEWOOD, CO 80110 | 303-789-3616

CALVARY Englewood   6

We believe that the Biblical pattern and model for pastoral leadership in the church is not that of CEO but of shepherd. Therefore, we are committed to leading people and community toward health and vitality through humble, caring, biblical shepherd leadership. Because it takes an extended period of time to bring revitalization and transformation to individuals, families, churches, and communities, Calvary pastors and our congregation are committed to each other for the long haul.

3. God-centered Worship

Our desire is to become a church where every believer experiences the sovereign grace of the Father, wholeheartedly treasures Jesus, and freely expresses their adoration of God individually and corporately through the power and leading of the Holy Spirit.

> **NOTE:** *Every weekend worship service in a Calvary congregation will include the following worship elements:*
>
> - *Along with singing, prayer, preaching, and giving, the Lord's Supper will be included as a biblical element of worship in each service.*
> - *Music style is not dictated, however excellence is. Whether pop/rock, country, or folk, it should all be leading in admiration and praise for our God.*

4. Expositional Preaching

We believe that expositional preaching is important because God's Word alone is what convicts, converts, builds up, and sanctifies God's people (Heb. 4:12; 1 Pet. 1:23; 1 Thess. 2:13; Jn. 17:17). Preaching that makes the main point of the text the main point of the sermon makes God's agenda rule the church, not the preacher's.

5. Healthy Families

God has designed the family as the foundation of society and as the primary mechanism to embody and advance His gospel in the world. Therefore, we are committed to encouraging and equipping families to more fully love and honor God, more faithfully love and serve one

CALVARY Englewood   7

another, and more intentionally pursue God's mission in their
neighborhood, city, and world.

> **NOTE:** To ensure that everything we do and say is understandable and
> transferred to all generations, we will create a culture of building the church
> up together as a priority. In other words, we desire to be "intergenerational"
> congregations,
>
> - Community Groups and DNA Discipleship Groups will not be separated
>   by age or stage of life but instead be diversified in order to have each
>   generation teaching and discipling each other.
> - We do not encourage "stand-alone" ministries that pull the family apart.
>   Our desire is for the family to grow up together at Calvary.

6. Authentic Relationships

The Gospel compels us to love one another because God, who first loved
us in Jesus Christ, has given us the ability to love our neighbors as
ourselves. Therefore, we are committed to becoming a community
marked by Christ-like love and service to one another.

7. Disciple-making

Scripture teaches that a live Christian is a growing Christian (2 Pet. 1:8-10).
Scripture also teaches that we grow not only by instruction, but by
imitation (1 Cor. 4:16; 11:1). Therefore our church should exhort our
members to both grow in holiness and help others do the same. Calvary
Church is committed to making disciples, not just converts.

8. Missional Living

Calvary Church is made up of people of all ages who Jesus has saved
and sent to be missionaries in the world. Missional Living is the primary
means of evangelism within our church. It is not a program we do, but a
life we live and the responsibility of every believer. God sends us all out to
be His witnesses. We see our webs of relationships as our primary mission
field but also desire to respond to God's call across the globe to
participate in the work he is doing.

9. Diverse Community

CALVARY CHURCH | 4881 S ACOMA ST | ENGLEWOOD, CO 80110 | 303-789-3616

CALVARY Englewood 8

At both the leadership level and within the congregation, Calvary seeks to reflect the makeup of the surrounding community ethnically, economically, and inter-generationally.

Common Family Networks

Southern Baptist Convention

Calvary Churches are part of the SBC (Southern Baptist Convention), CBGC (Colorado Baptist General Convention) and AVBA (Arkansas Valley Baptist Association). As such, Calvary Churches are required to give financially to the Cooperative Program and to be involved relationally with national (SBC), state (CBGC) and local (AVBA) ministry and mission partnerships.

Calvary Family of Churches:

All Calvary Churches are also a part of the Calvary Family of Churches. As such, all Calvary Churches will give a portion of their budget (1%) to help further the mission and vision of the Calvary Family of Churches. These monies will be specifically directed towards the planting, restarting, and adoption of new Calvary Churches.

Calvary Family Accountability, Encouragement & Support

Calvary Churches exist to glorify God by making joyful, passionate disciples of Jesus Christ (Matthew 28:19-20). In seeking to effectively carry out this mission, we recognize the extraordinary value in multiplying the reach of the ministry by planting local churches and by re-starting (re-planting) or adopting existing local churches. God is glorified when Calvary Churches and other churches cooperate with one another in order to foster relationships that edify, protect, encourage and support.

While it may seem messy, unnecessary, and overdone to some, we believe it is critically important for Calvary Churches to stay vitally

CALVARY Englewood   9

connected and accountable to Calvary doctrine, mission, core commitments, ministry philosophy and other Calvary Churches.

This relationship finds its primary expression through the Calvary Family of Churches (CFC) Board of Elders. Comprised of the lead pastor and one elder from each church, this elder board will meet regularly to provide a forum for ongoing accountability, encouragement, and support. These meetings will also be a time for prayerful, big-picture visioning and strategic planning for the family of churches and will be led by the CFC Executive Director, who will serve as a first among equals, and is responsible to lead forward the vision, mission and strategy of the Calvary Family of Churches. The CFC Elder Board oversees church planting and the relationships of Calvary churches so they may more effectively advance Christ's mission in order to build His kingdom.

This Elder Board will also help facilitate the mutual exchange and sharing of pulpit and music ministry, leader training, community demographic research, conferences, print materials and seed money devoted to church planting and pastoral education programs.

CALVARY Englewood   10

Frequently Asked Questions

Where will the core people for this new Replant come from?

The new core of people will come from three places:

a. From the people that are already a part of the existing congregation.

b. From other like-minded churches that live in the area or simply want to help this new location start up.

c. From the promotion we do via mailings, social media, advertising and word of mouth invitation.

What will happen to the people that are currently serving in ministry positions at the church?

We like to work with those that are already serving in the church and encourage them to continue on. A Replant will require as many able bodied people as possible to serve in various ministry capacities. Most of the ministry teams will need some training before the Grand Opening to accommodate younger families.

What will the leadership structure look like in the new start up congregation?

Typically the leadership team is composed of a lead legacy replanter-pastor, along with the eldership of the sending church, Calvary Church-Englewood. This team meets together regularly and serves as the primary spiritual leaders/shepherds of this congregation.

The Lead Replanter-Pastor does three basic tasks.

1. He loves and cares for the remaining members. He seeks to warm their hearts to the gospel. He seeks to help them lay down the idol of the past and cling only to Jesus through a fresh experience of the Gospel. He does this in many ways. He does it in his preaching and teaching. He does it as he spends quality time with the congregation. He does it by modeling a life of gospel-centered joy, not joy in numbers, or results or control but joy in Jesus. For many generations

CALVARY CHURCH | 4881 S ACOMA ST | ENGLEWOOD, CO 80110 | 303-789-3616

CALVARY Englewood   11

the members of dying churches have seen leaders who seem to find joy in results or control and not in the gospel. It will take considerable time to deconstruct this in the members. But it is time very well spent. It will be the foundation for trust and change that will be required

2. He does the work of a church planter in his community. He learns all he can, he volunteers and imbeds himself in his community. He understands his call is not just to the dying church but to the community. He seeks above all groups to located, evangelize and disciple millennial young men. He must make as a priority to discover, to lead to Christ and to disciple millennial young men. Dying churches have been unable to connect to millennials and especially to millennial men. Yet nothing can provide a more solid foundation for Replanting then a core of millennial young men who are making disciples. It is highly likely that when the dying church was just beginning and reaching its community it had an abundance of young men age 20-39 in key leadership roles.

3. He serves his community with radical generosity. While the dying church may not have many resources the Replanter is charged with the task of securing partner churches and networks to conduct ministry and meet needs in the community. Serving the community brings a new branding to a dying church. It serves to engage the millennials you are seeking to reach and it provides the older members with a reason for the church to exist. It is in the area of radical service that the older members and the new people who are reached begin to work together. It is around serving that new DNA is developed and new church life forms.

What can we expect in the first few months after the public launch?

You can expect growth, change and new people. Change is difficult for all of us. Most people in Replants enjoy seeing new faces and new families. With this comes a fresh sense of excitement and vision, but changes take some time to get used to. Much love, grace, and patience is needed from everyone.

CALVARY CHURCH | 4881 S ACOMA ST | ENGLEWOOD, CO 80110 | 303-789-3616

CALVARY Englewood   12

What will the worship and music be like?

Calvary seeks to sing the Gospel. Many of the traditional hymns share the Gospel boldly so we adapt a style of music that will minister to the existing people yet connect with the visitors from the community. In part, the worship style will depend on the people we are trying to reach and minister to from the community. We try to strike a balance between what the existing congregation was used to and outreach to the community and younger families. This is not always easy to do but we work hard at seeking to have a balance.

Does Calvary Church have a ministry that can help us reach the teens and young people?

Each Calvary Church location will have its own youth group but the Calvary family of churches work together in leadership development, special events and outreach. Calvary Church students can attend winter and summer camps with other Calvary Family Church's students at our Ponderosa Camp in Larkspur, Colorado.

What kind of support and help can we expect from Calvary Church's other Pastors and congregations?

Calvary Family pastors seek to work together to support and help the Replant. As a family network of churches, our pastors are significantly connected for the purposes of encouragement, dreaming, prayer, united ministry initiatives, etc. Specifically, each Calvary Pastor will announce the new Replant, pray for it, release people that are willing to go and help in whatever way is needed.

CALVARY Englewood   13

Specific Transition Steps
for Calvary Church - La Junta:

Calvary Church-Englewood recognizes the legacy of First Baptist Church of La Junta's Kingdom vision to see the Gospel be preached passionately in the La Junta community so the lost would be saved. Today, your desire has not changed. We feel this church can still be a lighthouse into the darkness of La Junta. Valuable funds are needed to help the success of this legacy replanting process, and Calvary Church-Englewood cannot fund this process without the help from NAMB (North American Mission Board of the Southern Baptist Convention). For funding to be received from NAMB, one of the following must occur:

Option 1. All day-to-day decision making is surrendered to an approved transition team and it calls an assessed replanter. In this scenario, FBC La Junta would come under the leadership of Calvary Church Englewood. Calvary would take over the day-to-day operations and make sure all financial obligations are met. FBC La Junta would take on the "doing business as" name of Calvary Church La Junta for legal purposes.

Option 2. They cease to exist and provide all assets to a Sending Church to become a campus of that church. In this scenario, real property and other assets would be turned over to Calvary Church Englewood and FBC La Junta would officially and legally cease to exist. Calvary would still take on the responsibility of day-to-day operations and meeting financial obligations.

Whichever option is chosen, we recommend the following steps:

- FBC La Junta officially votes to accept one of the options above.
- Upon official vote, begin the process of transferring property, funds, and other assets as needed based on the option chosen.
- Any transferred assets will be held in a sub-fund designated for First Baptist Church of La Junta when they replant as a healthy, interdependent, self sustaining, self-governing church.

CALVARY CHURCH | 4881 S ACOMA ST | ENGLEWOOD, CO 80110 | 303-789-3616

CALVARY Englewood   14

- During the transition time, FBC La Junta will become a campus of Calvary Church. Calvary, in addition to managing day-to-day operations, will provide for Sunday worship services and other activities which will prepare for launching Calvary Church La Junta.

- Calvary Church is in the process of training the nation's first replanting pastors. Until a replanter is trained, assessed and funded, the Elders of Calvary-Englewood will be making the decisions as the transition team for this campus.

- During the transition, a core team of existing and new leaders will be formed to prepare for launching Calvary Church La Junta.

- When the elders at Calvary feel our NAMB assessed replanter and the new core team is ready, we will launch as Calvary Church La Junta with one of our NAMB assessed replanters

We recommend *First Baptist Church of La Junta* approve the above recommendation from Calvary Church-Englewood to see a Lighthouse for the gospel in La Junta to continue for years to come!

Some Clarifications:

1. The name of the church will become *Calvary Church - La Junta* and will benefit this replant to reflect unison with Calvary's vision and values while recognizing First Baptist Church of La Junta's rich legacy and history in the community.

2. *Calvary Church - La Junta* will financially fund its Replanter-Pastor, along with other staff, with the help of existing members, Calvary Englewood, NAMB and other SBC partners.

3. Calvary's Governance, Constitution and By-laws become Calvary Church - La Junta's Governance, Constitution and By-laws.

4. Calvary integrates *Calvary Church - La Junta* into the Calvary Family of Churches as a new Calvary congregation.

5. The current members will serve as vital members of the replanting core team. Moreover, <u>EVERY</u> individual who is currently part of First Baptist

CALVARY CHURCH | 4881 S ACOMA ST | ENGLEWOOD, CO 80110 | 303-789-3616

CALVARY Englewood   15

Church of La Junta will have an important role to play in this replant. Those currently serving in the church will be encouraged to continue serving in the areas of their gifting and passion for the health and growth of this new congregation. We recognize many members may be tired and ready for a season of rest. Please know we will never force anyone from an area of service but if you recognize a desire to rest, we will help you transition and train a new member to serve in your capacity well.

6. *Calvary Church – La Junta* will be given the following tools and resources for health and growth of the congregation:

    a. Fellowship One church management software to manage

        i. Volunteer background checks,

        ii. Secure children's check-in system

        iii. Shepherding reports

        iv. Community Group/Sunday School attendance recording

        v. Congregation Assimilation tracking

        vi. Secure online giving for the congregation

        vii. Automated giving statements

        viii. Secure giving and recording of gifts to the Calvary-La Junta sub-fund

    b. Marketing materials (weekly bulletins, offering envelops, new visitor cards)

    c. Gospel Project curriculum available for children/students

    d. Children/Student Ministry oversight and training (if required)

    e. DNA discipleship plan and oversight for congregation

    f. Community Group scheduling, training, oversight

    g. Local community outreach planning, oversight

    h. Calvary Englewood may determine the need to invest financially in building renovations, signs, lighting, etc, to ensure the best potential restart.

CALVARY CHURCH | 4881 S ACOMA ST | ENGLEWOOD, CO 80110 | 303-789-3616

Replanting Blueprint

	PHASE 1: Identify (Month 0)	PHASE 2: Foundations (Month 1-2)
Leadership	- Conversation and prayer among the leaders to evaluate readiness of Legacy Congregation - Ongoing training of replanting pastor in Sending Church - Clearly identify the negotiables and non-negotiables	- Legacy team attend service at Sending Church and teachers shadow class - Calendar in place with replant pastors/residents, worship team, Sending Church volunteers loving on existing congregation - Begin identifying potential core team members
Systems	- Sending Church assesses current financial situation of Legacy Congregation	- Website up/email active/Facebook group - Pro-presenter install and training - Update the bulletin and info cards
Programs	- Assess the existing programs of the Legacy Congregation	- Weekly worship gathering as new replant - Sunday School continues - Outreach event - Vision night - Begin developing the four key ministry teams (Music, tech, hospitality, children's)
Building	- Assess the condition of the building	- Develop a game plan for signage - Sound system updated - Determine needed building renovation and their priority level
Legal	- Both churches must vote to move forward together and replant - Necessary leadership/officer changes - Decisions concerning property/banking details - Make name changes for church & register with SOS if necessary - Inform your denomination/network - Start/update corporate binder (with meeting minutes) - Determine finance plan/budget	- Finish denominational paperwork - Draft provisional budget

	PHASE 3: Soft Launch (Month 3-Public Launch)	PHASE 4: Public Launch
Leadership	- Begin weekly core team gathering - 1-3 relational evangelism strategy - Prayer walking - Revamp church membership	- Ongoing leadership meetings - Ongoing communication with the Sending Church and denomination or network - Replanting pastor develops & leads shepherding meeting
Systems	- Church management software integrated	- Improving existing systems and creating new systems
Programs	- Weekly worship service with lead replanter leading - Social media blitz to get the word out - Outreach events	- Weekly worship service - Community group launched - Outreach events
Building	- New, outside signage goes live - Create a coffee space - The Legacy Wall - Kids' space renovations including children's check-in set up	- Key spaces are ready for use
Legal	- Any remaining legal issues taken care of	- Identify any additional legal issues to be handled

V-TEAM
RESOURCES

G:

Sample V-Team Point Leader Letter

(The Calvary Family of Churches)

Point Leaders (QB),

Thank you for being part of our transitional volunteer leadership team (V-Team) for our Calvary *[fill-in-church-name-here]* replant, currently *[fill-in-church-name-here]*. We are excited to see Jesus made non-ignorable in this great community and you will be part of it!

As the point leader, you are in a sense the QB for the particular Sunday you are in *[fill-in-church-name-here]* You are the one to make sure doors are unlocked and then locked up again, that people are greeted warmly, that the worship service is ready to go, etc. *[fill-in-pastor-name-here]* will be your primary contact to help answer any logistical questions you have about this role and any specifics you need to know about the *[fill-in-church-name-here]* church.

5 IMPORTANT THINGS FOR YOU TO REMEMBER AS THE POINT LEADER:

#1: Recruit

The point leader each week is responsible for recruiting three individuals or families from Calvary to help lead the worship service and love on the people in [church name] for that particular Sunday. Please email mark@thecalvary.org and jeff@thecalvary.org the CONFIRMED names that will be joining you the Monday prior to the Sunday you will be serving.

#2: Sunday School

The church in *[fill-in-church-name-here]* has a weekly Sunday School class that begins at 9:30am. You and your team will need to be at the church by 8:30am to open the building, get coffee started, be ready to greet folks, etc.

#3: Worship Service

The worship service begins at 10:45am. Whoever is leading worship on that day should practice and do sound check during the Sunday School hour.

#4: Preaching

As far as preaching goes, you as the point leader have the option of preaching or finding someone else from Calvary (a resident, elder, deacon) to preach on the Sunday you are leading. Please run this person by Mark for approval and so he can help them prepare. For simplicity sake, you can choose a text to preach on. Use a sermon you have preached before if you would like. If you need help finding a text, or need help preparing your sermon, Mark is available to help however he can.

#5 Love.

The most important part of your role is to love the folks in the [church location] church like crazy. This means making sure you recruit team members who love people well. This will involve talking and listening to folks, encouraging them, hugging them, showing Jesus to them! It means from the moment they arrive at the church to the moment they are back in their cars leaving that they are being cared for and shepherded well by you and your team. What a joy it will be to minister to these sweet folks in this way!

Thanks again for your leadership! May God be glorified in and through you and your team as we lovingly lead this sweet congregation!

Sample V-Team Schedule

(Calvary Church La Junta)

March 6

Point Leader: Jeff Declue
Three Team Individuals/Families:

March 13

Point Leader: Jeff Declue
Three Team Individuals/Families:

March 20 (Palm Sunday)

Point Leader: Matt Whitt
Three Team Individuals/Families:

March 27 (Easter)

Point Leader: Matt Whitt
Three Team Individuals/Families:

April 3

Point Leader: Ricardo Cardenas
Three Team Individuals/Families:

April 10

Point Leader: Matt Whitt

Three Team Individuals/Families:

Find Point Leader and Individuals/Families for:

April 17, April 24, May 1, May 8. May 5, May 22, May 29

Sample V-Team Point Leader Checklist

(Calvary Church La Junta)

WEEKEND CHECKLIST

Before the weekend, recruit and communicate with:

1. **Worship leader** - remind them we would love to have one or two "classic" hymns (from what we normally do).
2. **Sunday School Teacher** - give them curriculum in advance.
3. **Preacher**
4. **Other Team Members**
5. **Sound Person**
6. **Slides Person**
7. **Offering Meditation**
8. **Child Care**
9. **Leadership** - Check in with Jeff about announcements and any new instructions

Before the weekend, prepare:

1. **Supplies** - *CHURCH KEYS!!!!! Offering Zippered Pouch, bulletins, computer, audio, communion supplies as needed.*

2. **Slides** - *(songs and announcements)*
3. **Print** - *song sheets in case projector dies (if you do not get to this beforehand plan to do it in La Junta on copier in office)*

Saturday Evening (if you are there) or Sunday Morning

1. Set up and check sound
2. Set up and check computer, projector and all slides. *Remember that at all times while the projector is on the closet door must be open and fan running!!!!*

Sunday Morning

1. Make sure you have three people for offering and two people for Communion (Jerry and Lorenz like to help)
2. Set up 40 communion servings (communion elements are located in the kitchen)
3. Make sure heat (or AC) is on downstairs (thermostat is in fellowship hall)
4. Make sure heat (or AC) is on in sanctuary (thermostat is in stage behind Calvary banner)
5. Unlock West facing door at 9:00 (re-lock at 10:00)
6. Unlock South Facing Door at 10:00 (re-lock after everyone has left church)
7. Make coffee in kitchen 9:00 (small green canister - 4 scoops - full pot of water)
8. Turn lights on in fellowship hall and sanctuary, and behind stained glass (stage left)
9. Greet outdoors if possible
10. Set up stair lift (key is normally in the closet at the top left of the stairs on the metal cabinet)
11. Sunday School starts at 9:30, teacher should be present and greeting and friendly by 9:15.
12. iTunes play list after sound check and rehearsal

After Service

1. Thank your team
2. Turn off all lights (double check: stained glass light and main lobby stair lights they are hard to see in daylight)
3. Reset all thermostats (flip to off then back to auto)
4. Check side doors and main entrance doors are locked and secured (west door needs to yanked hard)
5. Double check office door is locked and lights are out
6. Put offering into La Junta zippered pouch and put it in your stuff to come home
7. Bring any trash bags to the trash can in ally behind church offices
8. Spot vacuum any debris (especially if there were kids around)
9. Lysol wipe the toilets, and flush the urinals in the men's bathroom

At Home

1. Turn in offering to Calvary by Monday morning if possible
2. Return any equipment
3. Thank your team (email, cards, etc...)
4. Let Jeff know if we ran out of any communion supplies or other items.

SUNDAY MORNING SCHEDULE

- **8:00-8:30** - Arrive at the church

- **9:20** - Sunday School teacher is ready and welcoming downstairs

- **9:30** - Sunday School Starts

- **10:30** - Worship Music from comp or iPod is playing (Organ is nice too for now)

- **10:45** - Worship Starts

- **12:00** - Worship Ends

- Head Down the stairs and outside for talking, fellowship

- Keep an eye on the chair lift and if anybody needs help

- Clean up, lock up and head out

RESOURCES AND SUGGESTIONS

- Copier in office works, USB plug, generic print drivers (Matt connected easily)
- Library is a couple blocks south we think there is internet there but are not sure (closed on Sundays)
- Iron and ironing board are in the church offices
- If possible do childcare in the nursery. We have done child care in the overflow area behind the sanctuary this works but is not great. Katelyn Griffen is a teenager who is normally there and will gladly help watch kids if needed

Food
- In church: standard kitchen things, please clean up after yourselves
- Whitt's also left a toaster in the kitchen feel free to use it! Bring some bagels and cream cheese for you or your team if you want!
- If you want coffee for your team on Sunday morning bring some with you, the coffee there is not great

Restaurants:
- Copper Kitchen - Breakfast and Lunch is great cheap and a good way to get a feel for the town (couple blocks north of the church)
- Lucy's Tacos - big portions, cheap, and great tasting
- Boss Hogg's - cheap, massive portions and a great way to get the feel of town
- Sunday morning your best bet for a latte is McDonalds
- Felisa's (Mexican) - we have heard it is great but do not yet have firsthand knowledge

Sleeping

Paid Options
- **Hampden Inn** - Call ahead to make reservation, tell them you are with Calvary Replant for a discount
- **Holiday Inn** - allows pets

Free options (Bring your own bedding)

- Church offices - three cots and twin bed
  - 3 Cots
  - 1 Twin bed
- Church
  - Couches and futons in the unheated part of church. Move them at will but put them back.
  - Air mattresses in rooms off the fellowship hall also work
  - We now have a portable camping shower that can be used
- SBC house
  - 1 King bed
  - 1 Pull out sofa bed (unsure of size)
  - ~~SHOWER!!!!!! (not hot water yet)~~

POST-LAUNCH
RESOURCES

J:

How to Develop a New Church Membership Process

Church membership is common in most churches. However, it is rare to find churches that do membership really well. I would recommend waiting at least 3 months after the two congregations have officially voted to replant to launch a new membership process. This will allow you plenty of time to get to know and earn trust with the current members of the Legacy Congregation. This will also help you to better understand the Legacy Church culture, specifically the roles and responsibilities church members have had in the past. Once you determine the replant is ready, you will want to lead a very clear and effective membership process with the congregation. There are many books that have been written on this topic and many different ideas on how to do membership well. Regardless of the specific direction you want to go with membership in the replant, let me share two essential steps that I believe must be taken in order to do it well.

Step #1: Update the membership list

Now that the Legacy Congregation has voted to move forward as a replant, it is important to assess and evaluate the current membership list. Most likely, there are many individuals who are officially members of the Legacy Congregation, but who are no longer active. Perhaps some have moved away, some have passed away, some have simply stopped coming to church, and still others are now attending a different congregation. Whatever the reason, it is important the membership list be updated with those individuals who are active members of the congregation. There are different ways this can be done. My encouragement is to:

Write a Personal Letter

Have the replanting pastor along with other key leaders send a personal letter to each individual or family on the membership list who is no longer actively attending the church, letting them know the replant is happening. Tell them you are writing to see if they desire to be part of the new replant or not (due to a move, attending another church, etc.). Let them know that if they desire to be part of the replant, you would love to meet with them and tell them more about the new church.

Make a phone call or face to face visit

In addition to the personal letter, as is possible and appropriate, the replanting pastor should try to call or meet face to face with each inactive person or family on the membership list. If meeting face to face, the replanter should bring along at least one other key leader from the replant to meet with this individual or family. Ideally, it would be wise to bring a leader from the Legacy Congregation who most likely has some relationship with those you are meeting with.

The purpose of this meeting is threefold: First of all, you are going to love, encourage, and check up on this individual or family to see how they are doing and how you might be able to serve them. Secondly, you are going to share with them about the replant and to cast some vision about where this new church is headed. Thirdly, you are going to find out if they have any interest in being part of this new congregation as you are trying to update the membership list to see who is in and who is out. If they desire to be part of the replant, you should explain to them that there will be a new membership process the leadership is asking everyone to go through together. Let them know they are more than welcome to go through the new membership process with everyone else if they are interested.

Step #2: Develop a new membership process

Once you have clearly identified which individuals desire to pursue membership in the replant, it is important to lead them through an intentional membership process. This process is one the replanter and other key leaders should think and pray through together. The process should be clear and purposeful. Here is an example of what this kind of membership process could look like.

Membership class

The membership class is designed to give an overview of the replant, including it's vision, mission, core commitments, basic beliefs and theological distinctives. You want potential members to know exactly what it means to join this church and what is required before asking them to make a decision. The format and duration of this class is up to you. Some churches try to cover everything in one meeting time together, while other churches spread out the membership class out 4-5 weeks. Do what works best for the culture and rhythm of your church in your context.

Meeting with the replanting pastor

It is helpful to set aside some time for the replanting pastor, and/or other pastors, to talk with a membership candidate before he or she joins the replant. These meetings represent an extremely valuable opportunity for potential members to get to know even more about the church and for the leaders to hear more of the story and faith journey of the potential member. It's a chance to ask and answer questions, both directions and to help give a clear understanding of the role of a member in this congregation.

Baptism (for those who have not been baptized)

Baptism is intended only for those who have professed faith in Jesus Christ and can give sufficient testimony to the gospel and basic Christian beliefs. If a potential member has not been baptized, it is appropriate, as well as biblical, to ask the individual to take this step before becoming a church member. To help prepare them for this, a pastor should meet with them to help explain the biblical significance of baptism and answer any questions they might have.

Signing the Membership Covenant

The fourth step in becoming a member of your replant might be to sign a membership covenant. While some congregations may choose not to have a membership covenant, an increasing number of churches, especially church plants and replants, are finding it helpful and meaningful. For these churches, a covenant helps to bring a unified sense of healthy encouragement, accountability, and missional focus for members.

Being sent out as missionaries to the community.

The final step of this membership process is bringing the new members before the congregation in order to encourage them, pray for them, and send them out as missionaries to the community. This should be a fun and exciting event in the life of your replant. This could happen as part of a regular weekend worship service or a member's meeting. As far as frequency, it is recommended to schedule this time of commissioning regularly for new members. Membership in a church should never be about joining some club; it must be about joining the mission of God. Helping your members understand this will help to make membership in the Replant meaningful for both the individual members and the congregation as a whole.

K:

What Now?
Next Steps for the Replant

So, your congregation has replanted a dying church. Praise God! The question you are probably asking at this point is, *What now?* What is next? In order to serve you as the Sending Church and the new replant most effectively, we have launched a website where you can access free church revitalization training materials for use in helping replanting pastors, newly replanted congregations, and Sending Church leaders lead this new replant in a biblical and God honoring manner. You can access the video, audio, and teaching notes for these training resources at *nonignorable.org* or *churchreplanters.com.*

I highly recommend the replanting pastor working through the material for ten of these teachings in particular, which will hopefully be very helpful for his ongoing training and leadership of this new congregation. It might be wise and encouraging for leaders from the Sending Church along with some of the replant core team members to watch and discuss these teachings together with the replanting pastor. I am confident it will be a great learning experience for everyone involved.

TEN TEACHINGS:

1. Humble, Dependent Prayer *(Foundation #14)*

2. Building Trust and Winning Hearts in the Congregation *(Foundation #17)*

3. Leading and Shepherding Difficult People *(Foundation #21)*

4. Facing Criticism in a Godly Manner *(Foundation #36)*

5. Handling Conflict Biblically *(Foundation #37)*

6. Showing and Telling the Gospel through Strategic Relational Evangelism *(Foundation #30)*

7. Ministering Strategically to Children and Teenagers *(Foundation #27)*

8. Making Disciples through Intergenerational Discipleship Groups *(Foundation #29)*

9. The Necessity of Biblical Leadership: Pastors and Deacons *(Foundation #22)*

10. Membership Matters: How to do Membership Well *(Foundation #23)*

RESIDENCY
RESOURCES

Residency Application

(The Calvary Family of Churches)

Thank you for your interest in our revitalization and replanting residency program at Calvary Church. Our hope and prayer for this residency program is to encourage, educate, equip and unleash future pastors in their role of helping to lead revitalization in dying and declining churches for the glory of God. Under supervision, residents will gain knowledge and experience in the areas of pastoral leadership, shepherding, and preaching for a church revitalization context. We are excited about the possibility of you joining us!

There are three main parts to this application process. Please send each of the following via email to both **mark@thecalvary.org** and **jeff@thecalvary.org**.

1. An updated resume
2. Two letters of recommendation (one from a current or former pastor)
3. The included application

These letters should speak to your character, experience, and skills, and should discuss both strengths and weaknesses. Please ask your references to state how long and in what relational capacity they have known you. If you are married, one of your two recommendation letters should be a letter from a pastor who can describe your marriage and speak to its suitability for ministry. *Please type and email the following application:*

GENERAL INFORMATION

Name _____

Date of Application _____

Preferred Address: _____

_____

Preferred Phone: _____

Alternate Phone: _____

Email address: _____

Marital Status: Single/Married

Name of spouse: _____

How did you hear about the Residency Program?

EDUCATION BACKGROUND

Please list all schools attended and both degrees started and degrees completed (high school, technical college, university, graduate school, Bible institute or seminary).

THEOLOGICAL ALIGNMENT

Calvary Church joyfully partners in ministry and mission with both Acts 29 and the Southern Baptist Convention. Please read through the following doctrinal and philosophical statements for these two networks. *Please share any areas of disagreement you have and why.*

Acts 29 Overview *(Please read through this entire page)*
http://www.acts29.com/about/

SBC Baptist Faith & Message
http://www.sbc.net/bfm2000/bfm2000.asp

STRENGTHS & SKILLS

1. How would your friends and family describe you?

2. List your top three strengths and top three areas of needed and desired growth:

Strengths:
1. _____
2. _____
3. _____

Areas of needed and desired growth:
1. _____
2. _____
3. _____

PERSONAL STORY

1. What do you like to do for fun?

2. What kind of music do you like? Favorite bands or artists?

3. What are some of your favorite blogs or web-sites?

4. What books have had the greatest impact on your life and why (other than the Bible)?

Please answer the following questions in 2-3 paragraphs:

5. Please describe your faith journey. Include how God got your attention and some significant experiences and people that he used. How has this journey prepared you for this position?

6. How has your past ministry experiences helped prepared you for this position?

7. How does this position fit into your short and long-term goals? What do you hope to gain from this experience? Why do you want to do this?

Residency Syllabus

(The Calvary Family of Churches)

ATTENDANCE AND PARTICIPATION

Because presence is crucial to the work of church revitalization, residents are expected to be at **all** cohort meetings (1st and 3rd Thursdays: 4-5:30 pm, 2nd and 4th Thursdays: 4-6 pm on Thursdays, 5th Thursdays: OFF) and special events. They will also be required to attend Monday evening Shepherding meetings (5-6:30 pm) and Wednesday afternoon staff meetings (2-3:30 pm), unless other arrangements have been discussed and agreed upon.

READING REPORT

Each required text should be read reflectively, particularly focusing on how the material relates to the work of church revitalization. Residents will be required to complete four books per semester and submit a 2-3 page reading report for each. All four reading reports will be due by the end of the semester.

REVI ROUNDTABLES

Residents will participate in roundtable discussions of assigned readings and other material/special assignments. There will also be periodic roundtable discussions with successful church revitalization pastors. These will take place once a month on a Monday evening from 7:30-9:00 pm at Calvary Englewood.

JOURNALING

Residents will keep a journal throughout the residency. The expectation is that the resident will journal 1-2 pages each week. These journals should reflect the soul work the student is doing, and reflect on how lessons learned through the readings and discussions can be practically applied in a local church context.

DECLINING CHURCH VISIT

One of the special assignments is for residents to go spend a morning visiting a congregation that is declining and in need of revitalization. The purpose of this visit will be to go encourage the folks who are there, taking part in whatever activities they have going on that day (probably a worship service and Sunday School class) and observe *everything* that is going on…from the moment the resident steps out of your car to the moment they get back in to leave.

Residents will then write up a 3-5 page paper describing the experience. Be sure to include practical takeaways that can be applied to a future revitalization or replant ministry opportunity.

PASTORAL CARE/SHEPHERDING OBSERVATION OPPORTUNITIES

Residents will have some opportunity to observe and be part of pastoral care in action (hospital visits, shepherding visits, etc.) These opportunities will also arise through involvement in Community Group. Students should report on these opportunities in their journal.

PRAYER

Because the work of a revitalization pastor depends so much on the care for his flock, residents will be expected to pray systematically for the members of Calvary as part of their weekly shepherding responsibilities.

Residency Job Description

(The Calvary Family of Churches)

DESCRIPTION

The Calvary Family of Churches Church Replanting Residency is a developmental residency designed to help church replanting residents explore their vocational calling, be equipped for mission and ministry, being exposed to church replanting, and engage in missional living. The residency is a 12 month program, beginning in September and ending in August of the following year. The residency consists of three distinct experiences: pastoral cohort (1st Thursday of the month, 4-5:30 PM), preaching cohort (3rd Thursday of the month, 4-5:30 PM), and the church Replanting cohort (2nd and 4th Thursdays of the month, 4-6:00 PM). All residents will receive a mid-course evaluation designed to help steer the second half of the residency and provide direction for the resident post residency.

EXPECTATIONS

Church replanting residents will be expected to live and serve in a manner worthy of the gospel (Phil. 1:27), by God's grace, seeking to love God with all they are, love others sacrificially, and make joyful, passionate disciples of Jesus (Matt. 22:37-39; 28:18-20).

Church replanting residents will be expected to give 8-10 hours a week to their cohorts and supervised ministry and an additional 5-8 hours a week to their homework and living on mission. Each week, residents will be expected to attend the scheduled cohort meetings, complete all required homework, and engage in all required ministry/mission experiences. Residents will also be expected to engage in a supervised ministry experience, which will be defined and determined by the local elders at Calvary Church Englewood.

EVALUATION

All church replanting residents will participate in an evaluation, where the Calvary Family of Churches Church replanting director and 1-2 local elders from Calvary Church Englewood will work in concert with The North American Mission Board to assess the resident's progress and work with the resident to chart a course for the remainder of the residency and beyond. No Calvary Church replanting resident is guaranteed the endorsement of The Calvary Family of Churches to replant a church. However, pending the results of the evaluation, some residents will be endorsed and will be directed in next steps towards becoming a lead church replanter.

Sample Residency Schedule

(The Calvary Family of Churches)

REQUIRED READING

Christ-Centered Preaching, Bryan Chapell
Reclaiming Glory, Mark Clifton
Humility, C.J. Mahaney
The Shepherd Leader, Timothy Z. Witmer

NOTE: All reading assignments are due by the end of the stated month with the exception of Witmer's book. Have the Witmer chapters read and ready to be discussed for the Pastoral Cohort on the first Thursday of each month.

SCHEDULE (FALL 2016)

September

2nd:   Pastoral Cohort #1
9th:   Preparing for Revitalization Pt. 1
16th: Preaching Cohort #1
23rd: Preparing for Revitalization Pt. 2
30th: NO MEETING

Reading:
- Chapell – Chapters 1-2
- Clifton – Chapters 1-2
- Mahaney – Chapters 1-3
- Witmer – Chapters 1-5 (finish for pastoral cohort)

October

6th:   Pastoral Cohort #2
13th: Preparing for Revitalization Pt. 3
20th: Preaching Cohort #2
27th: The Heart of Revitalization Pt. 1

Reading:
- Chapell – Chapters 3-5
- Clifton – Chapters 3-5
- Mahaney – Chapters 4-6
- Witmer – Chapters 6-7 (finish for pastoral cohort)

November

3rd:   Pastoral Cohort #3
10th: The Heart of Revitalization Pt. 2
17th: Preaching Cohort #3
24th: NO COHORT - Thanksgiving

Reading:
- Chapell – Chapters 6-8
- Clifton – Chapters 6-8
- Mahaney – Chapters 7-9
- Witmer – Chapters 8-9 (finish for pastoral cohort)

December

1st:   Pastoral Cohort #4
8th:   The Heart of Revitalization Pt. 3

15th: Preaching Cohort #4

Reading:

- Chapell – Chapters 9-11
- Clifton – Chapters 9-10
- Mahaney – Chapters 10-12
- Witmer (Have finished by Pastoral Cohort) – Chapters 10-11

REPLANT ROUNDTABLES (2016- 2017)

(Mondays, 7:30-9:00pm, at Calvary)

2016

- September 26th
- October 24th
- November 14th
- December 12th

2017

- January 23rd
- February 20th
- March 20th, 2017 (Declining Church Paper Due)
- April 24th
- May 22nd
- June 26th
- July – OFF
- August 28th

P:

Replant Cohort Schedule

CORE COMPONENTS

Opening & Session Overview (5 minutes): Welcome, direct the cohort members to the desired objectives and outcomes for this session, prayer.

Instruction (25-30 minutes): Together watch the teaching video of the particular foundation(s) for the session. If the cohort leader would rather teach the foundation(s) themselves (not using the video) they can use the provided teacher's notes during this time. *NOTE: The actual instructional time should take roughly 30 minutes per foundation being taught.*

Quick Debrief (10 minutes): The cohort leader will lead the cohort in an initial discussion of key insights gained from the teaching/instruction time. (List on flip-chart or whiteboard.)

Discuss & Develop (30 minutes): Guide cohort through the discussion questions and exercises to stimulate thinking and work toward application.

Wrap Up (5 minutes): Review the key insights of this session and announce any assignments for the next gathering, pray and dismiss.

TIME ALLOTMENT

The time of each session will be directly related to the number of foundations being taught and discussed. **Leaders should plan for roughly 1-1½ hours of instruction and discussion per foundation.** The material can be used as a weekly gathering focused on one foundation (1-1½ session), a bi-weekly gathering focused on two foundations (2-3 hour session), or it can be used in a monthly cohort gathering format (4-6 hour session). Have the facilitator schedule in breaks as needed.

Replant Cohort Topics

40 Foundations

PART 1: PREPARING FOR BIBLICAL REVITALIZATION
(September – October)

1. What is church revitalization?
2. Why is church revitalization needed?
3. Understanding God's Heart for Revitalization
4. Counting the Cost: Potential Disadvantages and Challenges in Revitalization
5. Counting the Joy: Potential Advantages and Opportunities in Church Revitalization
6. Is this church ready for revitalization?
7. Am I ready for revitalization?

PART 2: THE HEART OF BIBLICAL REVITALIZATION
(November – December)

8. Heart Posture #1: Humility
9. Heart Posture #2: Love
10. Heart Posture #3: Patience
11. Heart Posture #4: Faith

12. Heart Posture #5: Passion
13. Heart Posture #6: Joy

PART 3: THE PRIORITIES OF BIBLICAL REVITALIZATION
(January – March)

14. Humble, Dependent Prayer
15. The Power and Necessity of Shepherding Preaching
16. Knowing, Serving and Networking in the Surrounding Community
17. Building Trust and Winning Hearts in the Congregation
18. Developing a Ministry Strategy
19. Leading Effective Change with the Word
20. Creating a Clear Shepherding Strategy
21. Leading and Shepherding Difficult People
22. The Necessity of Biblical Leadership: Pastors and Deacons
23. Membership Matters: How to do Membership Well

PART 4: THE PRACTICES OF BIBLICAL REVITALIZATION
(March – May)

24. Developing and Deploying Leaders
25. Designing a Gospel-Centered Weekend Worship Experience
26. Reimagining Adult Sunday School and Christian Education
27. Ministering Strategically to Children and Teenagers
28. Creating Transformational, Biblical Community
29. Making Disciples through Intergenerational Discipleship Groups
30. Showing and Telling the Gospel through Strategic Relational Evangelism
31. Redeeming Empty Space: Maximizing the Use of Your Church Building

PART 5: PERSEVERING IN BIBLICAL REVITALIZATION
(June & August)

32. Rooting Your Life and Ministry in the Gospel
33. Cultivating a Heart for Long-Haul Ministry
34. Putting your Marriage and Family First
35. Growing in Emotional Intelligence

36. Facing Criticism in a Godly Manner
37. Handling Conflict Biblically
38. Caring for Your Soul through Spiritual Disciplines – Resting Well----
    Bible and prayer
39. Managing Your Schedule
40. Training Up and Sending Out Church Revitalizers and Replanters

R:

Additional Growth Opportunities

Beyond the learning that happens in the cohort groups and serving in various capacities within the church, I would recommend offering some additional growth opportunities for your resident throughout the year. The following are some of the extra growth opportunities we assign our residents:

READING REPORTS

Our expectation is that each required text is read reflectively, particularly focusing on how the material relates to the work of church replanting and revitalization. Residents are required to complete the assigned books for the semester and then submit a 2-3 page reading report for each book. All reading reports will be due by the end of the semester.

REPLANT ROUNDTABLES

These are roundtable discussions that take place once a month on a Monday evening from 7:30-9:00 pm at Calvary Englewood. These roundtables serve as extra time to discuss assigned readings and other material/special assignments. Periodically we will use these roundtable discussions as an opportunity to meet or video-conference with successful church replanters around the country.

JOURNALING

Residents are expected to keep a journal throughout the residency. The hope is that the resident will journal 1-2 pages each week. These journals should reflect the soul work the student is doing, and reflect on how lessons learned through the readings and discussions can be practically applied in a local church context.

DECLINING CHURCH VISIT

One of the special assignments for our residents is to go spend a morning visiting a congregation that is declining and in need of revitalization. The purpose of this visit is to encourage the folks who are there, taking part in whatever activities they have going on that day (probably a worship service and Sunday School class) and observe EVERYTHING that is going on from the moment the resident steps out of his car to the moment they get back in to leave. Residents then write up a 3-5 page paper describing the experience. We ask them to be sure to include practical takeaways that can be applied to a future revitalization or replant ministry opportunity. We spend one of our replant roundtables discussing these church visits.

S:

Free Replant Cohort Materials

In order to serve you and your church most effectively, we have launched a website where you can access free replant cohort materials for use in your own church as you start a replanting residency. Everything you need can be found at *nonignorable.org* or *churchreplanters.com*.

Specific to the replant cohort gathering, you can access all of the teaching material for the 40 Foundations. Here you will find:

#1: VIDEO & AUDIO

Each of these Foundation teachings are between 20-30 minutes in length. These videos can serve as the primary teaching tool for your replant cohort group. If your pastor or another leader would prefer to teach rather than use the video teaching, the teaching notes are provided for each Foundation. The audio mp3 files are available here as well.

#2: TEACHER'S NOTES

These are the main teaching outlines to use for each Foundation. Again, leaders have the option of just watching the video teaching of this material, or they can use these outlines to teach the material themselves.

#3: STUDENT NOTES

These are the student notes that the resident and other cohort group members will receive for the teaching time. They have fill-in-the-blanks that will be filled in over the course of each teaching. You will notice that on the videos, the fill-ins come up on the screen. You can imagine that after the group concludes, the resident and other group members will have a very thick notebook of replant teaching material they can take with them for future use in their replanting context. The hope is this will be helpful material they can then share with other leaders wherever they go. *NOTE: I would recommend buying a binder for those involved in the cohort so they can compile their outline notes in one place.*

#4: DISCUSSION QUESTIONS

For each Foundation session, we have written discussion questions that can be used for group interaction and reflection during each cohort gathering. These questions are at the end of both the teacher and student outlines.

Preaching Cohort Evaluation

Text:

Title:

Preacher:

When rating a sermon, use the following 1–5 scale: "1" means "not at all" or "poor", 3 means "consistently" or "fairly competent" and 5 means "always" or "extremely well done." Add additional comments below each set of numbers.

GENERAL

1. The speaker grabbed my attention. I found myself thinking, "I need to listen to this."

    1   2   3   4   5

2. The sermon held my interest throughout.

    1   2   3   4   5

3. The speaker seemed to be in awe of God and full of the Holy Spirit.

    1   2   3   4   5

4. The end of the sermon was compelling and moved me to action.

     1   2   3   4   5

DELIVERY

5. The speaker engaged the audience with himself through an appropriate use of humor and self-disclosure.

     1   2   3   4   5

6. There was a balance of warmth, love and humility on one hand and confidence, power and authority on the other.

     1   2   3   4   5

7. The speaker avoided any annoying mannerisms or phrases (sticking hands in pocket, saying "you know," self-conscious references, repeating themselves, nervous laughter).

     1   2   3   4   5

CONTENT

8. The preaching points were clearly rooted in the text.

     1   2   3   4   5

9. The flow of the sermon was concise, clear and easy to follow.

     1   2   3   4   5

10. The main idea/theme of the message was clear and persuasive.

     1   2   3   4   5

11. The sermon was the right length.

    1   2   3   4   5

APPLICATION

12. The speaker applied the text throughout – they didn't just explain the text; they helped me figure out how to apply it to my life.

    1   2   3   4   5

13. The sermon was gospel-centered: Christ and his finished work were applied as the solution to any problem.

    1   2   3   4   5

14. The sermon was evangelistic – it called non-Christians to repent and believe the gospel in a compelling way.

    1   2   3   4   5

15. The speaker avoided Christian jargon and statements that exclude non-Christians ("we all know the story...")

    1   2   3   4   5

16. The speaker engaged Christians, and showed how the gospel addresses their fears, hopes, problems, etc.

    1   2   3   4   5

FEEDBACK

Give top 2-3 strengths and 2-3 weaknesses. Be specific.

Recommended Cohort Resources

PASTORAL COHORT

Leading with Love, Alexander Strauch
The Shepherd Leader, Timothy Witmer
Brothers, We Are Not Professionals, John Piper
The Reformed Pastor, Richard Baxter
Christian Ministry, Charles Bridges
Biblical Eldership, Alexander Strauch
Wisdom for Pastors, Curtis Thomas
On Being a Pastor, Derek Prime and Alistair Begg

REPLANTING COHORT

Can These Bones Live?, Bill Henard
Reclaiming Glory, Mark Clifton
The New Pastor's Handbook, Jason Helopoulos
The Conviction to Lead, Albert Mohler
Everyday Church, Tim Chester
Biblical Church Revitalization, Brian Croft
Humility, C.J. Mahaney
Comeback Churches, Ed Stetzer and Mike Dodson

The Advantage, Patrick Lencioni
Embers to a Flame, Harry L. Reeder, III
Church Planting is for Wimps, Mike McKinley

PREACHING COHORT

Expositional Preaching, David Helm
Christ-Centered Preaching, Bryan Chapell
Preaching, Timothy Keller
The Supremacy of God in Preaching, John Piper
Preaching for God's Glory, Alistair Begg
Saving Eutychus, Gary Millar and Phil Campbell
Preaching and Preachers, D. Martyn Lloyd-Jones

The Institute for Expository Preaching - It is highly recommended, if possible, for your church to send your resident to "The Institute for Expository Preaching," sponsored by One Passion Ministries. I know of no other training available today that better equips a pastor for his biblical preaching ministry. Even if your resident has a seminary education, this training will be incredibly helpful and encouraging in his development as an expositor of God's Word. Go to onepassionministries.org for more information.

SHEPHERDING RESOURCES

V:

What's the Difference?
Revitalization vs. Replanting

What exactly is the difference between church revitalization and church replanting?

CHURCH REVITALIZATION

Let's picture church revitalization and church replanting through an equation. Consider each of these four parts and their descriptions:

Revitalization = You + Existing People + Old Structure + History

You

When we think about leading a church revitalization, we're first looking at you (the pastor) and your wife and kids (if applicable). This is a calling God has placed on you, and you're all in this together.

Existing People

The pastor coming into this situation must seek to lead change and bring renewal to the congregation with whoever is present in the existing congregation. You don't get to pick those with whom you are doing this revitalization; your team is whoever is already there. These are the people who are already at the church and wanting revitalization, but they're typically not interested in being overwhelmed by a whole new group of people. They're not really interested in something radically new. They just want a pastor to help them become healthy and help them grow to love Jesus and their community.

A pastor then must seek to lead change in the congregation by bringing himself, his giftings, and his passions into the fold of the existing sheep. That's the team. And that's the team that God has given you to shepherd and come alongside to help turn this church around for the glory of God. That's revitalization. How long will it take? A long time! Revitalization takes longer than church replanting, which we'll discuss next. And revitalization requires the heart of a pastor who is patient and hopeful, who believes that God is in control, and who knows that God can change people.

Old Structure

In revitalization, the pastor must work within the old structure (bylaws, constitution, leadership structure, etc.) in order to lead change. This is certainly a challenge. You are going into the revitalization situation, looking at the bylaws and constitution through the eyes of the vibrant and visionary leader that you probably are, and you're realizing there's a lot you and the church *can't* do. The bylaws and constitution most likely met the needs of the church many years ago but may not allow for doing some things that you currently need to do to move the church forward. Therein lies the challenge: how to lead change when the bylaws, constitution, and leadership structure may be inhibiting it.

So in a revitalization, you are not only working to bring health to the people who are there, but you're also working to bring health to the church with the people who are there *under the old structure*. You must do your best with the structure that's in place, and over time, Lord willing, you can win the people's hearts and earn the right to make changes to bylaws, constitution, leadership, and polity. But, again, it takes time.

This is a big reason why pastors don't opt for revitalization. Because they want to bring change *now*. The pastor must have a long-haul vision of the church. This leads us to the fourth piece of the equation.

History

History can be both good and bad. Usually the people in the congregation really treasure their history. Effective revitalization is about entering into the story that God's been writing for this church for a long time. It's also about knowing what a humbling opportunity and privilege it is to shepherd these people who have this history.

At the same time, history can be a real challenge because it can be something that's hanging over the pastor's head all the time. "We've never done it this way before." "What's this new idea?" That's where history can sometimes be a detriment to helping a church get healthy again.

CHURCH REPLANTING

Now that you may have a better understanding of what church revitalization looks like, let's consider something probably lesser-known: church replanting. Church replanting is actually a strategy under the umbrella of church revitalization. What exactly is replanting, and how is it different from revitalization?

Replant = You + New & Existing People + New Structure + History

You

Again, you and your wife and children, if you have them, are an important part of this equation.

New People and Existing People

Unlike in a revitalization, for a replant there are the existing people and there are new people. The new people are probably excited about starting a new thing in a new place, building off the past of what this church has been, but definitely wanting to move in a new direction. At the same time, there are existing folks who have been a part of that church, but they're at the point where they're saying, "We know what we've been doing isn't working anymore. And we want to see God do something fresh and new. We're all in." So you are a replanter who is working as a leader to bring both new and existing people together in a common vision.

New Structure (bylaws, constitution, leadership structure, vision, & strategy)

Similar to church planting, in a replanting context, you have a new structure. You have new leadership structure, bylaws, and constitution. All of these things you have not inherited, but you have probably helped to develop. Maybe other churches and other leaders have helped you to develop these things. The advantage of creating new structure is there isn't a whole lot of red tape holding you back from being able to lead change (like there can be in a revitalization). You have bylaws and a constitution and leadership that are all visionary, and you're moving in the direction in which you feel God is calling you to go.

History of the Church

Unlike a new church plant, there is history with a replant. That history comes from those who have been part of this church and who are now a part of the new replant. As previously stated, history can be a good thing, but it can also be a bad thing depending on how folks approach history.

For most replant situations, history is a really good thing. It's a good thing to celebrate what God has done in the past and to build off those things the Lord has already accomplished. We don't want to get away from those great things that God has done. We want to build off of them as we move into the future.

Replanting in a Rural vs. an Urban Context

Compiled by Ron Klassen[1]

While the following lists speak in generalities, and while there are plenty of exceptions, these lists can be helpful in understanding some of the cultural differences when it comes to rural vs. urban contexts and values.

	RURAL	URBAN
How success is assessed	Survival is success. If the church maintains the numbers it had a year ago, it has been successful.	Advancement is success. The church must show an increase in giving, attendance, etc., to be a success.
How small is viewed	Small is attractive, large is threatening. Rural people are not sure they want the church to grow.	Big is better, small is inferior. Church growth is very important

	RURAL	URBAN
Degree of independence	Tend to live, work, and think independently. Therefore, consensus and cooperation are hard to achieve.	Are used to living and working in close proximity with others and thus are impatient with independent thinkers.
Preferred management style	Many are their own bosses and are, therefore, accustomed to single-tier management. They like to call the shots and have a say in all decisions.	Most are accustomed to multi-tier management. They want others to make decisions and are impatient when "bothered" with petty matters.
Unpredictability vs. predictability	Are used to unpredictability due to factors beyond their control (like weather). They might, therefore, see goal setting and vision as presumptuous.	Tend to only do one or two things in their area of expertise and hire the rest done. Therefore, the often have high standards and are perfectionists.
Degree of specialization	Tend to be jacks-of-all-trades but masters-of-none. They have few areas of specialization and, therefore, are not perfectionists.	Tend to only do one or two things in their area of expertise and hire the rest done. Therefore, they often have high standards and are perfectionists.
Perspective on finances	For many, income is cyclical and not guaranteed. Therefore, "budget" may be a foreign term. Assets are substantial but can't be sold because their livelihood is dependent upon them.	Income is usually regular and fixed. They have a hard time understanding the farmer who has no money for clothes one week but buys a new pickup the next. They want a church budget.

	RURAL	URBAN
Communication skills	Are intelligent, but often have weaker communication skills (because they mostly talk to animals or in local colloquialisms). They can be threatened by those with high verbal skills.	Typically can articulate pretty well. They might think people who talk haltingly or with weaker grammar aren't too smart. They could overpower them.
Homogeneity	Because of limited population to draw from, in certain areas achieving homogeneity is nearly impossible (areas like theology and church practices).	They can likely find a church with people who believe just like them and have similar tastes to theirs.
Outlook on life	A cloak of pessimism tends to hover over them – a defense mechanism protecting against dashed hopes due to circumstances beyond their control.	They cannot understand why rural people aren't gung-ho about the future, why they are seemingly always concerned about the "what-ifs," whey the don't want to take risks – even when times are good.
Perspective on time	They tend to be more task driven.	They tend to be more clock driven.
Definition of work	They might think "real" work is manual labor. Desk work, or mental work, is not viewed with equal respect as physical labor.	They can be real klutzes when it comes to physical work – they don't know how to do it or have the muscle or stamina for it.

	RURAL	URBAN
View of each other	They tend to view people in terms of how they relate to each other: "This is Bob, Jim and Nadine's' boy. He lives down at the old McPherson place."	They tend to view people according to functions and titles: "This is Bob. He is the chairman of our board. He is a senior partner in a law firm and serves on the town council."
Dealing with conflict	Conflict is too difficult to sort out and deal with because of a complex web of relationships.	While not pleasant, conflict is easier to confront because people only see each other on Sundays.
Decision making	They follow an informal and unstructured approach in meetings. Most decisions are made outside the meetings – in the café or in two pickup trucks sitting side-by-side on the road.	*Robert's Rules of Order* is their "Bible" for meetings. They want decisions made in an orderly fashion, with a formal proposal, discussion, motion, and a vote.

X:

How to Lead a Church Name Change

By Kevin Hanly

So you want to change the name of your church? Great idea! The receptivity of your church to a name change can actually be a good indicator of how ready they are for revitalization. But because it carries so much weight, it needs to be handled with care. If your congregation shows up Sunday morning and discovers that you've come like a thief in the night—torn down the old and put up a new sign out front—they aren't likely to notice or care how awesome the new name is. Here are some tips we learned from when we changed the name of our church a few years ago.

CELEBRATE THE OLD NAME

First of all, celebrate the old name. In our case this meant celebrating our denomination, because one thing we did was take our denomination's name out of the name of our church. The old name was "Community Evangelical Free Church of River Vale." Since the new name no longer included reference to our denomination, I tried to make a point to celebrate the great things about our denomination and was able to point out that even our denominational officials thought the change was a good idea. Secondarily, we kept the word *community* because that reflects a value we still very much hold. For you, it might be as simple as celebrating some of the ministry achievements that were accomplished under the old name. They key is to show respect for what has happened in the past and for the name with which all those great things are associated.

LOOK FOR HIDDEN SACRED COWS

It is important to note that a name change has a lot of ripple affects. Changing the name means changing a lot of other things. It means getting a new sign out front. It means revising the bulletin. It means redoing the website. It might mean repainting the sanctuary. What's important to remember is that someone in your church probably was responsible for putting up the old sign, designing the old website or bulletin, or originally painting the sanctuary. They may be less opposed to the name change per se and more disappointed that their work is being replaced. Be sure to recognize them for the work they've done and if possible seek to involve them in the new work as well.

PICK A NAME THAT HONORS THE HERITAGE OF THE CHURCH

Bringing change in ways that honor the heritage of the church is the key to just about every aspect of revitalization—including the name change. If you can pick a name that somehow accomplishes both your missional goals *and* honors the heritage of the church, you've got a win-win. In our case, we actually went back to what was the *original* original name of our church. The long name mentioned above which we were trying to change had previously replaced the much simpler founding name "River Vale Community Church." I was able to argue for the name "River Vale Community Church" much the same way Paul argues that justification is by faith—by going all the way back to the beginning—Abraham! In the same way, if possible, show how the new name will actually enable the church to be more, not less true to itself.

365 *Appendix X: How to Lead a Church Name Change*

SPELL OUT CLEARLY THE REASONS FOR THE NAME CHANGE

If you choose a name that inherently captures the essence of your vision (which is a good idea), be sure to spell out the connections for your people. More than likely, the main reason you want to change your name in the first place is for the purpose of *mission*. (Why else would you change it when the people who are already there surely don't mind the old name?) Explain how the new name will help to reach those outside the church. In our case, we pointed out that on one hand the word "evangelical" carries with it all kinds of mixed connotations to outsiders, and on the other hand some think "evangelical free" is to be taken the same way as "sugar-free" — i.e. "you mean there aren't evangelicals in your church?" If you don't have good reasons for your name change, you probably shouldn't be doing it. If you do, just be sure to take the time to spell out those reasons.

THE LEGAL SIDE OF CHANGING THE CHURCH NAME

A church name change can be done with a "DBA" or "does business as" so the constitution, articles of incorporation, bank accounts, building deeds, and other legal documents all stay intact. This is not a difficult process if handled properly when the church is voting to replant during their formal business meeting. It is crucial to communicate through this process that you are building off the legacy and history of the Legacy Congregation. The Legacy Congregation remains in existence and this name change will simply allow the new replant to effectively reach their community in a new way with a new identity.

Doing a DBA is a great way to communicate your love and respect for their history and legacy, while at the same time declaring to the surrounding community that a new church is being formed. When the Legacy Congregation is holding their business meeting to vote to replant, it is key to have the church make three separate motions to approve, which should be listed on the meeting agenda:

Motion #1: *We agree to enter the replant process with XYZ church (your church) and hand all day-to-day operation decisions over to them.*

Motion #2: *We agree to adopt XYZ church's bylaws as our own.*

Motion #3: *We agree to do business as (DBA) "new church name" (and be sure to list any variances that could be used).*

You may add a fourth motion that adds a person from your leadership team as a signer on their bank account but this is not mandatory at this time.

Following the vote, you will then go to your secretary of state website to submit the "statement of trade name of entity registered" required for a name change or DBA. While you are one the Secretary of State website, it is a good idea to go ahead and change the registered agent to a leader in your church. You will then want to take a copy of the business meeting minutes to the church's bank so they are notified of the name change for tithe checks to be deposited. If they voted for one of your leaders to be added as a signer on their account, add them. You may want to order new checks at this time as well.

Legally you are done with the name change. Lastly, make copies of the business meeting minutes and send a copy to your denominational state/national office so they are informed of the change. It is recommended at this time that a designated fund be set up in your church's budget so money can be transferred into the designated fund from the church's bank account.

Y:

Shepherding Older Members as a Younger Pastor

By Dan Hallock

TAKE AN INTEREST IN KNOWING YOUR OLDER CHURCH MEMBERS PERSONALLY.

Older people want to know whether you actually care about them or whether you plan to cater your ministry to young people and leave the elderly behind. Even though you're younger and they're older, you're not just their preacher—you're their pastor/shepherd. Care for them. Love on them, affirm them, and encourage them in the faith. Try to visit them at their homes or to call them on the phone, because that's meaningful to the older generations. Get to know them and discern how you can best minister to them through prayer and the ministry of the Word.

SOAK UP THE WISDOM OF OLDER CHRISTIANS.

Having lived many more decades of life than you have, most older people have lots of wisdom that will benefit you. Listen to their stories. Hear about how God has carried them through career changes, church difficulties, trials, parenting, marriage, and the joys of being a grandparent. Learn from their mistakes and also from their successes. Ask the Lord to help you apply their wisdom to your life so that you might avoid many unnecessary pitfalls and instead walk in the way of righteousness.

HONOR THE ELDERLY CHRISTIANS IN YOUR CHURCH.

You can honor elderly Christians both formally and informally. Perhaps you can honor them formally by having a weekly prayer time for seniors, by offering community groups or classes targeted toward issues facing the elderly, or by planning an annual dinner for them that's organized by the youth group. You can also honor older Christians by humbly seeking their counsel about important church decisions and the direction of the church. Even if you don't use all their ideas, most will appreciate that you took time to seek their input.

SHARE WHAT YOU LOVE ABOUT THE HISTORY OF YOUR CHURCH.

Instead of viewing your ministry as an undoing of the past, you want to view it as another chapter in the story God is writing for your specific church. Understanding this point will help you and the older people to see that you value, and perhaps want to reclaim, the historical, gospel-centered distinctives of your church. In order to do this, you first have to learn the church history. Some older churches have their history in writing. Additionally, learning the church history from older members is a great excuse to get together with them. After learning about the historical vision of the church, leadership changes, key transition points, and ministry successes, you can look for the central missional threads that tie your church's history together. Celebrate those historical themes and events with your church from the pulpit, at vision meetings, and in one-on-one conversations.

FIND WAYS FOR YOUR OLDER CHURCH MEMBERS TO SERVE IN MINISTRY.

I know a number of older saints who faithfully attend church and support the leadership, but they sadly feel that they are "old news" and don't have much to offer the church anymore with their limited energy and resources. We must counter this mindset by identifying service opportunities for our older members and by expressing our need for their help. Older members can thrive in ministry in the church through the greeting ministry, follow-up ministry, prayer ministry, card-writing ministry, sewing ministry, mentoring ministry, nursery ministry, and even the youth ministry! Think about ways that you can help your older church members connect the dots between their skill sets and the needs of the church.

DON'T ASSUME THAT OLDER MEMBERS ARE SPIRITUALLY MATURE.

While age can definitely be an indicator of spiritual maturity, it is not a definite indicator of spiritual maturity. Just as there are spiritually immature and mature young people, so also there are spiritually immature and mature older people. Regardless of age, all Christians are still in the process of sanctification, and we won't be perfected until Christ glorifies us in the future. While we surely want to shepherd and honor the elderly Christians in our churches, we must also realize that just like us, many of them still struggle with all the sins of the flesh, including gossip, lust, anger, bitterness, slander, and malice. The more experience you have in ministry, the less likely you will be surprised when you learn of sinful patterns and behaviors of those in your flock, regardless of their age.

REBUKE OLDER CHRISTIANS CAREFULLY AND GENTLY.

As a pastor/elder, God has selected you through the vote of the church to shepherd all the Christians in your flock. As a younger pastor, it can be quite stupefying and awkward to confront an older Christian man about his sinful behavior. In his letter to young Timothy, the apostle Paul writes in 1

Timothy 5:1, "Do not sharply rebuke an older man, but rather appeal to him as a father, to the younger men as brothers." Note that Paul does not say that it is inappropriate for young Timothy to rebuke the older men in his flock; rather, Paul instructs Timothy not to "sharply" rebuke and older man. In other words, young pastors should be prayerful and careful and gentle about when and how to rebuke an older Christian man. Sometimes, it might be more helpful to have one of your older elders to come alongside the older church member and rebuke him as a peer. Other times, depending on the type of rebuke, it might be most appropriate for you to meet with the older man and lovingly confront him in private. As much as it is up to you, take time to pray about the situation beforehand, to seek counsel from your other elders if appropriate, and to humble yourself before the Lord, so that you can work hard not lord your authority over any Christian, young or old.

INCORPORATE SERMON APPLICATIONS THAT WILL SERVE THE OLDER CHRISTIANS IN YOUR FLOCK.

It's a natural temptation for a preacher to find and utilize illustrations and application points that only pertain to people who are near the age of the preacher. Avoid this pitfall by putting yourself in the shoes of your parishioners, young and old. What are they going through in their lives? What are their fears? What questions are they asking about God and his Word? The more that you get to know the individuals in your flock the more precisely you will be able to apply God's Word to them. The last third of life is especially difficult for most people, because their bodies are wearing down, their energy level is far less than it used to be, their peers are passing away, and the reality of death and dying is ever-present. While you shouldn't pretend to know exactly what the older people in your church are thinking and feeling and experiencing, you can ask the Lord to help you point the older Christians in your care to the promises of the Bible that can best encourage, sanctify, equip them to use the remainder of their lives for the glory of God.

Z:
Recommended Community Group Resources

Community, Brad House

Life in Community, Dustin Willis

Everyday Church, Tim Chester and Steve Timmis

Why Small Groups?, C.J. Mahaney

Small Groups with a Purpose, Steve Gladen

Side by Side, Edward T. Welch

Leading Life-Changing Small Groups, Bill Donahue

Sticky Church, Larry Osborne

The Simplest Way to Change the World, Dustin Willis and Brandon Clements

Life Together, Dietrich Bonhoeffer

Total Church, Tim Chester and Steve Timmis

Activate, Nelson Searcy

Creating Community, Andy Stanley

Making Small Groups Work, Henry Cloud and John Townsend

GLOSSARY

Church Replanting: the process in which members of a dying congregation discern God's leading to joyfully submit their church's current and future ministry to an outside Sending Church and its leadership, working together to begin a new church for a new season of gospel ministry in their community.

Church Revitalization: a supernatural work of God in which He works to bring renewed health to a plateaued or declining church resulting in that congregation becoming a unified, vibrant, disciple-making body of believers on mission to reach their surrounding community with the gospel.

Core Team: the core team are those individuals who serve as the committed leaders and servants working together to launch this new replant. It is made up of men and women, boys and girls who are all-in with this replant. While there will be folks whose excitement and commitment may wane, the core team are those individuals who have made a commitment to be part of this new church regardless of the challenges that lie ahead. This is why we call them the core team—they serve as the core of this replant.

Denominational Leaders: in most cases, a denominational leader will be involved on some level throughout this process. This individual can be a huge help to both the Sending Church, as well as the Legacy Congregation. Denominational leaders bring a level of experience and leadership wisdom that is needed. For many Legacy Congregations that have strong ties with their denomination, these denominational leaders brings credibility and a level of trust that is beneficial in helping them navigate the journey.

Legacy Congregation: these are the remaining folks in the dying congregation that will potentially be replanted. In most cases, the majority of these individuals have been part of the congregation for many years and have a deep love for this church. Depending on the particular government structure of the congregation, these members of the congregation will have a say in whether or not the church is to be replanted. In congregational churches, these folks are typically the ones to give the final vote to either move forward as a replant or not. We use the term legacy to communicate our affirmation and desire to celebrate and build off of the God-honoring legacy of this congregation in the new replant.

Legacy Congregation Leaders: this group of individuals looks different depending on the church that is being replanted. Sometimes, it is whoever remains on the current deacon or elder board. In other cases, it may be the pastor who is trying to hold the church together and recognizes the church needs to be replanted. Still other times this group of folks may be made up of men and women who serve in various roles within the church. Whoever it is that makes up this group, these are the individuals who are representing and leading the Legacy Congregation, helping to discern whether replanting is the best option for the church and what it will mean and look like if the congregation decides to move forward with it.

Public Launch: the public launch is the official kick-off of the replant. This is the culmination of months of prayers and meetings and outreach events and worship gatherings. At the same time, it is really only the beginning of reaching this community with the gospel! At this point, the foundational pieces of this church replant should be in place and the core team is ready to lead and serve this new congregation.

Replant Core Team Members: in most replants, there is a group of new team members who will join the replanter along with the Legacy Congregation as they work together to begin this new church. These individuals will be long haul, committed members of this new replant. Typically, replant core team members come from a variety of locations including the Sending Church, the surrounding community where this new replant will be located, and from other nearby towns or communities.

Replanter: this is the pastor who has been trained up to revitalize and replant the Legacy Congregation. This is an individual who is being sent out from the Sending Church as the point leader to lead this new replant.

Sending Church: this is the congregation that will come alongside and help replant the Legacy Congregation. In a very real sense, the Sending Church serves as the sponsor or mother church for the replant. The role of this church is to pray for, encourage, and serve the Legacy Congregation, however they can. Moreover, this congregation will seek to support the replant over the long haul in various ways.

Sending Church Leaders: these are key leaders from the Sending Church who will help lead the replanting process. Often times this will be the lead pastor or an associate pastor, along with a handful of other key leaders who are invested in and committed to seeing this replant become a reality. While the entire congregation will be involved on some level, typically, these key leaders will be the ones most directly involved.

Soft Launch: during this phase, the core team of the replant begins to move forward together on mission, seeking to reach the community and build the tore Team. This is also an intentional season for trial & error as the leaders of the replant begin attempting and implementing new ministry systems and strategies in preparation for public launch.

Transition Team: the transition team could be a group of pastors, elders, deacons, or other leaders from the Sending Church. If there is not a clear Sending Church, this transition team could also be a group made up of pastors and leaders from different churches in the community, denominational leaders, or a combination of all the two. Whoever these individuals are, the dying church has agreed to give up day to day decision making to this outside group of leaders. They have surrendered to this transition team to help guide them and lead them into the future.

Volunteer Team (V-Team) Members: these are individuals from the Sending Church who will be serving the new replant in various ways at their weekend worship gathering. These folks are not permanent team members of the replant, but rather they are individuals who are eager to help out and serve during the transition time leading up to the public launch. This group may help with anything from leading music to holding babies in the nursery or serving on the greeting team. A key role the V-Team will play is training core team members of the replant to serve in various areas of ministry. For example, a V-Team member may be running slides for the worship service, but a volunteer from the replant should be with them learning how to do it. The same will go for the children's ministry, greeting ministry, and other areas of ministry. After you start seeing the core team members handling the various parts of the weekend worship gathering well, the V-Team can start phasing out.

BIBLIOGRAPHY

Abbott-Smith, George. *A Manual Greek Lexicon of the New Testament.* New York: Scribner's Sons, 1922.

"About." *Acts 29.* Accessed Mar 27, 2017. http://www.acts29.com/about/.

Allison, Archibald Alexander. "Biblical Qualifications for Elders." *Ordained Servant* 3, no. 4 (November 1994).

Baxter, Richard. *The Reformed Pastor.* New Edition. Banner of Truth Trust, Carlisle, PA: 1974.

Begg, Alistair. Preaching for God's Glory. Redesign Edition. Wheaton, IL: Crossway, 2010.

Bensen, Dan. "You Lost Me." *The Gospel Coalition.* Accessed May 3, 2017. https://www.thegospelcoalition.org/article/you_lost_me.

Bonhoeffer, Dietrich, and John W. Doberstein. *Life Together.* San Francisco: HarperSanFrancisco, 1993.

Bridges, Charles. *Christian Ministry.* London: FB &c Ltd., 2015.

Calvin, John. *Commentaries on The Epistles to Timothy, Titus, and Philemon.* Grand Rapids, MI: Baker Publishing, 1979.

Campbell, Regi. *Mentor Like Jesus: His Radical Approach to Building the Church.* Nashville: B & H Publishing Group, 2009.

Chapell, Bryan. *Christ-Centered Preaching: Redeeming the Expository Sermon.* Grand Rapids, MI: Baker Academic, 2005.

Chester, Tim. *Everyday Church: Gospel Communities on Mission.* Wheaton, IL: Crossway, 2012.

Chester, Tim, and Steve Timmis. *Total Church: A Radical Reshaping around Gospel and Community.* Wheaton, IL: Crossway Books, 2008.

"Church Replanting." North American Mission Board. Accessed May 3, 2017. https://www.namb.net/church-replanting.

Clifton, Mark. "Dying Churches Matter to God….and to NAMB." *Namb.net.* Accessed September 1, 2016. https://www.namb.net/send-network-blog/dying-churches-matter-to-god-and-to-namb.

Clifton, Mark. *Reclaiming Glory: Revitalizing Dying Churches.* Nashville: B & H Books, 2016.

Cloud, Henry, and John Sims Townsend. *Making Small Groups Work: What Every Small Group Leader Needs to Know.* Grand Rapids, MI: Zondervan, 2003.

Collier, Kevin. "How to Evaluate Your Pastor's Sermons." *9 Marks.* Accessed January 15, 2017. https://9marks.org/article/how-to-evaluate-your-pastors-sermons-2/.

Croft, Brian. *Biblical Church Revitalization: Solutions for Dying & Divided Churches.* Fearn, Train, Scotland: Christian Focus Publications, 2016.

Deeter, Justin. "Advantages of Established Churches." *justindeeter.com.* Accessed June 13, 2016. http://www.justindeeter.com/archives/1562.

Donahue, Bill. *Leading Life-Changing Small Groups.* Grand Rapids, MI: Zondervan, 2012.

Edwards, Jonathan. *The Salvation of Souls.* Wheaton, IL: Crossway, 2002.

Egeler, Daniel. *Mentoring Millennials: Shaping the Next Generation.* Colorado Springs, CO: NavPress, 2003.

Marty Giese, "A Pastoral Training Program for Rural Churches" (Master of Arts research project, Moody Bible Institute, Chicago, 1993).

Gladen, Steve. *Small Groups with Purpose: How to Create Healthy Communities.* Grand Rapids, MI: Baker Books, 2011.

Helm, David. *Expositional Preaching: How We Speak God's Word Today.* Wheaton, IL: Crossway, 2014.

Helopoulos, Jason. *The New Pastor's Handbook: Help and Encouragement for the First Years of Ministry.* Grand Rapids: Baker Books, 2015.

Henard, William. *Can These Bones Live?: A Practical Guide to Church Revitalization.* Nashville: B & H Publishing Group, 2015.

Hendricks, Howard and William Hendricks. *As Iron Sharpens Iron: Building Character in a Mentoring Relationship.* Chicago: Moody Press, 1995.

House, Brad. *Community: Taking Your Small Group Off Life Support.* Wheaton, IL: Crossway, 2011.

Howard, Brian. "How to Develop Leaders in your Church." *Context Coaching.* Accessed January 23, 2017. http://contextcoaching.org/develop-leaders-church/.

Hunter, Kent. *The Lord's Harvest and the Rural Church.* Kansas City, KS: Beacon Hill Press, 1993.

Keller, Timothy. *Center Church: Doing Balanced, Gospel-Centered Ministry in Your City.* Grand Rapids, MI: Zondervan, 2012.

Keller, Timothy. *Preaching: Communicating Faith in an Age of Skepticism.* New York: Penguin Books, 2016.

Lencioni, Patrick. *The Advantage: Why Organizational Health Trumps Everything Else In Business.* San Francisco: Jossy-Bass, 2012.

Lenz, Mark. "3 Keys to Managing Momentum in Ministry." *churchcentral.com.* Accessed March 14, 2017. https://www.churchcentral.com/blogs/3-keys-to-managing-momentum-in-ministry/.

Lloyd-Jones, D. Martyn. *Preaching and Preachers.* 40th Anniversary Edition. Grand Rapids, MI: Zondervan, 2011.

MacArthur, John. *First Timothy. MacArthur New Testament Commentary.* Chicago, IL: Moody Publishers, 1995.

Mahaney, C.J. *Humility.* Colorado Springs, CO: Multnomah Books, 2005.

Mahaney, C. J., ed. *Why Small Groups?: Together toward Maturity.* Gaithersburg, MD: Sovereign Grace Ministries, 1996.

McCheyne, Robert Murray. *The Sermons of the Rev. Robert Murray McCheyne.* New York, NY: Robert Carter and Brothers Publishing, 1854.

McKinley, Mike. *Church Planting is for Wimps: How God Uses Messed-Up People to Plant Ordinary Churches That Do Extraordinary Things.* Wheaton, IL: Crossway, 2010.

McKinley, Mike. "The Pros and Cons of Planting and Revitalization." *9 Marks.* Accessed June 13, 2016. https://9marks.org/article/journalpros-and-cons-planting-and-revitalizing/.

Millar, Gary, and Phil Campbell. *Saving Eutychus: How to Preach God's Word and Keep People Awake.* Youngstown, OH: Matthias Media, 2013.

Moher, Al. "A Guide to Church Revitalization." *The Southern Baptist Theological Seminary.* Accessed January 7, 2017. http://www.sbts.edu/press/a-guide-to-church-revitalization/#download.

Mohler, Albert. *The Conviction to Lead: 25 Principles for Leadership That Matters.* Bloomington, MN: Bethany House Publishers, 2012.

Mohler, Albert. "Training Pastors in the Church." *Tabletalk Magazine,* February 1, 2008. Accessed March 18, 2017. http://www.ligonier.org/learn/articles/training-pastors-church/.

Ogne, Steve, and Tim Roehl. *TransforMissional Coaching.* Nashville: B&H Publishing Group, 2008.

Osborne, Larry. *Sticky Church.* Grand Rapids, MI: Zondervan, 2008.

Piper, John. "Biblical Eldership" (Paper, Bethlehem, MN, May, 1999).

Piper, John. *Brothers, We Are Not Professionals: A Plea to Pastors for Radical Ministry.* Updated and Expanded Edition. Nashville: B & H Publishing Group, 2013.

Piper, John. *The Supremacy of God in Preaching.* Revised and Expanded Edition. Grand Rapids, MI: Baker Books, 2015.

Popper, Ben. "Nextdoor — a private, localized social network — is now used in over 100,000 US neighborhoods." *The Verge.* Accessed June 23, 2016. http://www.theverge.com/2016/6/23/12005456/nextdoor-100000-neighborhood-social-network-app-changes-business-plan-expansion.

Powell, Tyler. "The Importance of Assessment in Church Planting." Acts 29. Accessed February 20, 2017. http://www.acts29.com/the-importance-of-assessment-in-church-planting/.

Prime, Derek, and Alistair Begg. *On Being a Pastor.* Revised and Expanded Edition of *Pastors & Teachers* © 1989. Chicago: Moody Publishers, 2004.

Pue, Carson. *Mentoring Leaders: Wisdom for Developing Character, Calling, and Competency.* Grand Rapids: Baker Books, 2005.

Rainer, Thom. "13 Issues for 2013." *Church Leaders.* Accessed June 15, 2016. http://churchleaders.com/pastors/pastor-articles/164787-thom-rainer-13-issues-churches-2013.html.

Reeder, Harry L., III. *Embers to a Flame: How God Can Revitalize Your Church.* Phillipsburg, NJ: P&R Publishing Company, 2004.

Ridgaway, Toni. "Statistics Don't Tell the Whole Story When It Comes to Church Attendance."*Church Leaders.* Accessed September 12, 2015. http://www.churchleaders.com/pastors/pastor-articles/170739-statistics-don-t-tell-the-whole-story-when-it-comes-to-church-attendance.html.

Schmucker, Matt. "Why Revitalize?" *9 Marks.* Accessed August 5, 2016. https://9marks.org/article/journalwhy-revitalize/.

Searcy, Nelson, and Kerrick Thomas. *Activate: An Entirely New Approach to Small Groups.* Grand Rapids, MI: Baker Books, 2014.

Spurgeon, Charles. "Made Perfect In Weakness," *Truth for Life.* Accessed November 4, 2016. https://www.truthforlife.org/resources/daily-devotionals/11/4/1881/.

Stanley, Andy, and Bill Willits. *Creating Community: Five Keys to Building a Small Group Culture.* Sisters, OR: Multnomah Publishers, 2004.

Stetzer, Ed, and Mike Dodson. *Comeback Churches: How 300 Churches Turned Around and Yours Can, Too.* Nashville: B & H Publishing Group, 2007.

Stoddard, David. *The Heart of Mentoring: Ten Proven Principles for Developing People to Their Fullest Potential.* Colorado Springs, CO: NavPress, 2009.

Strauch, Alexander. *Biblical Eldership: An Urgent Call to Restore Biblical Church Leadership.* Revised and Expanded Edition. Colorado Springs, CO: Lewis & Roth Publishers, 1995.

Strauch, Alexander. *The Hospitality Commands: Building Loving Christian Community; Building Bridges to Friends and Neighbors.* Littleton, CO: Lewis & Roth Publishing, 1993.

Strauch, Alexander. *Leading with Love.* Colorado Springs, CO: Lewis & Roth Publishers, 2006.

Thomas, Curtis. *Practical Wisdom for Pastors: Words of Encouragement and Counsel for a Lifetime of Ministry.* Wheaton, IL: 2001.

Thomas, Scott. "Biblical Qualifications of a Pastor." *Acts 29.* Accessed August 3, 2014. http://www.acts29network.org/acts-29-blog/biblical-qualifications-of-a-pastor/.

Thomas, Scott. *Gospel Coach: Shepherding Leaders to Glorify God.* Grand Rapids: Zondervan, 2012.

Timmis, Steve. "Every Shepherd needs a Shepherd." *Acts 29 Blog.* Accessed September 4, 2014. http://www.acts29network.org/acts-29-blog/every-shepherd-needs-a-shepherd/.

"The 2000 Baptist Faith & Message." *The Southern Baptist Convention.* Accessed Accessed Mar 27, 2017. http://www.sbc.net/bfm2000/bfm2000.asp.

Ward, Ronald A. *Commentary on I and II Timothy and Titus.* Waco, TX: Word Publishing, 1974.

Warren, Rick. "The Five Stages of Renewal in the Local Church." Pastors.com. Accessed April 7, 2016. http://pastors.com/the-five-stages-of-renewal-in-the-local-church/.

Welch, Edward T. *Side by Side: Walking with Others in Wisdom and Love.* Wheaton, IL: Crossway, 2015.

Wells, Barney. "Leading Town and County Church," (notes from Doctor of Ministry class, Bethel Seminary, Minneapolis, Minnesota, 1999).

Wiersbe, Warren. *Be Faithful (1 & 2 Timothy, Titus, Philemon): It's Always Too Soon to Quit.* Chicago, IL: David C. Cook, 2009.

Wilson, Jared. *The Prodigal Church: A Gentle Manifesto Against the Status Quo.* Wheaton, IL: Crossway, 2015.

Willis, Dustin. *Life in Community: Joining Together to Display the Gospel.* Chicago: Moody Publishers, 2015.

Willis, Dustin, and Brandon Clements. *The Simplest Way to Change the World: Biblical Hospitality as a Way of Life.* Chicago, IL: Moody Publishers, 2017.

Witmer, Timothy Z. *The Shepherd Leader.* Phillipsburg, NJ: P&R Publishing Company, 2010.

Yackel, Meredith. "Replant Lab Aims at Reducing Number of Dying Churches."
    Baptist Press. Accessed May 3, 2017. http://www.bpnews.net/47483/replant-lab-
    aims-at-reducing-number-of-dying-churches.

NOTES

CHAPTER 1 – A MOVEMENT IS NEEDED

[1] Toni Ridgaway, "Statistics Don't Tell the Whole Story When It Comes to Church Attendance," *Church Leaders*, accessed September 12, 2015, http://www.churchleaders.com/pastors/pastor-articles/170739-statistics-don-t-tell-the-whole-story-when-it-comes-to-church-attendance.html.

[2] Ibid.

[3] Dan Bensen, "You Lost Me," *The Gospel Coalition*, accessed May 3, 2017, https://www.thegospelcoalition.org/article/you_lost_me.

[4] Thom Rainer, "13 Issues for 2013," *Church Leaders*, accessed June 15, 2016, http://churchleaders.com/pastors/pastor-articles/164787-thom-rainer-13-issues-churches-2013.html.

[5] Meredith Yackel, "Replant Lab aims at reducing number of dying churches," *Baptist Presst*, accessed May 3, 2017, http://www.bpnews.net/47483/replant-lab-aims-at-reducing-number-of-dying-churches.

[6] Ibid.

[7] "Church Replanting," *North American Mission Board*, accessed May 3, 2017, https://www.namb.net/church-replanting.

[8] Ibid.

[10] Al Mohler, "A Guide to Church Revitalization," *Southern Baptist Theological Seminary*, accessed January 7, 2017, http://www.sbts.edu/press/a-guide-to-church-revitalization/#download.

CHAPTER 2 – WHY WE MUST REPLANT CHURCHES NOW

[1] Matt Schmucker, "Why Revitalize?", *9 Marks*, accessed August 5, 2016. https://9marks.org/article/journalwhy-revitalize/.

[2] Ibid.

[3] Mark Clifton, "Dying Churches Matter to God....and to NAMB", *North American Mission Board*, accessed September 1, 2016. https://www.namb.net/send-network-blog/dying-churches-matter-to-god-and-to-namb.

CHAPTER 3 – UNDERSTANDING GOD'S HEART FOR REPLANTING

[1] Charles Spurgeon, "Made Perfect In Weakness," *Truth for Life*, accessed November 4, 2016, https://www.truthforlife.org/resources/daily-devotionals/11/4/1881/.

[2] Ibid.

[3] Ibid.

[4] Bill Henard, *Can These Bones Live?* (Nashville, TN: B&H Publishing Group, 2015), 2.

[5] Ibid.

[6] Mark Clifton, "Dying Churches."

[7] See Rick Warren, "The Five Stages of Renewal in the Local Church," accessed June 1, 2017, http://pastors.com/the-five-stages-of-renewal-in-the-local-church/.

[8] Ibid.

CHAPTER 4 – STEP#1: COUNTING THE COST & THE JOY

[1] Mark Clifton, *Reclaiming Glory: Creating a Gospel Legacy throughout North America* (Nashville: B&H, 2016), 23.

[2] Mike McKinley, "The Pros and Cons of Planting and Revitalization," *9 Marks*, accessed June 13, 2016, https://9marks.org/article/journalpros-and-cons-planting-and-revitalizing/.

[3] Clifton, *Reclaiming Glory*, 25.

[4] Justin Deeter, "Advantages of Established Churches," *justindeeter.com*, accessed June 13, 2016, http://www.justindeeter.com/archives/1562.

[5] McKinley, "The Pros and Cons".

CHAPTER 5 – STEP#2: RAISING UP A REPLANTER

[1] Brian Howard, "How to Develop Leaders in your Church", *Context Coaching*, accessed January 23, 2017, http://contextcoaching.org/develop-leaders-church/.

[2] Al Mohler, "Training Pastors in the Church", *CraigThompson.org*, accessed December 10, 2016, http://www.passionforpreaching.net/articles/training-pastors-in-church/.

[3] The time of each session will be directly related to the number of Foundations being taught and discussed. Leaders should plan for roughly 1-1½ hours of instruction and discussion per Foundation. The material can be used as a weekly gathering focused on one Foundation (1-1½ hour session), a bi-weekly gathering focused on two Foundations (2-3 hour session), or it can be used in a monthly cohort gathering format (4-6 hour session). Have the pastor or facilitator schedule in breaks as needed.

[4] Beyond the monthly preaching cohort, it is highly recommended that your resident is given the chance to preach in the main worship gathering at least once every four to eight weeks. Preaching in a "real" worship service will not only help the resident continue to grow in confidence and skill as a preacher, but it will be a blessing to both the congregation and the Senior Pastor.

[5] Steve Timmis, "Every Shepherd needs a Shepherd," *Acts 29 Blog*, accessed September 4, 2014, http://www.acts29network.org/acts-29-blog/every-shepherd-needs-a-shepherd/.

[6] Adapted from Steve Ogne and Tim Roehl, *TransforMissional Coaching*, (Nashville, TN: B&H Publishing, 2008), 69-70.

CHAPTER 6 – STEP#3: ASSESSING THE POTENTIAL REPLANTER

[1] Kevin Collier, "How to Evaluate Your Pastor's Sermons," *9 Marks*, accessed January 15, 2017, https://9marks.org/article/how-to-evaluate-your-pastors-sermons-2/.

[2] Jonathan Edwards, The Salvation of Souls (Wheaton, IL: Crossway, 2002), 51-52.

[3] Tyler Powell, "The Importance of Assessment in Church Planting," Acts 29, accessed February 20, 2017, http://www.acts29.com/the-importance-of-assessment-in-church-planting/.

[4] Adapted from Scott Thomas, "Biblical Qualifications of a Pastor," accessed August 3, 2014, http://www.acts29network.org/acts-29-blog/biblical-qualifications-of-a-pastor/.

[5] I am using "pastor" and "elder" interchangeably throughout this book as both speak to the same church office in the New Testament. For the sake of clarity, I have chosen to refer to this position as "pastor-elder" in this chapter. For further study, I recommend reading *Biblical Eldership* by Alex Strauch.

[6] John MacArthur, *First Timothy: MacArthur New Testament Commentary* (Chicago, IL: Moody Publishers, 1995), 96.

[7] Thomas, "Biblical Qualifications of a Pastor."

[8] Warren Wiersbe, *Be Faithful* (Chicago, IL: David C. Cook, 2009), 41.

[9] Thomas, "Biblical Qualifications of a Pastor."

[10] Ibid.

[11] Archibald Alexander Allison, "Biblical Qualifications for Elders," *Ordained Servant* 3, no. 4 (November 1994): 83.

[12] Ibid.

[13] John Piper, "Biblical Eldership" (paper, Bethlehem, MN, May, 1999).

[14] Alexander Strauch, *The Hospitality Commands: Building Loving Christian Community; Building Bridges to Friends and Neighbors* (Littleton, CO: Lewis & Roth Publishing, 1993), 43.

[15] George Abbott-Smith, *A Manual Lexicon of the New Testament* (New York, NY: Scribner's Sons, 1922), 38.

[16] Ronald A. Ward, *Commentary on I and II Timothy and Titus* (Waco, TX: Word Publishing, 1974), 55.

[17] Ibid.

[18] Robert Murray McCheyne, *The Sermons of the Rev. Robert Murray McCheyne* (New York, NY: Robert Carter and Brothers Publishing, 1854), 68.

[19] Thomas, "Biblical Qualifications of a Pastor."

[20] Piper, "Biblical Eldership."

[21] John Calvin, *Commentaries on The Epistles to Timothy, Titus, and Philemon* (Grand Rapids, MI: Baker Publishing, 1979), 83-84.

[22] Piper, "Biblical Eldership."

[23] Ibid.

[24] Thomas, "Biblical Qualifications of a Pastor."

[25] Ibid.

[26] These eight characteristics were identified and defined by the National NAMB Replant team in 2015.

[27] Brian Croft, *Biblical Revitalization* (Scotland, UK: Christian Focus Publishing, 2016), 34.

CHAPTER 8 – STEP#5: MARRYING SENDING & LEGACY CONGREGATIONS

[1] These will each be discussed in more detail in chapter 12.

CHAPTER 9 – STEP#6: GROWING A CORE TEAM & BUILDING MOMENTUM

[1] Mark Lenz, "3 Keys to Managing Momentum in Ministry," *churchcentral.com*, accessed March 14, 2017, https://www.churchcentral.com/blogs/3-keys-to-managing-momentum-in-ministry/.

[2] See chapter 12 for more explanation of the soft launch phase.

[3] The public launch is when the replant officially goes "public" as a new congregation.

[4] It is recommended that replanters train everyone in the replant to practice I-3 Relational Evangelism on a regular basis.

[5] In order to do this effectively, you must be intentional about taking attendance. It is recommended to find one or two leaders who can be responsible for taking attendance at each event that you do, particularly your weekend worship services.

CHAPTER 10 – STEP#7: DESIGNING GOSPEL-CENTERED ENVIRONMENTS

[1] Jared Wilson, *The Prodigal Church* (Wheaton, IL: Crossway, 2015), 46.

[2] Interview with Ben Haley in January of 2017.

[3] Interview with Dan Hallock in January of 2017.

[4] Interview with Steve Anderson in January of 2017.

[5] Tim Keller, *Center Church*, (Grand Rapids, MI: Zondervan, 2012), 49-50.

CHAPTER 11 – STEP#8: CREATING A STRATEGY FOR SUPPORT

[1] You'll want to meet once a year for a longer period of time (a 12-month period) to see the overview of care and support. This will help the team to properly plan for on-going as well as one-time care goals.

[2] There are many excellent, affordable, easy to use options for video calling. Two recommendations worth looking into are Skype and Zoom.

CHAPTER 12 – THE REPLANT BLUEPRINT

[1] Depending on the leadership and governance structure of the church, this will include your pastors, elders, and/or deacons. Whoever are the primary overseers of the replant should be at this meeting. For the sake of clarity, I am using the term "pastor" and "elder" interchangeably as representing the same pastoral office.

[2] See Chapter 10 for further discussion and instruction on how to design and lead effective community groups.

[1] Primary sources: (1) Marty Giese, "A Pastoral Training Program for Rural Churches" (Master of Arts research project, Moody Bible Institute, Chicago, 1993); (2) Kent Hunter, *The Lord's Harvest and the Rural Church* (Beacon Hill Press; Kansas City, 1993); (3) Dr. Barney Wells "Leading Town and County Church" (notes from a Doctor of Ministry class, Bethel Seminary, Minneapolis, Minnesota, 1999).

ACOMA PRESS

Acoma Press exists to make Jesus non-ignorable by equipping and encouraging churches through gospel-centered resources.

Toward this end, each purchase of an Acoma Press resource serves to catalyze disciple-making and to equip leaders in God's Church. In fact, a portion of your purchase goes directly to funding planting and replanting efforts in North America and beyond. To see more of our current resources, visit us at *acomapress.org*.

Thank you.

Made in United States
Orlando, FL
17 February 2023

30072212R00233